P9-ARS-493

WITHDRAWN

the series on school reform

Patricia A. Wasley	Ann Lieberman	Joseph P. McDonald
Coalition of Essential Schools	NCREST	Annenberg Institute for School Reform

SERIES EDITORS

School Work: Gender and the
Cultural Construction of Teaching
SARI KNOPP BIKLEN

School Change: The Personal
Development of a Point of View
SEYMOUR B. SARASON

The Work of Restructuring Schools:
Building from the Ground Up
ANN LIEBERMAN, Editor

Stirring the Chalkdust: Tales of Teachers
Changing Classroom Practice
PATRICIA A. WASLEY

Incorporating the following books from the
PROFESSIONAL DEVELOPMENT AND PRACTICE SERIES

The Contexts of Teaching in Secondary
Schools: Teachers' Realities
MILBREY W. MCLAUGHLIN,
JOAN E. TALBERT, & NINA BASCIA, Eds.

Careers in the Classroom:
When Teaching Is More Than a Job
SYLVIA MEI-LING YEE

The Making of a Teacher: Teacher
Knowledge and Teacher Education
PAMELA L. GROSSMAN

Staff Development for the 1990s:
New Demands, New Realities,
New Perspectives, SECOND EDITION
ANN LIEBERMAN &
LYNNE MILLER, Eds.

Teachers Who Lead: The Rhetoric of
Reform and the Realities of Practice
PATRICIA A. WASLEY

Exploring Teaching:
Reinventing an Introductory Course
SHARON FEIMAN-NEMSER &
HELEN J. FEATHERSTONE, Eds.

Teaching: Making Sense of
an Uncertain Craft
JOSEPH P. MCDONALD

Teachers' Work:
Individuals, Colleagues, and Contexts
JUDITH WARREN LITTLE and
MILBREY W. MCLAUGHLIN, Eds.

Team Building for School Change:
Equipping Teachers for New Roles
GENE I. MAEROFF

A Union of Professionals:
Labor Relations and
Educational Reform
CHARLES TAYLOR KERCHNER and
JULIA E. KOPPICH

Professional Development Schools:
Schools for Developing a Profession
LINDA DARLING-HAMMOND, Editor

Changing Teachers, Changing Times:
Teachers' Work and Culture
in the Postmodern Age
ANDY HARGREAVES

Chartering Urban School Reform:
Reflections on Public High School
in the Midst of Change
MICHELLE FINE, Editor

Unions in Teachers' Professional Lives:
Social, Intellectual, and
Practical Concerns
NINA BASCIA

Teacher Development and
the Struggle for Authenticity:
Professional Growth and Restructuring
in the Context of Change
PETER P. GRIMMETT and
JONATHAN NEUFELD

SCHOOL WORK

Gender and
the Cultural Construction
of Teaching

SARI KNOPP BIKLEN

Foreword by Maxine Greene

Teachers College, Columbia University
New York and London

Copyright Acknowledgements

Parts of this work were published earlier in sometimes substantially differ-ent form. The author gratefully acknowledges the generosity of the journals and societies cited below that supported her use of this material:

Portions of Chapter 2 appeared in a different form in S. K. Biklen, Can elementary schoolteaching be a career? A search for new ways of under-standing women's work. *Issues in Education, 3* (1985), 215–231; and in S. K. Biklen, Teachers, professionalism and gender. *Teacher Education Quarterly, 14* (Spring, 1987), 17–24.

A portion of Chapter 3 appeared in significantly different form in S. K. Biklen, Confiding woman: A 19th century teacher's diary. *History of Educa-tion Review, 19* (1990), 24–35.

Chapter 6 was published in similar form in S. K. Biklen and D. Pollard, Eds., *Gender and Education*, National Society for the Study of Education Yearbook. Chicago: NSSE, 1993.

Published by Teachers College Press, 1234 Amsterdam Avenue, New York, NY 10027

Library of Congress Cataloging-in-Publication Data

Biklen, Sari Knopp.
   School work : gender and the cultural construction of teaching /
Sari Knopp Biklen ; foreword by Maxine Greene.
     p.   cm. — (The series on school reform)
   Includes bibliographical references and index.
   ISBN 0-8077-3408-X (cloth : acid-free paper). — ISBN
0-8077-3407-1 (paper : acid-free paper)
   1. Women teachers—United States—Social conditions. 2. Feminist
theory—United States. 3. Educational sociology—United States.
I. Title. II. Series.
LB2837.B55   1995
371.1'00973—dc20   94-23659

ISBN 0-8077-3407-1 (paper)
ISBN 0-8077-3408-X (cloth)

Printed on acid-free paper
Manufactured in the United States of America

02 01 00 99 98 97 96 95   8 7 6 5 4 3 2 1

Contents

Foreword

This book startles and challenges in its call for a gendered understanding of women's work as teachers. Through its tapping of a multiplicity of perspectives, it sheds new light on the cultural construction of teaching in this country. The stereotypes are painfully familiar: the infantilized little person ground down by authority; the helpless agent of a normalization process; the guilt-ridden young mother trying to reconcile family obligations with a generally under-valued "career." Sari Biklen skillfully changes the lenses through which we look at teaching, particularly elementary school teaching; and she enables her readers, not only to see through the old stereotypes, but to understand how they became so central to our discourse.

Using vantage points as various as those provided by participant research in actual school rooms, a range of sociologies, nineteenth-century American history, and feminist theory, she shows us how traditional critiques depended on a "gaze" that almost always objectified teachers and their work. Moreover, the norms used in evaluating them have tended to be male norms linked to images of heroism or aggressive intellectualism. Because teachers themselves have so seldom been consulted over the years, the integral relations between their work as wives and mothers have been ignored.

One of the attractions of *School Work: Gender and the Cultural Construction of Teaching* is the making audible of so many voices. Out of interviews with parents and administrators, as well as teachers, the author is able to make clear the unique type of public positioning teachers experience. She is able also to place before her readers some of the complexities of teachers' power over the children they teach, the often contradictory possibilities in the use of that power, and the persisting effects of patriarchy on the way teaching is structured. Using novels and short stories, she opens perspectives on the imaginative construction of teacher identities. There is much to be discovered where teacher identity and a person's identity as a woman intersect; and there are important insights to be found when we are freed to think about the discourses that inform the creation of women in fiction. In addition to using fiction and the horizons opened by the imaginative, Biklen is able to make accessible a wealth of letters and diaries, especially from the nineteenth century. These tell us much about the adventure of teaching, particularly for those who left home for far-off places, survived loneliness and, often, maltreatment, in order to find themselves as individuals and define teaching projects for themselves.

Whether or not the readers of this text are teachers, they cannot but resonate to what is said about the tension experienced when teachers struggle to find their own voices while coping with institutional structures. Inevitably teachers find themselves influenced by existing social discourses and power relations; but they persist in seeking a kind of autonomy, a way of leaving a thumbprint they know is theirs. There is a concreteness about their search as presented here, in large measure because of the explicit effort to relate it to teachers' lived lives and to the role of work within those lives.

Feminist inquiries have been relatively slow in touching the complications and the richness of such narratives. There are the old dualisms to cope with: teaching as a matter of the mind or of the "heart." There is the problematic of professionalism and the often harmful results of the professional model. And, yes, there is the nagging issue of whether teaching is a career, and the related issue of how it compares to other careers at a moment when opportunities are opening up that were never open before. Are there indeed commitments to children and their growth that women understand more deeply than men? What is, what ought to be the relationship between teachers and the mothers of the children they teach? What difference does it make if the teachers themselves have children? What does social class have to do with what parents ask of teachers and what teachers ask of themselves? Questions like these are sparked by engagement with this book. Sari Biklen emphasizes the importance of dialogue among teachers, the need for what she calls "connecting talk."

Fully aware of how teachers draw on a variety of discourses in order to explain their work—to themselves as well as others—Biklen has the rare capacity to draw her readers into the forever unfinished conversation. Readers may well end with multiple unanswered questions about rules and controls, about service and commitment, about autonomy and community. They will surely find their gendered understanding enhanced in domains that may have seemed to exclude it in time past. They will grasp the power of institutional constructions in a new way; and, moved to reflect further on their own work, they may even be provoked to resist when the pressures become too much. But Sari Biklen's good work will make their own more enticing. This is a book that may conceivably alter a few lives.

Maxine Greene

Acknowledgments

This project has taken me a long time to complete. I began it as a feminist, in reaction to how the sociological literature treated women in teaching. Over the fourteen years I have been working on this book I faced my need to become more theoretically engaged. A progressive political and feminist perspective seemed inadequate. At times I postponed writing because of the importance of theoretically defining myself, a location it was difficult for me to find. Asserting a theoretical eclecticism several years ago freed me to finish this work. This eclecticism meant that I could draw on different and sometimes not directly compatible theories to explain particular aspects of the work.

I have been helped along the way in many intellectual, personal, and material ways. The National Institute of Education, now defunct, funded my first two years of research. Ursula Casanova, my project officer there, was supportive, enthusiastic, and engaging. Small grants from Syracuse University supported my archival research and my reading of fiction.

Lyn Yates has been very important in my intellectual thinking about feminism, post-structuralism, and methodology in relation to teachers and education. I have learned a lot from knowing her.

Other friends, colleagues, and relatives have been supportive, stimulating, and challenging; they have pushed me to think in new ways about education. Jan and Bob Bogdan always made me explain myself. Thank you. Shanti Menon, Pat Russo, Linda Steet, and I had the kind of group I wish I had had as a graduate student. I profited greatly from our talk. Diane Murphy is the kind of friend I want to be to others. Discussions with Nan Stein, Sandra Acker, Marj DeVault, and Jerry Grant have always made me think differently about what I was doing.

Many people read and commented on different chapters. I am grateful to Linda Alcoff, Nancy Beadie, Leslie Bender, Doug Biklen, Bob Bogdan, Janet Bogdan, Joan Burstyn, Marj DeVault, Fay Dudden, Jerry Grant, Mustafa Kiziltan, Sally Kohlstedt, Shanti Menon, Emily Robertson, Pat Russo, Mary Sheerin, Linda Steet, Ann Watts-Paillotet and the members of the 1988 Gender, Education, and Culture Seminar.

Earlier drafts of these chapters were given at annual meetings of the American Educational Research Association, where discussions with so many people, like Patti Lather, Charol Shakeshaft, Deborah Britzman, Jean Anyon, Maxine Greene, Geraldine Clifford, and Diane Pollard pushed me to consider alternatives I had not seen.

I appreciate support I have received from David Tyack and Michael Apple, and what I have learned from their work. I have benefited from other discussions about theory and practice with Felicity Nussbaum, Joan Brumberg, Mara Sapon-Shevin, Nirmala Erevelles, Raji Swaminathan, Susan Bordo, Lynne Arnault, and the first Multi-Cultural Narratives and Educational Change seminar.

Marcella Stark at Bird Library, Syracuse University, was especially helpful in locating historical material on teachers and fiction. Carole Saltz at Teachers College Press has such a good eye, and is so direct and supportive. I benefited as well from the advice and work of editors Susan Liddicoat and Carol Collins. Susan Kelly at Cultural Foundations of Education was a wonderful worker with the computer. And Loraine Kotary was a great support early on. I'd also like to thank Daisy Mak for her excellent bibliographic work.

Other kinds of support were priceless. Honey and Burt Knopp were present and intellectually keen on my topic. Patricia Numann and Jane D'Antoni made me feel surrounded by a brilliant and supportive women's health community when it was so important.

Doug Biklen is such a good person and mate. In addition to his intellectual comradeship, I appreciate all the ways in which he is not a small person in his soul, his physical labor, and, most important, his emphasis on the language of possibility. Molly and Noah Biklen changed during the years this book was written in ways that make me feel privileged.

Chapter 1

Introduction: Reconsidering Women Teachers

The popular films *Stand and Deliver* and *Lean on Me* constructed the educational figure as hero. In each of these Hollywood films, a male educator—a teacher in the former and a principal in the latter—set out to do his version of good by improving the conditions of schooling and education for their students. They took a Lone Ranger approach (acting out their authority solo) because they had a job to do and others (teachers, principals, staff) did not, from the hero's perspective, take their work seriously enough.

Both films tagged the failure of American education to adequately serve its students, particularly its least privileged, to frame why the heroes broke away from the pack. These educators had a vision of what might be accomplished, and they set out to enact their vision. The films offered several critiques of schooling: First, many teachers do not expect enough of their students because of race or class prejudice; second, too many teachers see their work as jobs and do not want to do anything extra to overcome inertia; and third, the leadership in some schools does not provide enough sustenance, safety, organization, or resources for teachers to do their best work.

These critiques came at a time of popular concern about schools, children, and the quality of American education. They dovetailed with fears about the American economy, the stability of our institutions, and shifts in how childhood is socially constructed. For whom was the public school system working? The films argued that the schools did not serve the underdog, not because schools were unable to do so, but because teachers and administrators were not doing their jobs. The work of the modernist hero was constructed against a domestic view of the traditional teacher as one who attended to the small, everyday issues (and not very well, either). The films conserved the school as an institution: Change the workers in the institution (and their motivation, energy, expectations, and so forth) to make the system work better.

This popular construction of the teacher-as-hero wrests the teacher from the safety and constraint ordinarily associated with the role (Waller, 1932). These films suggest that hope for American educational improvement lies with educators who act as heroes, willing to take risks and move beyond constraining and contractual boundaries. They construct heroes as men who swim against the stream; therefore, these men do not collaborate with others, do not work to build strong workplace cultures. I want to explore this metaphor of the teacher as hero for its use in understanding the work of teachers and for its gendered strategy of speaking against teachers. (A strategy [or conversation, activity, behavior] is "gendered" when particular socially or culturally shared understandings about relationships between men and women inform it. The term refers to the predominant practice of characterizing men and women in relationship to each other. The statement, "men are selfish," for example, carries the unspoken addition "in relation to women." This relationship is not static in every situation, and it is influenced by the class and race of the specific men and women involved, but it is coherent because men and women are unequally configured by power. If elementary schoolteaching is culturally constructed as domestic, or as a job for women, then it can be criticized, controlled, and organized as women's work. This criticism can come from both women and men, but it is anchored in a gendered understanding that dismisses, discounts, or takes authority over women's work.)

This issue of heroism is complex: The attractions of the heroic over the domestic are significant during national moments of cynicism with schools, in spite of the occasional warning that we need newer narratives than the "dreary cycle of individual heroism or self-blame" (Britzman, 1991, p. xiii). The story of heroes is a modernist tale (cf. Van Maanen, 1988) that assumes a linear relationship between consistent institutional historical memories and the purposes of education. Not only are these effects doubtful, but women, as feminist historians have shown, get written out of these tales. I explore how critiques of teachers and teaching rest on gender but are not acknowledged as doing so.

The heroic metaphor has several uses. Teaching has suffered because of its reputation as a haven for the ordinary and unambitious (Biklen, 1987b). Conceptualizing teaching as heroic acknowledges how work with children makes extraordinary demands on those involved with them as well as revealing how inadequate our understanding has been so far of the place of work in the lives of women teachers.

When teachers are seen from a sympathetic perspective, we study them as if their work were central to their lives. Teachers act heroic, according to the model of Jaime Escalante in *Stand and Deliver*, when they give more than other teachers to their students and do more for the school than others.

Framed in this way, teachers act as heroes when they legitimize the lives of their students, when they teach so that students feel that what goes on in the classroom is important, and when they adopt some sort of collaborative teaching approach that gives students a chance to participate in determining what is important. Teachers who validate their students' ways of knowing or who sacrifice their complacency to take risks with students—whether in Appalachia, New York City, Roxbury, or on reservations— exemplify this approach. These teachers embody "going beyond the call of duty." Their approach to their work is not limited to their "job description." Teachers take risks by serving children with AIDS, by integrating children with severe disabilities into the classroom, by teaching with devotion and commitment in inner-city schools. Teachers reveal commitment to teaching and to children when they insist on redefining the analysis of their work.

It is not only in places where the underclass, the marginalized, and the dispossessed live that teachers can be resisters. Those teachers who work in suburbia, in working-class sections of small towns, or in rural villages have many opportunities to act in this definition of the hero. The importance of resisting the conventional and moribund can be practiced anywhere. The possibility of heroism is inherent in teaching.

Another advantage of the heroic model is that it can be used to examine best practices as it honors those who practice them. It makes children important because it shows teachers taking risks for children's benefit and welfare. It underscores the need to attend seriously to children.

There are disadvantages to the heroic model as well. First, the idea of the heroic is so gendered as to be useless. People are heroic in isolation from others. The traditional hero is entrepreneurial (Gilder, 1989), individualistic, free to travel, works with little sleep. Lines between public and private life blur. Heroes are single-minded. So the heroic life takes over, and a family life is possible only if someone else can undertake child care responsibilities. Also, we may label men's and women's activities "heroic" for different reasons: men's when they are active and accomplish something, women's when they are able to accept and survive harsh realities. Women can become heroes just by defying the odds. In reference to female survivors of family violence, for example, Linda Gordon (1988) has said that our culture tends to "romanticize forbearance" (p. 289).

A second disadvantage is the historical construction of the hero as conservative. This kind of hero is represented by men like Rambo or Oliver North who enact mythical adventures to preserve a mythical America. Heroes are not necessarily revolutionary resisters; they can be individualistic adventurers who trample on the rights of less privileged peoples in the name of an American fantasy. While the disadvantages outweigh the advantages, particularly for understanding gender and teachers, there is a history of critiquing teachers from this perspective.

American activists have a long history of criticizing teachers. They have described teachers as promoters of conformity, and as part of racist school structures. In the late 1960s Jonothan Kozol charged that teachers participated in students' *Death at an Early Age* (1967). Herbert Kohl (1976), John Holt (1964), and James Herndon (1968) positioned students at the center of their stories, showing how they were victimized by insensitive teachers. They also implied that people interested in social activism could fight racism and inequality by being a different kind of teacher. Earlier in the century, John Reed decried teachers who, he argued, focused on memorizing facts, dulling the senses (Rosenstone, 1975).

Reed was involved in the dynamic of revolution and was attracted to the revolutionary hero. He wrote in "Almost Thirty," an unpublished memoir of his early life, that teachers continually held back change, and that their

> chief qualification is that they can plough steadily through a dull round of dates, acts, half-truths and rules for style, without questioning, without interpreting, and without seeing how ridiculously unlike the world their teachings are. (Rosenstone, 1975, p. 17)

In his view, teachers were mired in discourses of domesticity, and to domesticate the world was to destroy liberty. Neither did he see teachers as subjects who dared to question or interpret. Rather, they were bureaucratic figurines.

If heroism is partly defined by commitment, it becomes difficult to measure it for women in teaching. How do you determine the centrality of work in women's lives (Biklen, 1987a)? The teacher who leaves for five years to take responsibility for caring for her children does not necessarily indicate by her action that teaching is not central

to her life. In a society where work and family have been oppositionally constructed for women, work commitment is measured on historical models that have bound women in particular ways. Consider the
teacher who has two positions in order to earn enough money to support her family: the teaching position during the day and the salesper-
son position at the department store at night and on weekends. Is she
committed to her work—not, that is, to work to support a family,
but to the specific activities of teaching? Economics and professional
ideologies shape the concept of commitment.

Heroic tropes, even when redefined around commitment and resistance, contribute to constructing rather than deconstructing teaching
as a gendered activity. They do not provide insight into the rich and
complex ways in which teachers' lives in schools are constrained by
institutional discourses and at the same time expanded through their
interactions with children. The hero is constructed against the feminine. In occupations sex-typed as feminine, "each individual worker is
replaceable, or *defined as replaceable . . .* " (Coser & Rokoff, 1970).
The heroic trope, by its very nature, suggests that the hero is irreplaceable and makes a unique individual contribution. When applied to
education, the implication is that this contribution is invaluable in a
way that regular teaching is not. This book rejects the heroic as an
entry point to study women who teach, and instead takes seriously the
events of their daily lives.

The recent explosion of research on the lives, perspectives, and
voices of teachers has drawn attention to what teachers do, pedagogically, and how the sites where they work influence their activities
and beliefs about teaching. Another recent approach representing a
particular kind of critical work in education—including critical and
feminist theories, Foucauldian post-structuralism, and cultural studies—examines how teachers' work in schools and our understandings
of it are produced and reproduced. This book is located among these
approaches; it explores how social and cultural constructions of teachers and teaching as work are part of a teacher's subjectivity. How a
teacher understands the meaning of teaching and the discourses she
draws upon to understand and explain her choices and actions are
shaped by what it means to be a teacher in our culture. In particular,
this work examines how these cultural constructions are connected to
gender.

Different chapters explore the cultural constructions themselves
as well as how teachers understand them. The data drawn from participant observation suggest that, particularly with elementary schoolteaching, the cultural constructions of teaching are so gendered, so

connected to teaching defined as a woman's activity, that it is nearly impossible to reform teaching without examining and confronting the gender question.

The school, like other institutions, is not a gender-neutral site. It has been historically and occupationally structured around a particular understanding of women's loyalties and time. Feminists have studied how curricula, interactions with teachers, and opportunities, to point to only a few concerns, are gender-differentiated (American Association of University Women, 1992). Teachers may reproduce and/or contest gender arrangements in their teaching in considered or unexamined ways.

Gender, as "a system of culturally constructed relations of power, produced and reproduced in interaction between and among men and women" (Gal, 1991, p. 176), is also present in the lives of teachers as adults working in schools. That is, teachers do not have to focus on gender for it to significantly mark their lives.

The gender question, however, is not simple. First, researchers' politics shape constructions of gender. The particular feminist theory informing the ethnographer's work influences whether we look at Lacanian or psychoanalytic structures, material conditions, or work or school cultures. Second, gender is not isolated from the daily work of teaching. Problems connected to discourses about gender are also embedded in discourses about professionalism, regulation, and pedagogy. While at some moments it is useful to separate these, the connections are important as well. Additionally, teachers do not always articulate their concerns about gender even when their speech, centered around the vocabulary of "mothers," "she," and "women," suggests that gender is the central issue.

PROJECT HISTORY

In 1976, as the only known feminist professor in my school of education, I was asked to organize a conference on women and educational leadership. I immediately accepted, even though I knew very little about women and educational administration, because the conference offered me the opportunity to do work on women and because the literature on feminism and education was so small that I did not worry about my ability to learn it and quickly become "expert." The success of the conference fostered our efforts to edit a book based on the papers from the conference (Biklen & Brannigan, 1980).

Writing the first chapter of that book introduced me, for the first time, to the sociological literature on teachers, who comprise the "pool" from which most educational administrators come. In all the literature I could find written during the 1950s, 1960s, and 1970s, women teachers appeared as objects of social scientists' gaze. I use the word "gaze" here and throughout this book to signify how social scientists look upon and "capture," through their writing and through the theories they apply, the women they write about. I am appropriating the "gaze" from film criticism, which uses this term to explain how the technology of the camera, as well as the content of the film, works to influence the viewer to see the film from the point of view of the male characters (Mulvey, 1975). Mulvey identified the "system of the look" to describe not only how the female characters become the object of the camera's (male) gaze, but also how it constructs the gaze of the audience to be a male gaze as well.

In relation to the study of women teachers, the social scientists not only examined women teachers as objects by talking about them rather than having them talk, but also through using an understanding of women's work theorized only in comparison to a gendered normative model. Etzioni's *The Semi-Professions and Their Organization* (1969), Lortie's *Schoolteacher* (1975), and Dreeben's *The Nature of Teaching* (1970) were among the works that framed women in schoolteaching against theories of careers and work that not only took the lives of particular men as normative, but also generated models of teaching to reflect these particular lives. They related teachers' humble status to the public's low respect for a teacher's intellectual endeavors, the lack of professional autonomy, the low degree of professionalization, and the large number of women in the field (Etzioni, 1969). Teaching, said Dreeben (1970), was one of the women's occupations that "appealed more to the heart than to the mind." Simpson and Simpson (1969) reflected this language: "The main intrinsic appeal of the semi-professions is to the heart, not the mind" (p. 203). Teachers, one of these "semi-professional" groups, reflect a "lack of drive toward intellectual mastery" (p. 239). Another sociologist who had studied the careers of medical men compared the schoolhouse to a harem: "In some ways, the school principal resembles, not so much the administrator in the world of business and industry, as the patriarch presiding over a harem. The duties differ but the structure is similar" (Hall, 1966).

This literature emerged from a discourse that accepted as appropriate the traditional image of woman as family-centered; as subordinate in the organizational hierarchy because of pliable, deferent, passive attitudes; and who elected to work for financial reasons. This literature focused on middle-class women without acknowledging it,

Table 1.1. Women Teachers on Their Work

% OF WOMEN	ONE OF THREE MAJOR REASONS
73.9	Want to work with young people
37.4	Value of education to society
28.2	Interest in subject matter (most important to secondary teachers)
22.0	Opportunity for lifetime of self-growth
12.1	Long summer vacation
8.0	Need for second income
3.2	Stopgap until marriage
2.4	Employment mobility

(NEA, 1972)

ignoring the many (working-class) women who did not have the luxury to choose.

At the time, few qualitative or interpretive studies investigated teachers' perspectives on their work and lives to counteract this kind of positioning. Lortie's *Schoolteacher* (1975) took seriously what teachers did and how they thought about their work, but left unproblematized the question of gender. Surveys conducted by the National Education Association contradicted the sociologists' framework. Their 1972 publication, *Status of the American Public-School Teacher*, reported results of a survey that 1,007 women responded to about different aspects of their work. In response to a question asking informants to indicate on a checklist their three main reasons for choosing teaching, the major reasons women gave for why they had chosen teaching were not primarily related to their family lives. Table 1.1 lists reasons women gave in response to the question. The women surveyed framed their answers around their interests and desires, emphasizing service and social good along with access to knowledge. The traditional family-oriented reasons reported in the literature—the last four listed in Table 1.1—ranked much lower than those having to do with self-fulfillment or societal need. Though these answers also reflected gendered constructions of subjectivity, they emphasized personal interest rather than the needs of others.

This contrast between the demeaning of women in the sociologists' gaze and the skimpiest, most meager form of talking back, that is, "speaking as an equal to an authority figure" (hooks, 1989, p. 5), that the surveys represented occasioned my interest in studying women teachers.

Settings, Subjects, and Texts

I received funding from the National Institute of Education in 1980 to do a participant observation study of women teaching elementary school, in order to develop a feminist analysis of women's perspectives on their lives as teachers. The purpose of the study was to examine what perspectives women who taught elementary school held about their work, what they valued and criticized about their occupation, and how these views were constructed by discursive processes in schools. I chose elementary over secondary teaching because, as a generally sex-segregated worksite, it is so much more the province of women.

My interest in teachers had been generated by my reading of the sociological literature on the occupation of teaching and its female members. As I have said, this literature suggested that female teachers lacked commitment to their work, that they were more interested in affairs of the heart than of the mind, and that they might be more profitably compared to members of a harem than to workers in a business. The literature also treated commitment to work and family as oppositional. Hence, teachers who wanted families lacked work commitment. I determined to "rescue" women in teaching from the hands of these social scientists (e.g., Biklen, 1985).

I did not think of women in teaching as indistinguishable by race and class, undifferentiated from one another. I did not imagine, that is, that there was only a single story to tell; the story would have many strands. I recognized the "importance," as Tanya Modleski (1991) argues, of "holding on" to the category of woman while at the same time "recognizing ourselves to be in the *process . . .* of *defining and constructing the category*" (emphasis in original, p. 20). At the same time, while I observed and interviewed European-American, African-American, and Latina teachers, and did not try to collapse the differences in their perspectives to some generic category of "woman," the category of "woman teacher" was foremost in my thoughts. I wrote against the social scientists' gaze in order to reveal its technology, and to help make teachers subjects in, rather than objects of, their stories.

I predominantly conceptualized the problem as one in which

women teachers were victims. They were victims of sociologists, who talked about them. And they were victimized by a public that demeaned their work and seemed to dismiss their commitment, considering teaching an ordinary job for ordinary women.

In order to see women teachers only as victims, I had to avoid seeing them in relation to children, with whom they were in a position of power. Therefore, I observed them outside the classroom. This way of proceeding also permitted me to speak to teachers about their understanding of their work without the interference of my judgments about their treatment of children.

The empirical work influencing this book is all interpretive, but of three different types: participant observation, historical archival research, and analysis of fictional texts.

Participant observation. The first part of the research consisted of intense participant observation at one elementary school in a medium-sized northeastern city during the 1980–81 school year, and interviews with teachers and parents. I visited the school three to four times a week, in addition to interviews. I also observed and interviewed at another elementary school in the city for comparative purposes, but on a much less sustained basis. The teachers whose lives appear in this book (in Chapters 2, 4, 6, and 7) taught at the first elementary school, a school I call Vista City Elementary. The name of this school, as well as the names of teachers and administrators who worked there when the fieldwork was carried out, are pseudonyms. In addition, I changed, in one other circumstance, a husband's occupation so that this teacher could preserve her anonymity if she so chose.

Vista City Elementary School, serving grades kindergarten to six, looked like a nice old-fashioned school—at least from the front. The school was actually divided into two parts, each of which was built at different times. The front part of the school sported a stucco exterior and a tiled gabled roof. Large bay windows identified the kindergarten rooms on the south side of the building. This part of the school was constructed in 1912. In 1932, what everyone called "the new building" went up. In contrast to the old building, the new building was a functional brick rectangle. The old building's beautiful dark, polished wooden floors, always kept shining, contrasted with the new building's linoleum floors, which always showed scuff marks in spite of the janitors' efforts. The school was divided so that the primary-age children occupied the old building and the older students were in the new building, where lockers lined the hall.

The school was due for renovation efforts to save on heating and modernize the facilities. A committee planned for these changes while I was doing this research, and the work commenced the next year. The shiny wood floors in the old building, which became slippery when wet, were covered with indoor-outdoor carpeting, the cafeteria was moved up from the basement to the first floor to become a "cafetorium" (combined cafeteria and auditorium), and other significant changes occurred.

Vista City Elementary served 800 students during the 1980–81 school year. The instructional staff, including aides and "specials," numbered 60. Of these, only two were male classroom teachers, although men held the positions of gym teacher, school psychologist, and several special nonteaching positions. In spite of the significant number of African-American students in the school, most staff members were of Euro-American descent. On the instructional staff a teacher, a reading specialist, a librarian, and an instructional specialist were African-American women. The vice principal and a gym teacher were African-American men. Several of the support staff, including a social work aide and a special education aide, were also African-American women.

The school, located in a middle-class community populated predominately by professionals and academics, had many children bused in from poorer neighborhoods; thus it served a wide variety of social classes. Unlike some other schools in the city whose students were primarily Italian or Polish, it was not known as a school that served particular ethnic populations. Vista City Elementary had an outstanding academic reputation. When achievement test results were published in the local newspaper each spring, the school always boasted the highest scores.

The situation for Vista City teachers during the period of this study was a bit peculiar. This period was a time of declining enrollments, and many schools in the district had staffs that were almost entirely tenured. But at this school particular circumstances had created a comparatively high percentage of untenured teachers. Job insecurity was high for these teachers; they did not know whether they would have a job the next year. The untenured teachers found these circumstances constraining.

The teachers ranged in age from their early twenties to late fifties. Many were married, although most of the youngest teachers and two of the oldest were single. There were a couple of divorced women on the teaching staff, and one of the male "specials" was also divorced. Teaching experience varied widely, from first-year teachers to those with 20 years' experience. Most, however, had taught for between 5 and 13 years.

Central to these teachers' lives was their picture of teaching as a form of spectacle and display that offered few emotional protections when their personal lives could not be put aside. During the course of the year I spent at the school, one teacher's father had a heart attack, another broke up with her boyfriend, another was slow to recover from an operation, another's child was experiencing serious trouble in school, and still another discovered that her husband was having an affair. These parts of their lives and the feelings generated from them were difficult to lay aside in the classroom. Teachers had to be on show, to "give fully" even in sorrowful times. Teachers felt that they could not occupy themselves with paperwork, an option they envisioned as available in other occupations.

The school's location in a community of "professional" parents put the teachers under a specific kind of pressure. Teachers read the expectations of these parents as particularly high. They were consequently sensitive about being observed in their classrooms. The issue was intensified for me as an observer because I had a child who had just started at the school. I was known as both a researcher and a parent and considered part of my early task to confront how I was examined.

How researchers and writers portray women who teach relates not only to their ideological and material relationships to informants, schools, and educational authority—or, put another way, to "contexts of power, resistance, institutional constraint and innovation" (Clifford, 1986, p. 2)—but also to how those relationships affect research design. We position ourselves in relation to our informants, and then write about them against or parallel to other ways of considering them.

Feminist legal theorists, for example, have based their work in recent years on cases of women as marginalized people. They concern themselves with women as excluded and devalued. When women are excluded from equal access; when they are subjected to the effects of the drug DES; when they are unable to have the law directly benefit their pregnancy, unless it is considered a disabling condition, and hence based on male norms of wellness: then, in some ways, women are always "the good guys" (see Bell, 1988). Women are identified as victims of an unjust system and in need of redress.

When participant-observers study teachers, our relationship to them is shaped by the particular historical issues of the period (not unlike feminist legal theorists) and by issues of power. Feminist interest in the nature of teachers' work (as opposed to training teachers to do antisexist work) began during the mid-1970s, when teachers were not taken very seriously by most groups. My concern was to study these teachers as women whose work was significant to them, however they configured it, and to understand the discourses they drew upon to explain their situations. Data from this fieldwork informs the discussions of teachers' careers (Chapter 2), the narratives of women's agency and their entrance into teaching (Chapter 4), the portrayal of the relationship between mothers and teachers (Chapter 6), and the description and analysis of teachers' talk (Chapter 7).

Archival material. At the end of the year of participant observation and the completion of the research report I felt dissatisfied with what I had learned about teachers, because I could not connect them with other teachers historically or culturally. There was a larger story to tell with my data. This search led me to explore the perspectives of nineteenth- and early-twentieth-century teachers as they were revealed in letters, diaries, autobiographies, and unpublished or locally published manuscripts. I had studied the perspectives of current teachers; how did teachers in the nineteenth century talk (or write) about their work? The Schlesinger Library (Radcliffe), the Bancroft Library (University of California at Berkeley), the Olin Library (Cornell University), the Library of Congress, and the National Archives had collections that provided access to the changing rhetoric and shifting identities of women who taught.

I was curious about the relationship between women who taught currently and those who were among the earliest in the occupation. What perspectives did earlier teachers have on the occupation? Did the opportunities that teaching offered women in the nineteenth century apply to all women? The "natural" connections between women and children, on which early arguments of opening teaching to women rested, must have been taken up by women in different ways. I was concerned about the range of those ways. I chose the nineteenth and early twentieth centuries rather than the mid-twentieth century because I wanted to maintain my focus on ordinary women. The temptations to examine those leaders who organized for women teachers' rights did not seem consistent with my fieldwork efforts.

The larger story about teaching that interested me concerned the ideas and understandings about teachers that were socially available. Fieldwork taught me some of the ways teachers themselves described teaching. What went unmentioned or was ignored? Historical data offered the opportunity to explore both the shifts in teaching as an occupation, and the traces left by earlier women teachers. Contemporary teachers stepped into a dialogue about teaching already in progress (Bakhtin, 1981). Archival data offered access to earlier participants. Chapter 3 makes use of these materials to study the perspectives of these women.

Analysis of fiction. Pupils gain years of experience as they move through the grades observing and coming to know teachers. Their experience and way of knowing teachers are interpreted not only through first-hand engagement, but also through reference to other interpretive frames. These frames include parental advice and admonitions, social and educational policies, peer cultures, and popular culture. It is through this latter discursive way of coming to know teachers that I explored how teachers are culturally constructed. I read magazine fiction, short stories, and novels written during the nineteenth and twentieth centuries where a teacher was the main character to examine how the construction of what it means to be a teacher is anchored, represented, and negotiated in popular culture.

Thinking of fiction as a narrative form that handled evidence differently from social science scholarship (Krieger, 1984), I was curious about how teachers were represented in imaginative writing. In a continuum that reached from the stereotype (the spinster teacher, or the woman waiting for a husband) to complex characterization (the deep, perhaps contradictory, woman), the contributions that fiction would make to images of the teacher might become a shorthand for referring to taken-for-granted assumptions about them. How connected were these representations to particular historical periods? Were some images so powerful and dramatic that they carried lasting effects? The teachers I interviewed never mentioned reading fiction about teachers, so I was not looking to fiction as a source for Vista City Elementary teachers' understanding of teaching's cultural reputation. I was interested in how issues of agency and connection, resistance and regulation—concerns of current teachers—were represented in a fictional approach to the world. These data engendered discussions of autonomy (Chapter 4), and the relationship of gender to race and identity in the 1950s (Chapter 5).

These three forms of data—participant observation and interview fieldnotes; diaries, letters, and other unpublished archival material, as well as published autobiographies and biographies; and fiction—lent themselves to different kinds of stories about teachers and raised questions about methodology.

METHODOLOGICAL PERSPECTIVES

The cultural visibility of teachers raises methodological concerns when feminists study them. When we study a socially exploited or marginalized group, we have some relationship to them. We may share experiences with our informants based on classification by race, gender, class, sexual orientation, and/or disability that sensitize us to their interpretations of their situations. Our personal experiences attract us and define our projects. We may, for example, come from a working-class background; we may have a disability; or we may have an intellectual and emotional understanding of oppression that draws us to our informant's situation. Our own histories locate us as they provide avenues of identifying informants who experience social mistreatment or silencing. Our projects aim to create noise (as opposed to silence) around our informants.

Teachers as Public Figures

Teachers have not, however, suffered from cultural invisibility; all of us who have been allowed to attend school, who have our own children in school, whose relatives or friends are in school, "know" teachers. We know teachers when we are pupils, when we are parents, when we are community members. We can see teachers as allies who promote education for people we love and care about; we can see teachers as rescuers who insist that their students resist succumbing to unjust circumstances; we can see teachers as promoters or resisters of social change efforts for school integration for young people with disabilities, for example, or for curriculum transformation around issues of race, gender, class, and disability; we can see teachers as mean, boring, nice, great, bad, racist. However we see them, teachers are more powerful than students. When they use that power in students' behalf, students benefit, but when they oppose students unjustly, when they mistreat them or use their authority to cover up incompetence, students suffer.

Teachers are such public figures, their work so central to our lives (either positively or negatively), that if, as ethnographers or as feminist social scientists, we want to know them, we must take their cultural position into account. Several matters take on importance. First, we take teachers for granted as fixtures in our lives. Second, we often have difficulty separating what happens or happened with actual teachers with whom we or our children or our friends' or relatives' children have daily contact from the teachers we study. Our own relationships with teachers shape our understanding; the relationships of our reading audiences with their teachers shapes their understanding. Teachers cannot be extracted from ordinary life.

While they are public figures, their lack of occupational status and power affects how the public knows and characterizes them. Many of us may have had good experiences with individual doctors, for example, but have little problem categorizing the medical profession as power-centered, insensitive to the needs of patients, and a vehicle for status mobility. This analysis does not ignore the presence of good individual doctors. It argues that the occupation of doctoring carries a different reputation from that of its individual members. While consumer movements have changed the relationship of many doctors and patients, doctors continue to hold power. Doctors are positioned differently from teachers vis-à-vis the public.

These features of women teachers—that they are publicly positioned, with authoritative power over the lives of children, and quintessentially representative of a gendered occupation for women—account for the lack of research about them during the 1970s. The lives of women teachers held little interest during the 1970s for feminists studying women's work (important exceptions include Lightfoot, 1977; Sklar, 1973). Teachers' work represented rather than challenged the position of women in the society. Women who had been seriously exploited or who were unusually successful attracted more interest. Collections on women and work centered on working-class women who had been marginalized in American culture (e.g., Baxandall, Gordon, & Reverby, 1976). Feminists explored what the lives were like of women who were intensely supervised and monitored, like telephone operators (Langer, 1972), and the more unusual cases of women who were successful in fields of science and mathematics (Kundsin, 1974). In feminist scholarship on work, administrators attracted more attention than teachers, although in practice anti-sexist teaching training was important and ongoing (Biklen & Brannigan, 1980; Estler, 1975). The focus on teaching was first expanded by the work of sociologists of education and feminist historians (Antler & Biklen, 1990; Apple, 1986; Hoffman, 1981; Kaufman, 1984; Perkins, 1987; Sterling, 1984).

Sociologically, teachers were conceptualized as neither workers nor management. Not only were they not exploited workers, they sometimes rejected the notion of being considered workers at all, preferring to be considered professionals, a circumstance that raised questions of voice. Teachers are a central feature in the everyday lives of any family with school-age children. This mainstream location offers a plurality of possibility. They can coproduce cultural containment as well as reproduce their future selves in girls in their classrooms. They can also coproduce liberation, not just by explicitly countersexist teaching, but in their central work of developing educated women who are later in a position to see through some of the contradictions of their lot.

Representing Gender

Feminists have searched for ways of studying how gender works for teachers, and how teaching has worked for women, without making these meanings constant. Feminist historians, for example, have argued that in contrast to its meanings during the past 30 years, teaching during the nineteenth century was a radicalizing activity for women (Clifford, 1981, 1987; Shakeshaft, 1985). Teaching provided Lucy Larcom, author of *A New England Girlhood* (1889/1961), with an occupation that centered around learning and knowing. Before one could become a teacher,

> one must know something first. I must acquire knowledge before I could impart it, and that was just what I wanted. I could be a student, wherever I was and whatever else I had to be or do, and I would! (p. 161)

It took her six or seven years to learn enough to break away from mill work and become a teacher (Woody, 1929, p. 490). Both Lucy Stone and Susan B. Anthony first entered the public world through teaching, Susan B. Anthony in 1835, at age 15, teaching a summer session, and Lucy Stone in 1834, at age 16, for $1 a week and "boarding around" (Barry, 1988). Both pioneers of women's rights left teaching, however, because the occupation came to frustrate them. Even as they rejected it, teaching had expanded their futures.

A current methodological issue for feminists studying women teachers centers around the difficulties of studying the meanings of gender through the work of individual teachers. I have stated that my approach was to spend time with teachers when they were working with other adults. I chose this frame because the work of ordinary teachers interested me. Another important approach has been to study women teachers who are also feminists (Casey, 1993; Middleton, 1993; Weiler, 1988).

Weiler studied the struggles of women teachers to do what she called "feminist counter-hegemony" (1988, p. 101). Her teachers were conscious of being gendered subjects, that is, persons who were shaped by discourses about gender. These secondary school teachers described their classrooms as places "where consciousness is interrogated, where meanings are questioned, and means of analysis and criticism of the social world as well as of a text or assignment are encouraged" (p. 114). These teachers engaged with their students over questions of experience, interpretation, and action. Weiler argued that as multilayered subjects, the teachers had contradictory understandings of oppression, and were sometimes unable to disentangle the "conflicting" demands of race and class with gender (pp. 126–127).

Middleton's study of New Zealand feminist teachers used a life history approach to explore the meaning of feminist teaching at many levels and in different contexts. Her self-interrogative study examines how women who became teachers were regulated as students in the discursive practices of their secondary schools. She sets up contrapuntal dialogues between different voices, including feminist teachers in secondary schools and academic feminists teaching teachers. Middleton's own voice as negotiator, teacher, and actor engages in this dialogue.

Casey also focused on women working for social change, though here, social change refers to more than feminist work. She framed her work around the life histories of three groups of teachers: Catholic women religious, secular Jewish women, and black women. She explored their identities, most coherent as a group among the Catholic women religious, and their politics. Central to her discussion of the language her life history informants use is her analytical debt to Bakhtin (1981). While she examined language to see how social discourses intersect, she did not strip the teachers of their intentions and consciousness. Life events carried different meanings for her informants. Some of the African-American teachers she studied described their own education as a form of resistance. Themes among secular Jewish women articulated how their experience of "the best" segregated schools triggered their own opposition to the many different forms of segregated education.

The examination of feminist teachers freed Weiler, Middleton, and Casey from considering how teaching is enacted in women's lives. I did have this problem because I was studying teachers who were not only progressive, but who were also conservative, temporary, traditional. The range of teachers' perspectives and situations made it more difficult for me to suggest feminist revisions.

Their research, like mine, is connected to the explosion of recent work on gender, teaching, and voice. Grumet (1988) explored contradictions in the lives of women teachers, how teaching was structured by patriarchy, and pedagogical issues, based on materialist and psychoanalytic theory. A collection of chapters edited by Acker (1989) on gender in the working careers of teachers emphasized how teachers' work is constrained by institutional structures and how teachers resist and negotiate these structures (see also Miller, 1990). The centrality of gender to teaching is illustrated in Altenbaugh's (1993) collection on *The Teacher's Voice;* the first section of the book is entitled "Women's Work."

Issues of Power and Resistance

I did not frame this study of teachers around the ways teachers resisted injustice. Resistance is not central to the definition/occupation of teaching, although many teachers have resisted others connected to their site of work in order to teach well. Teachers have opposed unions in order to fight racism and enable students of the Ocean Hill-Brownsville district in New York City to have an education. Individually, teachers have opposed administrators, parents, and other teachers in order to teach justly and well. But it is not just through resistance that teachers can express their commitments to equality or to a good education for all of their students. Teachers can experiment with new practices, insist on including children who have been excluded from school, spot children who need attention and give them the kind of attention they need, or provide stimulating education to demanding students.

Teachers have power over children; they use this power, ideally, to help children develop incrementally. They focus on the daily, specific details: the shape of the letter L, the crook of the 'f.' They do this, however, with an eye toward the future. Learning how to write an L is valuable when it goes with other letters, words, and sentences that enable students to express themselves and influence others.

Teachers do not always use their power over children well. Teachers need to manage many children in a class, and sometimes they show insensitivity to particular children. Like other street-level bureaucrats, they often do "the best they can" within a structure that disempowers students; the best they can do in the situation is bad. They participate in the school's role in reproducing social relationships.

Willard Waller (1932), in fact, pointed to the problem of control and to the conflict-ridden relations of teachers and students as the cause of this problem:

> In analyzing the opinion people have of teachers, it is necessary to reckon with the teacher stereotype which partly reflects and partly determines that opinion. This stereotype apparently represents a caricature of the methods used by the teacher to maintain control over children. . . . This problem of control arises, of course, out of the necessity of conducting schools along the lines of teacher domination and pupil subordination. From the means which the teacher has to use to obtain control and to keep it arises a generalized conception of the school teacher which perdures in the minds of all the graduates of the school. The idealized conception tends to become a caricature, and an unpleasant and belittling caricature, because a real enmity exists between teacher and taught, and this enmity transmutes the

work of memory into irony. In accordance with this theory, each generation of teachers pays in its turn for the sins of the generation that has gone before; it would require some decades of sensible and friendly teaching to remove the stigma from the occupation. (pp. 58–59)

This stereotype portrays teachers as defenders of order and control.

As the women I studied worked, and negotiated the process of making meaning of it, my concern centered on how to examine their words and the contextual frames that gave their words particular meanings. Toni Morrison (1987) captured in her novel *Beloved* the tensions I encountered between studying the teachers' voices as their own (emphasizing their agency) and attending to the social discourses that influenced what the voices represented (emphasizing structural regulations). She describes how Sethe tried to assert some ownership over her work:

> she who had to bring a fistful of salsify into Mrs. Garner's kitchen every day just to be able to work in it, feel like some part of it was hers, because she wanted to love the work she did, to take the ugly out of it, and the only way she could feel at home on Sweet Home was if she picked some pretty growing thing and took it with her. The day she forgot was the day butter wouldn't come or the brine in the barrel blistered her arms. (p. 22)

Even though she was a slave caught in an oppressive world, she wanted to make what she created meaningful to her as well as assert some ownership over it. She soon realized its impossibility: "As though a handful of myrtle stuck in the handle of a pressing iron propped against the door in a whitewoman's kitchen could make it hers. As though mint sprig in the mouth changed the breath as well as its odor. A bigger fool never lived" (pp. 23–24).

This idea, that one tries to claim a hostile environment by decorating it or putting one's own things in it to shape and change it, captures the uneasy position of contemporary women teachers. They are caught between the institution, which is not theirs, and the desire to do important work with their own stamp on it. There is also the issue of how teachers contribute not just to the education of the students in their own classrooms, but also, at some times, to shaping the institution in ways that might contribute to a better social practice.

Our scholarship needs to attend to the complexity of this relationship. We need to study the placing of the sprig *and* the sites and discourses that define the need for sprigs. In this book I attempt to examine how women in teaching try to make teaching their own, without ignoring the discourses that shape how they represent teaching to themselves and each other.

ORGANIZATION OF THE BOOK

The chapters in this book draw on the very different sorts of data I have described, so that my discussion of gender and teaching might benefit from both their range and differences. Chapter 2 uses fieldnotes from participant observation and interviews to discuss women's work commitment. Chapter 3 depends on archival texts for its description of how teaching served women in the nineteenth century. Chapter 4 explores the question of autonomy and agency in the lives of nine-teenth- and twentieth-century teachers through fictional and autobio-graphical texts as well as through the words of contemporary teachers. Chapter 5 considers two novels about teachers written in the 1950s, one the well-known *Good Morning, Miss Dove*, the other the un-known *Aggie*, to investigate questions about teaching, identity, and race in the fictional representation of teaching. Chapter 6 returns again to the participant observation data to analyze the conflicts between mothers and women teachers in a school located in a highly pro-fessionalized community. Chapter 7 continues the reflection on the qualitative data to study how teachers talk about and through their relationships with each other, particularly around conflicts and com-munity-building. In the concluding chapter I discuss other educational discourses that intersect with those of gender which teachers draw upon for their own analytical frames. In addition to my examination of talk and assumptions that constrain teachers, I end with a focus on feminism and other discourses of possibility.

The image of teaching as a domestic occupation reflects more the gendered ordering of social relationships and the social position of children than it does the work itself, or the way women in this occupa-tion talk about their work. Meanings are created in the contexts of the informants' and writers' worlds. These contexts are both historically specific and capable of change. When particular popular constructions (such as the asexual teacher) last through generations, only the strength of the image is revealed, not its immutability.

CHAPTER 2

Can Elementary Schoolteaching Be a Career?

Clare Fox, a 1984 Brown University graduate, wanted to become a teacher but found little support for the idea from family and friends. Upon graduation, she wrote a letter seeking advice from a former well-remembered teacher, Margaret Treece Metzger:

> I am told that I didn't have to go to Brown University to become a teacher. I am told that teaching is a "wonderful thing to do until you decide what you really want to do with your life." I am told that it's "nice" that I'm going to be a teacher. (Metzger & Fox, 1986, p. 349)

Her own advisers equated a teaching career with a failure of ambition: "Why does it seem that the decision to teach in our society is analogous with the decision to stunt one's growth, to opt out intellectually in favor of long summers off?" (p. 349) Why, in other words, are teachers not taken seriously? Clare Fox herself shares these cultural constructions when she agrees that "going to work for a big corporation — whether an advertising firm, a bank, or a publishing house — impresses me. It would seem 'real,' 'grown-up,' as teaching never will" (p. 350). Metzger's response contrasts the internal rewards of teaching with some of its external problems (and aggravations) as she describes the stimulation of the work. Her advice reflected these tensions: "Although you have to come to some terms with the outward flatness of the career, I want to assure you that teachers change and grow" (p. 351).

Both Fox and Metzger struggle with the nature of teaching as work as well as with the quality of teaching as a career. They both confront the inadequacy and limitations of the sociological vocabulary to describe the nature of this work. Fox insists that teaching does not appear "grown-up." Metzger advises that the external structure of the occupation does not reflect its internal rewards. Is teaching a real career? Is it grown-up work or does its relationship to children forever infantalize it?

This chapter investigates these questions to explore the nature of teaching as work, first examining the fit of teaching within the sociological definition of career, and then comparing the meanings of career the social science literature and society produce with those constructed by women who teach at Vista City Elementary School. Informants' life stories suggest that the prevailing concept inadequately frames and reflects these women's lives. Teachers recognize that the work they do does not add up to a professional career. Those at Vista City saw, as the only corrective, more recognition for their work and heightened social position. To these ends, many wanted their professionalism expanded and enhanced. This chapter explores as well as critiques this attraction. What concepts do career and professionalism take for granted? How does the relationship to children shape the occupation's definition? What do teachers understand about the teaching reputation? Why does teaching not seem like grown-up work? These questions help focus the discussion of career and professionalism.

DEFINING A CAREER

Professional careers that carry high social status are made possible by domestic and occupational social relationships that depend on certain uses of time. We measure careers by the stages they go through, by the training they require, and by the success (whether monetary, prestigious, or fame-related) they achieve. Calling on Hall's (1948) study of medical careers, Becker describes how careers are commonly understood as

> the patterned series of adjustments made by the individual to the "network of institutions, formal organizations, and informal relationships" in which the work of occupations is performed. This series of adjustments is typically considered in terms of movement up or down between positions differentiated by their rank in some formal or informal hierarchy of prestige, influence, and income. (Becker, 1952/1970, p. 165)

Becker distances himself from endorsing the traditional definition by describing careers as a "series of adjustments." This phrase almost belittles a career; at least it whittles it down to a kind of mechanical process. Bledstein (1976), on the other hand, calls on shared social acceptance for the status of the career when he describes it as "a pre-established total pattern of organized professional activity, with upward movement through recognized preparatory stages, and advancement based on merit and bearing honor" (p. 172). This view emphasizes the coherence of the career and the goal orientation of the career occupant.

"Career" has also been used to describe a sequence of changes in people's—any people's—lives. In this use it refers to various positions, stages, and ways of thinking that people pass through in the course of their lives. It emphasizes the participants' perspectives on life. In this mode, one can refer to the career of a juvenile delinquent, a waitress, a drug user (Hughes, 1937). Qualitative researchers have been attracted to this use of career because it offers a handy organizational scheme to understand how changes in subjects' lives are related to each other. It is also a democratizing concept because anyone can have a career. Although the traditional definition has been applied to the structure of particular careers, such as the medical, the legal, and the academic (e.g., Hall, 1948; Lortie, 1959; Wilson, 1942), this alternative way is both deregulating and deflating—it deflates the importance of separating some kinds of work from others by professional qualification. It deregulates because it pushes scholars to take all kinds of work seriously.

Several important features of professional careers predominate. First, careers take place in the public sphere and are measured by an individual's participation in the wage-labor system and the status that accrues from that participation. These definitions of career make no mention of family life because family life was not considered intrinsic to the career. Work and family, in other words, are separate. Men's instrumental role in families has enabled them to participate in the family structure by working; hence, enhanced career commitment could be read as family devotion. Wives who never saw their husbands and children who missed their fathers may have read their work orientations differently, but sociologically, the father's role as family man was not necessarily in conflict with career mobility. And when we speak of a man's family problems slowing down his career advancement, or point to different responses of ethnic groups to this model— such as Italian American men who resist moving away from communities where their extended families reside—we are simultaneously acknowledging the existence of a real-life problem and reinforcing this definition of career.

The situation is turned on end for women. Their work and family life are oppositional, positioned at opposite ends of the same continuum that frames a woman's contribution to the workforce in relationship to the family. Even though the woman's financial contribution is essential to the lives of many families, her reputation as a mother bears little relationship to her contribution. Single working mothers, for example, always strive to be "good mothers," meaning attentive to their children, even as they work full-time. Evaluations of the relationship between one's ability to provide for a family and one's participation in family life are embedded in historically specific circumstances. We now tend to discriminate between a father's ability to generate income for a family and the amount of time he is at home or sets aside for family life.

A woman's career commitment is measured by the amount of time she devotes to work as opposed to family. Some occupations are said to enable the meshing of these worlds more easily than others, though this understanding is in question (Glass, 1990; Huber, 1990). As more women have entered professional careers, they have had to find ways to integrate family and work life, give up family life as they knew it, or change their workplaces (unless they drop out of or slow down their careers).

A second feature of this definition is career commitment. "Commitment" means dedication to and identification with one's work. Career commitment has two major aspects, both of which relate to time. The first aspect is long-term commitment. Here, career commitment refers to the decision to undertake a career in the first place. Careers are envisioned as trajectories that may start at some lower stage or position but always have a higher goal in mind. Hence, when Clare Fox decides to become a teacher rather than a corporate executive (or even a teacher rather than a school principal), she will not only find herself in a less lucrative position, but she must face criticism because she is said to have lowered her career commitment (Nieva & Gulick, 1981). Researchers who study this form of career commitment are interested in the length of time a woman plans to work and in her career goals. Ward Mason, for example, measured teachers' career commitment by asking them where they planned to be, professionally, five years hence (Mason, 1961). In this frame, those who wanted to remain in teaching had more commitment than those who dropped out to raise a family; those who saw themselves as principals had more commitment than those who saw themselves remaining in the teaching role.

Another aspect of career commitment relates to the short-term use of time for work. One common yardstick for differentiating occupations from professional careers, for example, is the career's tendency to spill over the nine-to-five time slot. Jobs are defined by hours, the saying goes, but not careers. Medical careers exemplify such demands:

> Central to the status of a profession is a field's ability to induce members to do their job no matter how long it takes and no matter what other demands are made on their lives. These requirements are stringent in medicine, where lives may be at stake in the physician's decision about how high a priority should be given to finishing a job. (Bourne & Wilker, 1982, p. 122)

Current notions of the professional career include heavy workloads and large time commitments. Women breaking into professional careers must understand these requirements and give them priority in their lives in order to succeed (Fox & Hesse-Biber, 1984; Kahn-Hut, Daniels, & Colvard, 1982).

The perspective just described positions women in tension with a stable, coherent phenomenon called a "career" that can be described, envied, and vetted. When women express and exhibit career commitment, they must reckon with both these perspectives and their position (as newcomers or intruders, depending on one's point of view) and consider the implications: Their biographies rather than the structure of the career are expected to alter. How will they handle their families? How will they reconcile the masculine world of work with feminine identities? How can they remove gender from evaluations of their work? All of these questions assume that the structural foundations of careers are stable though flexible.

Against this external and traditional view, elementary schoolteaching measures up as less than a full career. It has been described both as "careerless" and as an occupation of "lateral careers." It has been labeled "careerless" because until recently (and even now not nationally), the occupation of teaching was structured without the possibility of promotion within teaching. Advancement meant becoming an administrator and leaving teaching. Additionally, teaching is structured to accommodate the in-and-out patterns of women's employment. That is, "to persist in teaching is, in a sense, to be 'passed over' for higher position or marriage" (Lortie, 1975, p. 89; see also Becker, 1952/1970). In the framework of career, elementary schoolteaching, as Clare Fox discovered when she looked to friends and relatives for advice, does not loom large.

Part of the problem in establishing elementary schoolteaching as a career is its precarious position in relation to the elite professions. Teaching, nursing, and social work, labeled "semiprofessions" (Etzioni,

1969), are differentiated from "full" professions by shorter training, a lack of control over technical knowledge, lower status, less right to privileged communication, and decreased autonomy from supervision or societal control. Teaching, like other semiprofessions, is women's work.

TEACHERS AND THE REPUTATION OF TEACHING

When comparing this categorization of career to how women who teach understand their working lives, some discrepancies emerge. Most of the women who taught at Vista City Elementary School understood the social reputation of their work, as I will show shortly, but they did not conceptualize their working careers, particularly their career commitment, in a way that reflected the traditional categories sociologists use. DeVault (1990) has suggested that categories of language "are often incongruent with women's lives." Because of this "linguistic incongruence," we can have difficulty finding categories that fit certain kinds of work. Studying women's work helps to expand and change the categories and vocabulary available to analyze work. In her research on all the processes and meanings connected to the work women do in feeding their families, DeVault moved from categorizing her topic as "housework" to "providing food" to "the work of feeding a family" to "feeding." She could take from the sociological literature no category that fit her topic, although she examined an activity central to the lives of those she studied: "Looking back, I can see that I identified in a rough way a category that made sense to my respondents because it was a category that organized their day to day activity" (p. 99). Roberts and Barker (1989) found similar difficulties when they asked people to rank women's work. "The level of information given to respondents asked to grade men's occupations is seen as insufficient when people are asked to grade women's work" (p. 130). Is the housewife, for example, engaged in full-time or part-time work? The incongruities and inconsistencies this lack of fit suggests emerge in the reputation of teaching.

How do teachers view the social value of their work? Some of their methods of evaluation are direct. They compare how much less money they make in relation to other professionals in society. Some are less direct. They consider how their work looks in the eyes of others. Here I want to examine how teachers see their work reflected in the perspectives of two groups: the public at large and those who supervise teachers.

The Public Perspective

Feminism helped to create rising expectations among women for job opportunities with higher status and better pay. Teachers, too, were caught up in this tide, including some of those at Vista City Elementary School. The popular press (e.g., "Teachers Are in Trouble," *Newsweek*, April 27, 1981) has carried articles noting teachers' low social esteem; education scholars have noted it as well. Women studying to be teachers at Yale, for example, before the university dropped its master of teaching program, revealed that while they were interested in the program, they "dreaded the 'intellectual insult of being undergraduate education majors'" (Sarason, 1982, p. 65). Their dilemma, as Metzger noted in her letter to Clare Fox, reflected an internal appreciation of teaching that conflicted with its external devaluation.

One Vista City teacher accounted for why "teachers usually get a lot of bad press" from the public at large. The public did not understand the work of teaching:

> How difficult it is to be a teacher. Teachers are underpaid and
> undervalued. How many people end the day after working
> nine to five at some corporation and go home and just sob be-
> cause their work was so hard. Nobody understands what it's
> like to work around children all day—how hard it is and what
> it does to you.

This kindergarten teacher felt that the public did not realize how emotionally draining it was to work with children. Children are a special population.

The appearance of the work could deceive if it were measured only by the required hours of work:

> Teaching looks easy from the outside. I went into the bank
> the other day at a little after two [o'clock] and the teller said
> to me, "Ha, how do you like that—two o'clock and here you
> are out and my wife has to stay downtown and work until
> five." I said, "Yeah, but you don't know what I do all day."
> That's what it looks like from the outside: the hours, the sum-
> mer vacation—and people don't know what it's like to be re-
> sponsible for thirty kids for six hours every day. It's very, very
> difficult.

This first-grade teacher reflected the position that many teachers find themselves in, always explaining to others how their work is more demanding than it looks. They feel on the defensive.

Teachers also feel that public sympathy for teachers centers too heavily on school problems such as violence, drugs, and race relations. This focus detracts attention from the struggles that arise even in a school where morale is high and relations among people are good. As one second-grade teacher said, "People emphasize the bad part of teaching too much these days. You know, it's hard enough teaching a class when you don't have discipline problems. That's what the public doesn't understand." From the elementary schoolteacher's perspective, the public lacks understanding of what the costs are of constant attention to children.

The teachers' resentment arose from their uncertainty as to whether the public viewed them as serious workers. Teaching well, as one of the teachers said, is challenging even when the class has few discipline problems. Vista City teachers did not want teaching to be undervalued (or underpaid). They wanted recognition that they worked diligently at challenging positions, and they wanted the status such a reevaluation would bring.

The discourse of reform emphasizes changing, by many means, the ways in which teachers are perceived by transforming the vocabulary for, and hence public perspectives of, their work. This approach reflects progressive efforts as well as more mainstream approaches. Henry Giroux (1988), for example, calls for teachers to be "transformative intellectuals," a label that builds on higher-status mental powers rather than lower-status nurturing ones. One might argue, as Sara Ruddick (1989) has done, that nurturing as a maternal act involves thinking and theorizing, which are intellectual activities, but Giroux does not suggest by his writing that this is what he means. The effect of this emphasis is to defeminize teaching and hence to raise its status.

Teachers at Vista City rarely suggested that the status of elementary schoolteaching was related to the categorization of their occupation as women's work. Usually they were too busy defending and explaining the seriousness of their work. So although they gave examples of how their work was gendered, they did not name it as such. Other reasons they offered for the lower status of teaching included the view that teachers were powerless public servants (in contrast to politicians). They also argued that the many mediocre people in teaching detracted from the reputations of those were "more professional," that is, better at their work. Some teachers did suggest that working with children was not socially valued and that consequently it was difficult either to make money in teaching or to receive social recognition.

Increased consciousness about women's roles also affected teachers' occupational evaluations. A second-grade teacher, for example, said that the women's movement made her more conscious that teaching had low status as a profession and that she could do something "better," such as finding a position in "business management" or administration, where the "pay is more and the status is better." She felt uncomfortable that the public looked down on women who taught "now that there is an impetus for women to do more."

A music teacher felt torn between her recognition of this negative evaluation and the pleasure her occupation brought. She knew, she said, that there was "very little status in teaching," and that if she were to choose a career again, she did not know if teaching would be it. She said: "It's a funny thing. I'm caught in this. I love my work. I love teaching, but I wish teaching had more recognition and that people cared about it more."

Teachers developed strategies to handle themselves with the public. Some tried to convince themselves that self-evaluations were most important. A kindergarten teacher said: "Other people don't consider us professionals like doctors or lawyers. But I do!" Others complained and wished for an alternative: "I want respect from others about what I do. I'm in my forties now, and I know I can do this well. I want other people to value what I do." Another strategy was to argue with friends who denigrated teaching. One teacher challenged her friends who teased her about short hours and long vacations:

> You get to go to the bathroom whenever you want to. If you're not feeling so great one day, or if you're feeling down in the dumps, you can take a two-hour lunch. We don't have the flexibility to arrange our lives that way. When we're in bad spirits, we still have to come in and be 100 percent there for the kids.

These teachers tended to compare up to elite professions rather than down to working-class positions. They see increased talk of accountability and diagnosis, combined with public and governmental discourse on the importance of education, as indicative of the increased professionalization of the field. Apple suggests that teachers have confused managing students and making technical decisions with increased professionalism (Apple, 1983, p. 620).

One of the most dangerous strategies to handle public disdain was occupational camouflage. Some teachers never revealed their occupation in settings and with people they did not read as receptive. One teacher whose husband was a corporate executive lied about her occupation when people discussed work at parties. She said, "When people make terrible comments about teachers, the last thing I'm going to do is tell everybody I'm a teacher." This strategy rendered her an invisible worker.

Reading the Administrators' Perspectives

Teachers read their relationship with the central administration as well as with the public as indicative of their devalued status. Most if not all of the teachers at Vista City viewed the low level of staff development programs as evidence of "downtown's" view of teacher competence. During the year I observed at Vista City Elementary, most teachers referred bitterly to a particularly demeaning in-service session as symbolic of their position.

All elementary schoolteachers had met in a large auditorium for a session on the importance of writing in the curriculum. At the start of the session, a new curriculum was handed out to the "one thousand or so" teachers sitting in the audience, and they were told to open to the table of contents. They did so, and the speaker on the stage then read the table of contents out loud. After he finished that, he read the curriculum for the fourth-grade level. The teachers, with the material resting on their laps, had listened to almost forty-five minutes of reading, and "were beside [themselves] with wrath." From where the audience sat, "downtown" must see them as incompetent and illiterate; otherwise, why would the sessions be so unsatisfactory? While teachers saw downtown as incompetent, they recognized that "downtown" administrators had once been teachers. Since most of the teachers I interviewed did not clearly perceive movement into administration as advancement, their dissatisfaction suggested that poor teachers must be promoted. However, they still read their own devaluation into this treatment.

This view that they were not valued was echoed widely around the school. Teachers felt that good in-service training should provide "stimulation" and "rejuvenation" for teachers. One teacher commented that because she took her job seriously, she wanted these sessions to stimulate her, to give her "new ideas." But the session in which an administrator had read the curriculum out loud offended her: "We obviously know how to read. What is it? They think we can't read? They don't respect us. Part of the reason for that is that people who go into administration are usually neither good teachers themselves nor very fond of teachers. And they run the show!" Teachers felt that central administrators were "out of touch" with what teachers did in classrooms because they did not respect them.

Special education teachers also felt devalued by how the administration treated them. Teachers complained of a variety of circumstances and policies, including lack of feedback for hard work or innovative programming, as well as the high paperwork demands. After a teacher had spent substantial time preparing a detailed "write-up" on each child in her class, she was asked by the downtown special education office to fill out a short checklist on the same issues. The checklist "did not reveal anything at all about a child." She was convinced that her earlier painstaking descriptions would sit unread in a drawer. The central office did not respect teachers' time.

Teachers did not suggest an alternative view of their treatment by the central administration. For example, one could read the in-service programs and the special education paperwork as resulting from increased bureaucratization of schooling or administrative incompetency. But even if teachers did read it this way, they would do so against their image of the elite professions. I want to look at the contrast between the external vocabulary for career and teachers' resistance to it. While they understood their low status, they had an alternative understanding for the structure of their work lives. They resisted the definition of career, in other words, by an alternate picturing of their work histories.

The Teachers' Perspective

From the start of this study, a contradiction emerged between teachers' descriptions of their work histories and the actual details of those histories. Asked to describe their work experiences, teachers would often begin with the statement, "I have always worked." In the early stages of my research, I would form a mental picture of a person who had worked continuously in a full-time position and had a career goal in sight. Yet, as informants provided chronological details of their work lives, they almost always described a discontinuous pattern: full-time teaching that had been interrupted for childbearing and/or part-time work, followed by reentry into the full-time employment market. Surprisingly, they often ended their work histories by reiterating that they had always worked.

Redefining commitment. Kate Bridges, a Vista City teacher in her mid-forties, described her occupational commitment in these words: "I have felt passionately about teaching for twenty years." She had not taught continuously, however, for twenty years. She "loved" her first two years of teaching, which took place in an "inner-city kind of school." After she had children of her own, however, she sought part-time positions in a nursery school, a college education department, and a drug rehabilitation center, all in different cities. During this period, she also earned a Master of Arts in Teaching degree.

As her children grew older, Kate noticed the shrinking job market for elementary teachers. A job opportunity arose, and although she had been planning to go to Europe with her husband, an architecture professor on sabbatical, she decided to take it. "If I don't accept this job now," she felt, "God knows if I will ever get my foot in the door." In resisting pressure from her husband to arrange her own work plans around his schedule, Kate communicated the importance of her work in their lives. Although the position restarted a full-fledged teaching career, she also considered that she had been interested in, involved with, and thinking about teaching for twenty years. In this frame of reference, she had shown internal occupational consistency in a world in which for middle-class white women, working and mothering were not socially facilitated. She had always thought of herself as a teacher.

Kate had worked hard for two decades, and some of this work had involved teaching children in schools. But she had not always been able to translate her passion for teaching into occupational reality. Although she had always considered herself a teacher, she had not always been engaged in full-time teaching. As Kate and her colleagues saw it, however, bearing and caring for one's own children did not necessarily reflect on one's career commitment. When these women were not actually engaged in teaching, they kept in touch with colleagues at their former workplaces and thus remained informed about school events, they sometimes ran day care centers in their homes or engaged in other kinds of educational work with children, they kept their subscriptions to their teaching journals, they continued to think of themselves as teachers, and they planned to return to teaching. In other words, their internal conceptions of themselves as teachers remained consistent.

When the time came to return to work, many of those women who had been out of the classroom for five or more years found that locating a teaching position was not their only problem. Husbands had a major impact on how married teachers made decisions about work. Some teachers used Kate's method and spoke to their husbands directly about their career interests. But other women had husbands who obstructed their return to work. The case studies of three such women reveal the strategies they developed to overcome their husbands' resistance.

Sylvia Richardson, now in her fifties, taught seventh graders for five years, followed by a nine-year hiatus devoted to childrearing, after which she returned to teaching. Her husband had opposed her return. "We're not for this women's lib thing," she explained. But he supported her decision to become a substitute teacher, a port of entry she figured provided her an opportunity to ease her way in, since she would be able to turn down opportunities to work when it suited her (him?).

A teacher friend offered invaluable advice: "Don't substitute in the seventh grade, because the students have really changed since you were there." Sylvia decided that if seventh and eighth graders were more troublesome and if substituting would, therefore, offer frequent occasions for her husband to say, "We don't need this aggravation. Come on home," she had better pick a group that would be less demanding.

So Sylvia began to substitute in the elementary grades. Gradually she escalated her availability until she was substituting daily, a circumstance that caused her husband to relent and endorse her return to full-time teaching. "At least we'll know where to find you," he told her.

Sylvia Richardson strategized in order to return to teaching. That is, she chose certain ways to act and rejected others so that she could get her way, overcome her husband's resistance, and continue her work as a teacher. The economics of our times also affected the material conditions of her life and made her choice more attractive. First, she chose a grade level that would be less "difficult" than junior high school, so that she would not be tempted to burden her husband with her occupational concerns. Second, she started as a substitute teacher, an action that provided him some time to adjust to her working outside the home.

Jessica Bonwit's strategy was more determined but perhaps more personally costly. She had also left teaching to rear her three children (though she operated a day care program in her home during this period). "Something went 'click' after six years," and she knew that she had to return to the classroom. Her husband shared neither the household work with her nor her interest in her continuing teaching. Jessica promised him that her return to work would not require increased effort on his part. "He didn't mind so much when I went back to work because his life didn't change at all," she explained.

Jessica paid a price for her return to full-time teaching, and she resented her husband's selfishness. "I love my husband, but sometimes I don't like him very much," she said. She valued teaching enough to shoulder full responsibility for both classroom and home.

Carrie Amundsen did not work outside the home before her children were born. Like Sylvia and Jessica, however, she had to develop a strategy in order to enter the workforce as a full-time employee later on. Because she had never completed her bachelor's degree, she enrolled in a mathematics course at a local university. Her goal at the time was only enrichment, but she enjoyed the course and "ended up taking more of them." After completing an undergraduate degree in reading, she earned a master's degree in special education.

By this time Carrie was eager to put her training to use. However, when a former professor who was starting a special program in the schools offered her a position, she responded, "My husband will never let me work full-time." "Let me worry about your husband," her future employer responded. So Carrie and her professor "worked out a deal" whereby she would tell her husband that she intended to try working for just one year. At the end of that first year, Carrie "weaseled" her way into one more year, and then another, and another. She and her ally, the professor, had developed a way to handle her husband. The family was intact and Carrie was working as a teacher.

All three women developed methods that allowed them to engage in full-time work as teachers and remain in intact families. When the time seemed right, each translated her mental commitment into an occupational reality. While they were away from the classroom, two of these women ran day care programs in their homes. These two stayed in touch with their colleagues and discussed classroom and organizational life with them. They continued their subscriptions to magazines such as *Instructor* that concerned primary instruction. All of them planned to return to full-time work, and they developed strategies to overcome their husbands' obstructionism.

To the outsider, these women appear to lack career commitment because of the incongruence between the social science concepts and their positions. From traditional sociological perspectives, these teachers balanced teaching responsibilities on the fulcrum of family life. These perspectives, however, have taken male working patterns as normative. Measures of career commitment do not take realities of women's lives into account. By contrast, the women see themselves exhibiting both commitment and coherence in their working lives.

Gender and race at work. The teachers in the above examples were European American. They thought about, negotiated, and constructed their relationships to their families around cultural, class, and community norms. Even when they complained about or attempted to resist constraints on themselves as participants in the public economy, they did so around particular understandings of the good mother, good child care, and women's responsibilities. This pattern, connected to sanctioned understandings of childrearing sensibilities, was not reflected in the lives of all the women who taught at Vista City Elementary. An African-American teacher did not share either the same organizational strategies for juggling childrearing and work, or the same constraints on family organization.

Before becoming an instructional specialist, Barbara Timmitts had been an outstanding teacher at the school. Teachers with very different beliefs about teaching continually mentioned her name in connection with her exemplary work, her high standards, and her accessibility. Her promotion to instructional specialist related to her reputation as well as to her eventual interest in becoming a principal. Barbara discussed in interviews her ambivalence about the principalship; she had already rejected such an offer once because she felt she was not "ready." Like other teachers, she was worried about work that took her "too far away from children." At the same time, she was interested in advancing in the school system.

Barbara was very interested in the study, and I spoke with her on many occasions. Unlike all the other teachers I interviewed, however, Barbara always referred to our children at the beginning of each meeting, each time she saw me. We spent significant amounts of time discussing babysitting, day care, and the benefits and disadvantages of different child care arrangements. She was the only teacher I came to know through this research whose children's names I knew. She always asked after my children by name as well, particularly after my daughter, who was then in day care.

I read these interchanges at the time in a particular way, and I think I read them wrong. Then, I did not want to talk about child care with Barbara; I was interested in her perspectives on her work. I also wondered if these conversations might signify that she did not take me and my work seriously. My frustrations with how central our children were to our relationship were real, but I did not investigate them, as I should have done, as a source of data. Barbara's outstanding reputation as a teacher marked her, for me, as an unusual "source" of information about working conditions at the school, how she negotiated with parents and other teachers, and other aspects of themes that were rapidly emerging as significant. If I had considered Barbara's discussions about our children as meaningful for, rather than peripheral to, the research,

I would have realized how similar my position was to Barbara's: the only teacher in the school whose very young children were cared for by others. Barbara may have spoken to me about these issues because she did not trust speaking about them to other teachers, with whom she shared some values but not others, without receiving criticism.

It was not that she would have received criticism, necessarily, but that she was hesitant. Her career pattern was unbroken; she had always worked as a teacher. She planned to be an administrator. I misread her continual talk with me about children as evidence of a flattened interest in the content of her work rather than as a signal of our similar strategies of managing work and family: we both depended on day care, our husbands were active, in different ways, in child care responsibilities, and we both loved our work.

How race works in institutions was an issue in this research. Race did not personally come between Barbara and me around our views toward the relationship of work and family, for in fact we held comparable perspectives. Rather, my insensitivity to its significance at the worksite flattened my portrayal of teachers' work histories. I offer some examples. First, in Barbara's case, I did not explore the role her mother, who lived in the south, played in the child care arrangements: She came north to stay for an extended period of time when the babies were born so that Barbara could return to work after her maternity leave was up. Second, I was not determined enough to interview the other young African-American woman who taught at the school. She was an acquaintance and seemed adverse to talking to me. My holding back from asking her directly to speak with me meant I could not talk to her about her plans for organizing work and family life. Though she did not yet have children while this study was underway, she later did, and gave significant energy to developing a day care center in the school.

Arrangements for child care, the significance of work to one's identity, and the negotiation of home- and school-work are embedded in different cultural, ethnic, class, and familial patterns. These patterns shift for women through different historical moments. Race is significant to these arrangements and should not be overlooked.

The contradictions of upward mobility. We have been accustomed to thinking about coherence in worklife in terms of upward mobility as well as continuous employment. Just as the teachers at Vista City Elementary School questioned why breaks for the bearing and rearing of children should be equated with a lack of career commitment, so they brought a different perspective to the issue of upward mobility.

Those teachers who had reputations as outstanding practitioners brought a high level of idealism to their work. This idealism caused them to work hard to accomplish their goals and thus contributed to their reputations as excellent teachers. At the same time, the work setting frustrated these teachers because it was not ideal. Some of these excellent teachers responded by focusing more strongly on their own classrooms and isolating themselves from other adults in the building. Others brought their idealism to bear on other aspects of the job, such as committee work. In neither case, however, did the idealism of teachers further their careers. On the one hand, teaching affords few opportunities for advancement. At the same time, Vista City teachers placed higher value on teaching ability than on administrative ability. Teachers found few administrators they admired. Most felt that teachers who were promoted to administrative positions were poor or mediocre teachers. Teachers also felt that administrators at the building level were caught between the regulations of the central administration on the one hand and the demands of parents on the other. Vista City teachers tended to think the principalship a powerless position. It was not anchored to great opportunity.

These views reflected limited career opportunity for women as well as their commitment to the individual management of their lives. When they thought about such working patterns as a "career path," they categorized them by the actual practices the work entailed rather than by their viability as signal posts for career advancement. Educational careers as a "series of adjustments" took on, for most women in their positions, the patina of careerism and incompetence. They made judgments based on how the positions looked to them in their situations rather than as positions more generally defined. They looked for alternate forms of career commitment.

One way teachers showed career commitment was through commitment to children. Christine Bart, head of the first-grade team, voiced criticism, not of Barbara Timmitts, the instructional specialist, but of what promotion to an administrative post had accomplished for her. "She was about the best teacher in this school, and she was promoted to pushing a cart down the halls. She walks around with requisition slips and a pencil in her hand. Now what is that?" Bart scorned the effects of this promotion.

One could interpret these comments in several ways. One interpretation critiques Timmitts; she could effectively handle a teaching position but was inadequate to master an administrative post that required more initiative. Hence, she was reduced to "pushing a cart down the halls." An alternative reading of the statement provides a structural criticism of administrative positions; administration is removed from children and wastes the talents of those skilled practitioners who are needed and valued. This was the view to which Vista City teachers subscribed: Children are the core of teaching. One might also see a wholesale rejection of administration here, arising from stereotyped defenses of the status quo or justification of Bart's own immobility. And herein lies a part of the contradictory way in which these teachers represented the career path to themselves. In the same breath, they spoke high praise for excellent administrators and considered them middle managers caught in a giant bureaucracy.

These teachers revealed commitment to teaching well in their daily work by organizing their schedules to benefit children at their own expense. Roberta Blake, a special education teacher, gave up every free period, including lunch, so that her class could be mainstreamed for art, music, and physical education. The teachers for these subjects would only take her students if she were present. Kate Bridges spent a majority of her lunch hours in her classroom correcting the papers that her class had completed during the morning. She asserted that this approach provided "infinitely more mileage" for the children, even though it is taken "out of the teacher's skin." The members of the sixth-grade teaching team asked the principal to schedule all special classes for their students first thing in the morning, so that teachers could have as much continuous time to work with students as possible. Sandra Miller, a first grade teacher, gave up her lunch hour and her time after school for a month in order to administer individual "levels tests" without "stealing" time from her reading groups. Many Vista City teachers attended to teaching well rather than to positioning themselves for a "series of adjustments."

As they saw it, a great teacher had a schoolwide or even districtwide reputation for excellence. That reputation was not determined by style. Great teachers could be strict or lenient, interested in or opposed to, say, learning centers. Great teachers were admired in schools by students, other teachers, parents, and the administrator.

This is not to say that the teachers were uninterested in power. Those who had reputations as great teachers were able to wield more power and thus to strengthen their autonomy. These were important benefits. Power increased formally through such rewards as election to the faculty council or nomination to serve on a districtwide committee, and it increased informally when the principal solicited their views or gave them greater leeway to organize their classrooms and curricula. Given the manner in which schools and school districts are organized, they were not convinced that being a great administrator carried equivalent weight.

TEACHERS AS SOCIAL RESISTERS

Vista City teachers were resisters in many areas of their lives. They resisted framing their worklives to fit social science definitions; for example, they refused to visualize the bearing and nurturing of children as signifying a lack of career commitment. They resisted their husbands' obstructions to their working full-time; and they resisted the view that one could most effectively gain power through upward mobility, which meant distancing themselves from children. Securing a reputation as a great teacher provided an alternative path to power.

One could legitimately ask whether the teachers envisioned themselves in any way as social resisters. Did they have a sense of themselves as a group with shared antagonisms or an articulated rebellion against conventional social norms? No teacher described herself as a resister or presented herself in opposition to group norms. Yet in their individual statements they rejected "commonsense" and sociological methods of evaluating the place of work in their lives. It was as if they had come to think about their work in a way that did not follow convention. Hence they resisted the discourse of work for women even though they did not attempt to pursuade others to act as they did. One can be a resister without making a clear ideological case for what one does.

At the same time that teachers did not see work and family life as oppositional, they were vulnerable to the social devaluation of teaching. This public attitude caused them to doubt their worth as important workers. They desired higher status and wished a firmer footing in the professions would get them there. They were not alone in this wish. Both the Carnegie Commission Report, *A Nation Prepared* (Carnegie Forum on Education and the Economy, 1986) and the Holmes Group report on *Tomorrow's Teachers* (Holmes Group, 1986) wanted to change how Americans think about teachers by creating cadres of professional teachers to improve the quality of teaching and, therefore, of American education. In the process teachers would gain more status and hence more autonomy, higher pay, and greater career opportunities.

IN SEARCH OF A PROFESSIONAL MODEL

In a speech entitled "Is Social Work a Profession?" delivered to the National Conference of Charities and Correction in 1915 (Flexner, 1915), Abraham Flexner argued that social work ought to be considered a profession, but that to become one, it would have to change. In his famous report on medical education published five years earlier, Flexner (1910) had developed, from his visits to individual medical schools around the country, standards that medical education had to meet. These visits generated a model of professional behavior that included what he called "objective standards" to which he could hold up other occupations. One could understand what professions were, he told the social work audience, by looking at the characteristics of professions that were "universally admitted to be such . . . " He suggested that they examine law, medicine, and the ministry and "by analysis extract the criteria with which, at least, one must begin the characterization of the professions" (Flexner, 1915, pp. 577–578). Others have expanded, critiqued, and evaluated this model, some attending to its accuracy, others focusing on the privileges that professionalism brings to those so positioned. Functionalist sociologists of the 1950s who attempted to establish these objective criteria included Cogan (1953), Goode (1957), and Greenwood (1957). Less sentimental views of professions are represented by Becker (1962/1970) and Roth (1974). In addition to Bledstein's (1976) history there is Larson's (1977) Marxist critique.

The arguments around professionalism grew out of the lives of nineteenth-century men engaged in occupations from which women were originally excluded. As so many occupational sociologists and historians have shown, occupations diminish in status as more women populate them. The more elite professions had fewer women. As more women pursued professional positions, they had to negotiate their personal lives with work in a way that men did not. Their social and gendered positions raised different questions for them regarding demeanor, language, action, and family relations. The professional model is a gendered model of privilege; teachers, like those in other borderline professional occupations, have aspired to its privileges. Here we want to look at how teachers made meaning out of professionalism.

Vista City teachers, like many nationally, regretted social devaluations of their occupation and wanted to appear in a different light. Professionalism seemed to be an answer. They were attracted to a certain image of the professional. To them, the autonomous professional makes a socially recognized contribution. Special training is necessary, and the service that is provided is often not easily evaluated by the client to whom it is provided. This was the professional that the teachers had in mind.

This image seemed more related to an ideal than the reality of professional life. Teachers sometimes compared themselves to doctors, but their image of the medical profession seemed to be viewed through a time warp. As they saw it, doctors had absolute control over their clients, doctors always kept their patients waiting, and doctors' patients never complained to them about their behavior. In more recent years, however, the consumer movement has challenged doctors' control. Patients will "shop around" for the doctor they like, challenge the doctor's decisions, and request second opinions. Also, medicine has become bureaucratized, more controlled by the dictation of insurance companies. Even in the past, doctors did not live up to the professional ideal. As critics of professionalism have suggested, that ideal has always been so far from the reality it pretends to describe that its usefulness is damaged:

> The symbol systematically ignores such facts as the failure of professions to monopolize their area of knowledge, the lack of homogeneity within professions, the frequent failure of clients to accept professional judgment, the chronic presence of unethical practitioners as an integrated segment of the professional structure, and the organizational constraints on professional autonomy. A symbol which ignores so many important features of occupational life cannot provide an adequate guide for professional activity. (Becker, 1962/1970, p. 103)

The symbol had great meaning for Vista City teachers, however, in its representation of greater autonomy and power.

If teachers occupied the kind of professional status they envisioned, they would not, from their perspective, always have to be available. As the chapter on relationships between teachers and middle-class mothers suggests, the expectation of these mothers that teachers would always be available to their needs and queries made teachers feel powerless. Teachers felt themselves positioned as passive subjects not in the face of parental demands, which they expected, but in the specific and intense focus of the mothers on the needs of their own children as well as in mothers' ability to press these demands when they wanted. Teachers wanted to limit mothers' space for making their demands. Were they professionals, teachers argued, they would be able to limit this space.

What these teachers meant by "professional" included their expertise and their specialized training, although the specialized training was debated. The kind of professionalism toward which Vista City teachers gravitated was a traditional model that offered them greater respect. When their conflicts with middle-class mothers over grades or a particular diagnosis of a child's behavior problem seemed particularly disturbing, teachers would defend their decisions with reliance on their professional expertise: "I have the files, so I know the real story." They turned to the trappings of professionalism for rescue, to the window dressing of files, records, and labels.

Teachers did not argue that all teachers were professionals. Good teachers were professionals, but poor teachers were not. "There are teachers who are here for their paycheck only and who really don't put in a lot of extra time and really don't care. They're not professional." This view is common in occupations striving for professional status. When the transition occurs, people in these occupations become self-conscious about many work-related issues. They become "dreadfully afraid that some of their number will not observe company manners and so will hurt the reputation of all" (Hughes, 1971, p. 311). Sloppy teachers did not observe company manners. The test of a professional was how well you taught the children: "Being able to know differences in kids and develop a plan for them to learn well and follow through on that plan is the test of whether or not you are a professional." If you were a professional, said one teacher, "then parents had to realize that you had to take responsibility for the decisions you made for children."

Teachers' definitions emphasized both status and autonomy.

> A professional is someone who's had some special training
> and contributes some service to the country. It's not like having a job like an assembly-line worker. It has to be more than
> a job. Professionals are not just concerned about pay, and
> many of them would work for low salaries because they have
> an intrinsic interest in their work.

This view emphasizes service, central to how professions are traditionally defined (though challenged by many who configure the professional–client relationship in the language of power). It ignores the clustering of the elite professions at the highest end of the pay scale.

Teachers wanted autonomy as well. "Acting like a professional means that you look at the objective and then you decide yourself what content you're going to use to get there. You make these decisions." Though her definition portrays her making decisions about how to get "there," this teacher appeared to take "the objective" as a given. She did not question the there, reflecting Apple's assertion that teachers mistake making technical decisions for increased professionalism. A student teacher who had spent time in England did not take "the objective" for granted:

> In England, teachers have much higher standing as professionals because they make all the decisions about the curriculum. Here, the state makes the decisions about what the curriculum is going to be every year, rather than the headmistress in every school making these decisions. There, teachers really get to teach things they like. The things they don't like, they don't have to teach. In those ways, they end up being like a doctor—they get to make those kinds of decisions.

In her view, English teachers were held in more respect because they were allowed to make those decisions.

The traditional model distinguishes between professional and nonprofessional occupations in ways that attracted teachers. In this model, a nonprofessional occupation:

> has customers; a professional occupation has clients. A customer determines what services and/or commodities he wants, and he shops around until he finds them. His freedom of decision rests upon the premise that he has the capacity to appraise his own needs and to judge the potential of the service or of the commodity to satisfy them. . . . In a professional relationship, however, the professional dictates what is good or evil for the client, who has no choice but to accede to professional judgment. (Greenwood, 1957, p. 48)

While Greenwood dramatically overstated the case for the professional's inviolability, it was just this authority that attracted the teachers. When teachers talked about parents visiting classrooms to observe them in order to submit a preference for their child's teacher for the following year to the principal, they described the practice as "shopping around for the teacher." Most teachers rejoiced when the practice ended. Teachers wanted the parents to act like old-fashioned clients rather than like customers, for the parents' behavior said to the teachers, "You are not a professional." By and large the parents who enacted this practice were white and middle-class. When the practice ended, they lost a privilege.

Teachers' attraction to the professional model can be read in several ways. First, as women they are conscious of the obstructions they have faced in the workplace. Excluded from powerful roles in the social order by gender discrimination, women who teach elementary school seek the power professional status would secure. Second, as members of a fringe profession, their insecure social location makes them vulnerable to what they read as interference and demands of middle-class parents. If they were more securely positioned in professional privilege, they would be able to handle parents more easily and feel greater satisfaction with their occupation's reputation.

Teachers tended to associate social stereotypes about teaching with problems they had in their work, that is, with parents, curriculum controversies, the principal, and the district—in sum, with a host of intra- and extraschool concerns that they related to their low power as teachers. One teacher suggested that teachers do not have built into their occupational image the expectation that they will have control over their working lives. In her words, teachers do not expect to feel that:

> this is my school. And what I think about, and the values I think are important, and the teaching approaches that I think are important, and the ways of relating to parents that I feel are important are going to be taken seriously. . . . And that as a staff we will come to a decision about what this school means to us and what it will be like.

She wished teachers in her school would develop this sense as a group.

Unfortunately, the professional model many teachers at this school sought in order to dignify and enhance their social status formed a wedge that will actually stunt long-term development of a satisfying work setting. The professional model has three harmful results. First, it interferes with the construction of cooperative relationships with the lay community (parents, particularly mothers), so that parents and teachers become adversaries rather than partners. Second, it feeds the tensions that, for many teachers, arise out of the uneasy coexistence of love, concern for, and interest in their students on the one hand, and on the other, feelings of dissatisfaction with certain working conditions of schools, particularly bureaucracy, and teachers' vulnerability and powerlessness. Third, it leaves unresolved the basic question of gender. Use of the traditional professional model to change the condition of women who teach elementary school cannot question the social devaluation of women's work. It simply attempts to change the nature of the category by constructing the occupation more closely to the gendered model of the professions.

The incongruence between traditional definitions of career and teachers' thinking about their working lives suggest that teachers live in a double world. Measured against categories that divide life into public and private realms and privilege the public realm while excluding women from leadership in that realm, teachers appear not to have careers. In this frame, women lack both career commitment and coherence in their working life. Looked at away from this backdrop, however, elementary school careers take on an alternative coherence and reveal commitment. In this alternative frame, work and family are not oppositionally positioned. Teachers refuse to accept that interest in family life detracts from commitment to work.

At the same time, however, they do see that their work lacks social status and power, both of which they want. They accept the social stereotypes about teaching even as they dislike them. Their own analysis tends to emphasize their powerlessness in relation to bureaucracy rather than around the definition of elementary school-teaching as women's work. In their view, working with children does not necessarily infantilize a person. To struggle against the demeaning definitions of teaching, Vista City teachers desired to be professionals who could fend off intrusions by parents and ineffective school officials. This quest for professionalism took more of a defensive than an assertive stance.

Of the problems connected to the kind of professionalism teachers wanted, the largest concerns the danger it poses to children, as Chapter 6, on relationships between mothers and teachers, describes. If the model of professionalism to which the teachers are attracted is risky, what possibilities are there which will help to restructure the teacher's role, and to bring them the greater status they need? Chapter 8 discusses some possibilities.

CHAPTER 3

Women's Rewards in Nineteenth-Century American Schoolrooms

Abolitionist Charlotte Forten wrote to her father in 1855 for permission to attend normal school in Salem, Massachusetts, to train for teaching. First denied that permission, she managed, with the help of friends, to turn him around. It appears that Charlotte's father worried she would be unable to find a teaching position in Salem because she was African American. But the principal of the normal school assured her of his absolute confidence in her ability to obtain a post, and Charlotte must have communicated these assurances well. Normal school was as intellectually stimulating as she expected it to be. She expressed even greater enthusiasm to her diary, however, when, on June 18, 1856, her principal told her that she had been offered a schoolteaching position in Salem. She was to begin the next day. So far her relationship to actual pupils had been almost purely theoretical.

The actual practice of teaching shook her. On June 21st, 1856, two days into her first teaching position, she confided to her journal that she found "the children rather boisterous and unmanageable; but Mr. Warren [the school principal] thinks there is slight improvement in them. That is some comfort . . . " (Forten, 1961, p. 82). A week later she was still not reconciled to the work, though determined to be:

> The weather is hot; the children restless, and I find a teacher's life not nearly as pleasant as a scholar's. But I do not despair. Oh! no! I have faith. Ever shall my motto be, *"Labor omnia vincit."* [Work conquers all]—I found my scholars very pleasant and obliging. They bring me beautiful flowers every day. Many of them interesting children. Others very far from being so.—May I be granted strength to do my duty in the great field of labor upon which I have entered! (p. 82)

What she had liked about normal school was learning; about teaching she was less certain.

Charlotte continued, throughout her teaching career, to waver back and forth in her feelings. She usually equated good teaching experiences with children's good behavior. Take Monday, September 7, 1857, in her second year of teaching: "First day of school. 'Tis pleasant to see the bright young faces again; — but it *isn't* pleasant to go to work" (p. 109). Eleven days later she complained, "A hard day at school. This constant *warfare* is *crushing*, killing me. I am *desparate* to-night" (p. 111). On the last day of the term, November 21, 1857, she remarked that the "scholars [sang] most sweetly; it was very pleasant to hear them and to see so many beaming, happy little faces . . . " (p. 121). But when school started again nine days later, she criticized the children as "wild and unmangeable [sic], as usual after vacation . . . " (p. 121). These entries suggest that Charlotte had little patience with the actual conditions of teaching.

Her experiences teaching in the South suggest this tension. She went to the South Sea Islands off the coast of South Carolina to participate in what was called the Port Royal Experiment, an effort to transform the South and promote abolition through educating black people, from whom literacy had been officially withheld (Clinton, 1984; Rose, 1964). When she first arrived to teach the freedmen, Charlotte commented, "How bright, how eager to learn many of them seem. The singing delighted me most." Two days later she taught a class for Laura Towne, an abolitionist educator, remarking how much she enjoyed it. "The children are well-behaved and eager to learn. It will be a happiness to teach them" (p. 146). But on November 5th, when she began her "first regular teaching experience" there, she confided that "it was *not* a very pleasant one. Part of my scholars are very tiny, — babies, I call them — and it is hard to keep them quiet and interested while I am hearing the larger ones. . . . Well, I must not be discouraged. Perhaps things will go on better to-morrow" (p. 148).

Charlotte Forten balanced her ideal of serving humanity, particularly through some form of antislavery work, with the need for a supporting wage. She chose teaching as the avenue to accomplish these goals, but had to continually negotiate the actual circumstances of teaching with her concept of what it ought to be, and with the purposes that she meant it to serve.

While Charlotte Forten may have been an unusual person, her story reflects that of many other nineteenth-century women. The tensions she experienced between her interest in becoming a teacher and her difficulties with children were not atypical. A teacher's relationship with her "scholars" was central to but not solely responsible for the rewards the occupation provided.

Teaching served nineteenth-century women in many ways. It expanded their personal and occupational horizons, since teachers who went West tended to marry later and maintain more independent and egalitarian marriages (Kaufman, 1984, p. 43). Women who went into teaching became less likely to accept prescribed assumptions about women's value to society. Teaching served as a radicalizing activity for nineteenth-century women (Clifford, 1981, 1987; Shakeshaft, 1985). Women made more out of teaching than many educational reformers may have wanted them to make out of it.

The occupation of teaching came to want women, and women came to teaching. How can we understand the larger meaning that teachers made of their work in nineteenth-century America? To get at this question, I will examine two major aspects of their experiences. The first concerns the attractions teaching held for women: What purposes did teaching serve? The second concerns the criteria teachers applied: How did women evaluate their teaching situations?

SOURCES AND METHODS

The sources for this study are teachers' diaries and letters, as well as recollections, reminiscences, autobiographies, and biographies. Readers bring particular perspectives to these pages, and their perspectives partially shape what they take from them. In this case I use these materials to understand the meaning that teachers made of their situations. How did they interpret their own lives? What order did they give to their experiences? What stories did they develop to understand the positions in which they found themselves? I use the word "story" here to suggest that people not only *need* to develop a way of looking at the world in order to account for their situations, for the things that happen to them, but also that they, in fact, *do* develop ways. Symbolic interactionists call these stories "perspectives" (Bogdan & Biklen, 1992). I do not mean to suggest that the women are telling "lies." Rather, I use this word to portray the importance of developing a worldview to give one's life a certain meaning. Nancy Cott, for example, argues that women's religiosity during the first thirty-five years of the nineteenth century enabled them to take time away from service to others to write in their diaries and reflect on the meaning of their lives. Their religion gave them the opportunity for self-reflection and self-focus even as it demanded service to others. The stories the women developed about the importance of this activity in no way diminished their religious devotion (Cott, 1977, p. 140).

Writing about their experiences meant that teachers translated their activities, conversations, and interpretations into texts. They described and pronounced themselves vexed or excited about some aspects of their lives while ignoring, at least in writing, others. These texts had authors, in other words, who shaped a particular picture of experience. While it is these pictures that will constitute the major focus here, they can be fully realized only in relation to structural conditions that influenced the interpretations teachers made of their experiences. Biography intersected with social structure around opportunities available for women and particular life histories. I have reproduced the diary entries for all the teachers cited in this chapter as I found them, errors included. The sources are indicated in the numbered notes at the end of this chapter.

HISTORICAL BACKGROUND

Society, roles for women, and teaching changed dramatically over the course of the nineteenth century. An industrializing society saw economic production transposed from households to factories; though an increase in wage labor brought increasing autonomy to women, it did not significantly raise their status (Sklar, 1973). This increase in wage labor coincided with the development of an ideology of domesticity emphasizing women's nurturing abilities and providing a rationale for their role as teachers. The century also witnessed the gradual feminization of teaching. That is, women began to teach in publicly supported schools in addition to the private schools to which they had already gained access (Clifford, 1983; Prentice, 1975). Their numbers swelled by the 1860s, and they predominated by the 1880s. The 1900 census reported that women constituted 74.6 percent of the teaching force (Matthaei, 1982, p. 206).

This development was by no means uneventful or equally applicable to all groups. Black literate Southern women who wanted to teach faced economic difficulties when they had to count on a poor black community to support them, and racial difficulties when they sought support from Northern organizations dedicated to fostering the education of freedmen, because those organizations preferred to employ white teachers from the North. Jacqueline Jones (1985) estimates that in Georgia between 1865 and 1870, only about 75 black women found a "modest salary for at least a few months from a northern source" (p. 56).

Geography shaped not only the speed of women's entrance into teaching, but the quality and nature of schooling, and hence working conditions as well: School buildings and teaching positions varied by locale and, of course, over time. Rural and urban schools were organized differently, providing contrasting teaching experiences (cf. Fuller, 1982; Gulliford, 1984; Kaestle, 1983; Tyack, 1974). We have many more first-person accounts of rural and village schoolteaching than of urban teaching experiences even toward the latter part of the century, when urban centers were expanding so rapidly. New England education led the rest of the country, while the South lagged in its provision of public education until after the Civil War (and, in fact, no public high schools for black students existed in the South until the 1920s). This did not prevent women from traveling South to teach, however, either in plantation schools or in the subscription schools they generated. Subscription schools were organized and financially supported by groups of families for their children's education; teachers were paid a certain fixed rate that fluctuated according to attendance. Northern teachers who traveled South (except for those who taught freedmen) were often forced to behave entrepreneurially. Because towns did not mandate the provision of education, teachers who went South during the 1830s and 1840s had to visit families and solicit them for students, unless they worked on a plantation. Many teachers found this practice humiliating.

While education in the West developed later than in the Northeast, enthusiasm for it was high, and teachers commanded respect in the towns. Eastern women went West to teach, often lured by a spiritual mission or by the adventure the West held. Primitive conditions affected women differently, however. Some teachers took up the challenge willingly, learning to ride horses and, perhaps, wield shotguns, while others only grudgingly persisted. Some turned around and went home.

Throughout the country, financing schools was often accomplished by a combination of methods that included local funds, taxes, state financing, family and community contributions, and subscriptions (see, e.g., Kaestle, 1983; Tyack & Hansot, 1982). Some women taught in private schools, while others began by being hired by school districts, first for summer sessions, and then to teach in the winter schools as well. As the century progressed, the process of education became inextricably connected to the lives of women. How it served them is an important question.

HOW TEACHING SERVED WOMEN

Teaching was one of few available occupational choices for women. The range of women drawn to teaching varied enormously. As conscribed as opportunities were, however, women experienced the choice and labor of teaching differently. When they made meaning of their choices to themselves and their friends and families, they showed that teaching provided different rewards. But the rewards women reaped from teaching were not idiosyncratic. They cluster thematically around four types: financial, service-related, intellectual, and liberating—as a means to independence. While these four can be separated for the purpose of discussion, in actual practice they were most often tightly intertwined. Almost every teacher taught because she needed money, but some teachers left teaching to earn money in other ways if they did not receive other rewards as well.

Financial Rewards

Teaching provided a salary. Many who entered teaching had to support themselves or contribute to the support of others for a variety of reasons: They needed money, their families needed money, they finished training and had a few years before they would marry (Allmendinger, 1979), they had been orphaned or widowed or left destitute. Or they wanted financial remuneration in order to become independent, a choice they preferred over remaining the dependent spinster aunt in a relative's home. A nascent system of schooling permitted easy access to teaching.

Schooling lacked standardization, a condition that offered benefits and detriments, depending on the perspective from which it is examined. Looked at in terms of public benefit, discrepancies in qualifications, abilities, and quality of teachers stand out. Mary Bradford (1932), for example, a lifelong Wisconsin teacher and school administrator as well as a firm believer in the professionalization of the teacher, used her own experiences as a beginning teacher at the end of the nineteenth century to illustrate how poorly prepared and hence inadequate she was. During her second year in high school, in the spring of 1872, it became necessary for her to contribute to the maintenance of her family. She applied to take an examination for a third-grade certificate, the lowest grade that would enable a teacher to be permitted to teach, having had no training: "No better measure of general educational progress can be found than that resulting from the comparison of what preparation is required today before a girl is al-

lowed to try to teach, and what I have just described as my own. . . .
The salary was twenty-five dollars a month, a very poor salary, but I
was a very poor teacher" (p. 128).

The option of opening a private school—no matter what their
training—offered women in financial need an immediate opportunity.
Whether they were successful or not was another issue entirely. Jennie
Lines, a New York teacher who taught in Georgia, described her hu-
miliation when visiting families to attract students, an activity she
decried as "begging" (Lines, 1982, pp. 67–68).

These schools often began on a small scale, started, perhaps, in
one room of a family's home, moving to larger quarters as the number
of "scholars" expanded. During the 1820s, for example, John Whitall's
daughters planned to help their father overcome some recent financial
losses:

> They decided to move to Philadelphia, and open a school, which they
> were well qualified to do; and the change was accomplished in 1823.
> They sent around notes to all their father's creditors, stating their
> intention of trying to pay his debts, and proposed, where there were
> daughters in any of the families of the creditors, to educate those
> children as part payment. . . . They soon had a large and flourishing
> school, which enabled them not only to help pay their father's debts,
> but supported them and their parents in great comfort, and secured
> to them finally quite a little estate. (Smith, 1879, pp. 39–40)

The Whitall sisters took it upon themselves to rescue their father from
monetary ruin.

In Philadelphia, Mary Anna Longstreth and her sister opened a
school in their mother's home in September of 1829. The school gained
students slowly, but in 1836 the school moved to Cherry Street, where
it remained for 21 years (Ludlow, 1886). Miss Minnie Clark's Arkansas
subscription school started as a room in the Lee home during the
1830s, but when the school became too big, she moved to a two-room
log schoolhouse 100 yards away (Delta Kappa Gamma Society, 1955).

In Newton, Massachusetts, Elizabeth "Miss Lizzie" Spear, born in
1842, began, in her early twenties, to teach one or two pupils in her
own home. When the numbers increased to 10—which her mother felt
to be too large a group for the house in the winter—she rented rooms
and "Miss Spear's School" grew very popular. "Popular" may be an un-
derstatement. Woodburn suggests, in fact, that "practically all Newton
attended Miss Spear's School at one time or another" (Woodburn, 1937,
p. 29).

In New England as well as in the South, women could teach students and earn money. Elizabeth Payson Prentiss was the daughter of a minister who died in 1827, four days before her ninth birthday. Her mother moved the family from Portland, Maine, to New York in 1830, where Elizabeth's eldest sister opened a school for girls. At the end of 1831, however, the family returned to Portland. They moved from house to house, renting and living with relatives, until they finally bought one of their own. It was in this house that Elizabeth opened a school for little girls. "It consisted at first of perhaps eight or ten, but their number increased until the house could scarcely hold them" (Prentiss, 1882, p. 24). While the form teaching at home took was a little different in the South, the pattern was similar. Teachers gathered students around them in living quarters. Sara Fitch Poates, for example, taught in a school held in a plantation house in Mississippi during 1858 and 1859 (Marston, n.d.).

As all of these cases suggest, many teachers were middle-class women who needed to earn money to support themselves and/or their families. They chose teaching to meet their financial problems, but that did not mean that they were always successful; sometimes their schools failed, epidemics broke out, families could not be persuaded to send their children to the particular school, or the money available for education in the immediate locale was simply inadequate.

Financial needs, however, were not isolated from other concerns and rewards of teaching. Women continued to make choices about teaching opportunities that balanced monetary remuneration with religious or humanitarian concerns.

Harriet Cooke (1861), for example, was a very religious woman who had experienced great financial hardship in her life. She was born to a lower-middle-class family continually short of money. Harriet's father died when she was 12, and she began teaching at 16. She married at 22 and bore four children between 1808 and 1813. These were the only years of her adult life when she did not work (although teaching predominated, she also ran a boardinghouse for several years). With a husband who spent some time in debtor's prison and died of a stroke in 1820, Harriet had to bear the family's financial responsibilities.

As a devout woman, however, she mingled religious devotion with financial considerations to justify her decisions. In 1825, for example, Harriet "commenced" a school in Vergennes, Vermont, where she taught for four years, even though she experienced religious conflict with Vergennes residents. She felt their criticism of her religiosity, while she disapproved of their balls and dancing. However, offered a position in Middlebury, a town more congenial to her views, she turned it down because, in spite of her personal unhappiness, she could not relinquish the good salary she earned in Vergennes. When her finances improved a year or two later, she was able to take the Middlebury position (Cooke, 1861, pp. 84–97).

She continued to attend to these tensions between her religious commitment and financial need. In 1835, on a visit to her sister in New York, she was offered the editorship of a magazine, "designed expressly for the improvement of young ladies"; Harriet declined because "God had not then called me to engage in such an undertaking" (p. 172). But she also turned down the more religiously appealing invitation to become a missionary teacher in Illinois: "Having been satisfied that the compensation offered could not meet necessary expenses, and having no capital of my own on which I could fall back in trying emergencies, I was compelled to give the negative to this plan" (p. 172).

Like many other women, Harriet chose teaching to support herself and her family. She tried running a boardinghouse but was never successful at it, eventually deciding that "this was not my vocation" (p. 83). Teaching was:

> My mind had become more and more impressed with the belief that it was my duty to teach, and as circumstances all seemed to point to this as my future employment, most willingly, though with much fear and trembling, I assumed new responsibilities, and . . . commenced a school. (Cooke, 1861, p. 84)

As a teacher Harriet reaped both financial and emotional rewards.

Rewards of Service

Teaching could provide moral rewards as well. Women went into teaching who were not dependent on the salary they earned. Angelina Grimké, for example, wrote home during a visit to the Hartford Female Seminary in 1831 that many of Catharine Beecher's students, "though quite independent" financially, "had become teachers simply from the wish of being useful" (Sklar, 1973, p. 98).

Many women wrote about the rewards of teaching in terms of religious or humanitarian ideals of service. These ideals clustered chronologically. During the first three or four decades of the nineteenth century, women tended to articulate their goals as teachers around religious ideals, but they began employing humanitarian and less overtly religious language starting in the 1840s. I do not mean to oversimplify this change. It was not as though women never used religious language or declared religious motivations later. We know, for example, that many women who traveled South to teach for the Freedmen's Bureau held missionary attitudes, or worked for various missionary groups. It is rather that the tone of the rhetoric women used to describe their goals clearly changed between the first decades of the nineteenth century and by about the 1860s (cf. Jones, 1980; Small, 1979; Swint, 1967).

Service to God dominated the religious ideal of service. Women performed the labor of teaching for Him. Bringing education and culture to their students, however, was only one part of the religious orientation. Many of these teachers measured their work by the numbers of students they converted. This was particularly true from the period of the Second Great Awakening in New England (which started in the 1790s) through the early 1840s (see Cott, 1975). These conversions were encouraged to take place during prayer meetings and religious revival meetings held in communities and towns.

In the 1830s and 1840s, freed from the immediate care of her own grown children, Harriet Cooke became an active participant in the religious revival, attending frequent prayer meetings and documenting the numbers of conversion "cases." She often displayed great pride in how many "cases" her particular school contributed to the town totals. Like many other women of the period (Berg, 1978), she also deeply involved herself in missionary work, so that even when her "records" show that she did not convert anyone in a particular year, she still prided herself on how much she "accomplished for the missionary cause" (Cooke, 1861, p. 237).

Fanny Kingman Holmes professed similar ideals in her diary. Born in 1814 in North Middleboro, Massachusetts, she began teaching in January 1836. She opened her school in Fall River, and taught until 1841, when she married a widowed minister 26 years her senior and the father of two children. Her ideals helped her overcome her nervousness at her first educational enterprise. She "felt a delicacy about proceeding when the elder young ladies of the school entered," but did so anyway, "feeling God's help." Two months later she exulted that out of a class of five young ladies in her Sunday School class, four "are rejoicing in the hope that they have become reconciled to God." Also, two pupils in her regular school "are trusting in God." Four days later two more of her regular pupils "consecrate" themselves to God, and eight to ten more did the same the next month.[1]

Fanny Kingman Holmes and Harriet Cooke, like other teachers whose ideal of service was religious, spoke to God frequently in their diaries and criticized themselves for their worldliness (see also Prentiss, 1882; Sleeper, 1843). Fanny, for example, discounted her success at science and classical literature. Though her superiors praised her performance, she concluded that success simply filled her heart with vanity. Yet she recorded the praise, undoubtedly happy to have talents to use as a teacher.

Fanny enjoyed teaching and, unlike Charlotte Forten, found it easy to combine teaching with her ideals. She wrote in her diary on May 20, 1838: "Again I have been permitted to meet with my school to instruct immortal minds & prepare them in some measure to go forward in the various duties of life. Oh that I might so instruct them, that they may become useful members of society—doing much good in their day & generation." Fanny, like Charlotte, wanted to be useful in life.

One difference between them centered on how they represented their pedagogical skills in their diaries. Charlotte was a scholar and intellectual who was committed to improving the living conditions of African-American people. Teaching provided a means for her to do so, both in her work in the Southern schools and in her appointment to a position in a school that served white students in the North. Normal school was important to her because of the intellectual stimulation it offered. She continually wrote in her diary, as the examples I gave in the opening of this chapter suggested, of the difficulties she had in managing a classroom of children and of her equivocal feelings for her students. Fanny, on the other hand, saw teaching as an opportunity to instill religious feeling in her students. She was rewarded in her efforts by her promotion to preceptress of the Bedford Grammar School. Teaching increased Fanny's confidence as she experienced success in the classroom.

Fanny conceived her role as a sort of gardener of the mind: "To be sure I have not that delightful 'nursery' of fruits, flowers, & shrubs here, but then I have a nursery of immortal minds which require constant care and watchfulness, lest seeds even more destructive than those of natural weeds & briars, be sown in their minds."[2] Fanny's teaching abilities reinforced her religious ideals of service to God through the schoolhouse.

Other teachers found rewards centered more on humanitarian goals. Social change and service to people marked this orientation. These teachers were moved by social problems, and responded to them through efforts to help participate in processes of change. Charlotte Forten, for example, wanted to "live for the good that I can do my oppressed and suffering fellow creatures." To do this she would "prepare" herself "for the responsible duties of a teacher" (Forten, 1961; see also Ames, 1969; Jackson-Coppin, 1913; Swint, 1966).

Middle-class black women teaching during the late nineteenth century in Southern cities saw teaching as "genteel" work. More importantly, however, they defined it as a form of social activism that contributed to building equality (Jones, 1985, p. 143). Teaching was a form of service around racial uplift. Fanny Jackson Coppin's address to the 1879 graduating class of the Institute for Colored Youth underscored this value:

> You can do much to alleviate the condition of our people. Do not be discouraged. The very places where you are needed most are those where you will get least pay. Do not resign a position in the south which pays you $12 a month as a teacher for one in Pennsylvania which pays you $50. (Perkins, 1987, p. 136)

Work made people independent, but it should not separate them from their communities.

Intellectual Rewards

Another reason teaching appealed to women was its connection to books and to knowledge. Before the Civil War, teachers received most of what training they got at teachers' institutes. This was true after the Civil War as well in some parts of the Midwest, particularly Kansas (Fuller, 1982, pp. 169–177). They would attend these institutes, depending on the location of their schools, for two to three weeks between some school sessions. There they would meet with others who struggled with similar issues, discuss strategy, and read. Charlotte Forten valued her Normal School education because it enabled her to learn languages and provided a framework for her to master mathematics and classics. She was not alone: "And many a Midwestern farmer's daughter through the years dreamed of reaching great intellectual heights by graduating from the state normal" (Fuller, 1982, p. 168). These teacher training institutions offered intellectual as well as practical knowledge.

Mary Mudge, a Lynn, Massachusetts, teacher whose diary for 1854 reveals many details of her daily activities, attended many lectures on literature, politics, and religion, and thus fed her intellectual life. In addition to extracurricular community activities, Mary and her teaching friends joined together to talk about work. This talk, whether it happened informally between two or three teachers or on a larger, more formally organized scale, provided educational and intellectual stimulation. On October 14, 1854, for example, Mary and Miss Newhall, a friend and teacher, "went up to the High School house. There were about 15 or 20 there. Met to see about forming an Institute for the Teachers to meet for self improvement. We had quite a pleasant time." The Institute was established. Mary attended meetings again on October 23, October 30, and November 27. In addition to this group, Mary also attended a "school" to teach teachers how to teach writing. Mary took her work very seriously.[3] This richly endowed life was common among New England village schoolteachers of this time.

Another sort of intellectual reward came from the challenge of "scholars" and their situations. Figuring out a problem and remedying it was satisfying. Clara Burt, who started teaching in 1875 in San Joaquin County, California, exemplified this perspective. She relished the challenge of difficult students:

> So many say the children are getting along fast. There is one boy thirteen yrs. old who entered four weeks ago lacking a day. He had not been to school a whole month in all put together before. He read dreadfully in the Third Readers didn't know a figure or letter in writing. I took him in hand and showed him how to write. Now he can read quite nicely, reads and writes No. adds them and next Monday will commence subtraction with the rest of the class. Every day he writes 15 hard words from his reader, on his slate as a spelling lesson. Wed. he missed only 1, today 3. They were the words *believe, deceive,* and *threaten.*[4]

While Clara recognized the boy's intelligence, she also admitted her own role in his development. This kind of work stimulated her.

Developing successful ways to teach students excited these teachers. While some teachers picked up methods of teaching from teachers' institutes or from their normal school training, others observed children, talked with colleagues, or corresponded with friends who taught at other locations. Thinking and talking about such concerns created great satisfaction. Elizabeth Hatheway, for example, decided to encourage her students to teach each other in algebra class. Even though her students had all started at the same place, they had progressed differently. If the students rather than she first corrected those with wrong answers and tried to explain the right process, she discovered, and if, at the same time, she could impress on students that doing mathematics well was not a matter of the right answer so much as the process of doing it, then her students progressed faster. As she wrote to her sister, "Another week of my teachership has taken itself off, leaving the comfortable reflection that I have succeeded in my profession so far beyond my hopes."[5] The intellectual challenges of teaching provided their own reward.

A Means to Independence

In May 1880, during the last week of the term, Clara Burt's suitor, George, brought her back to school after a weekend with her family. He wanted her to marry him and give up teaching. Clara wondered: "He hoped that this was the last time I should ever come over to school. I can not tell. I wonder sometimes if I am not full as happy as those who are tied down by family cares." By Christmas she had broken off her relationship with him. She remained a teacher and school principal for the rest of her life.[6]

Independence was an important reward of teaching for those who wanted it. Some women did not want to marry, but neither did they want to remain dependent on and beholden to family members for their livelihood. Others wanted freedom during a particular stage in their lives; hence the attraction of going West to teach with the National Popular Education Board. Frances Jane McCulloh (Bartlett), a California native, wrote home to her family from the normal school she attended in the early 1890s about a fellow student's illness. "Miss Drake is her name and is an only child. Her parents live in Maine. It shows her ambition to do something in the world to be away out here teaching."[7] Elizabeth Hatheway's friend expressed similar sentiments in a different vocabulary when she wrote to Elizabeth, who had left the North to teach in Tennessee, that her move away from home and family showed her firm and independent spirit.[8]

Choosing to marry or stay single was not the only way teachers defined independence; many teachers spoke of marriage as attractive only if it were connected with love. The feminization of teaching coincided with the development of the notion of romantic love, the economics of which were significant (Matthaei, 1982, pp. 108–114). Hence many teachers insisted that they would never leave teaching for any offer of marriage; they had to love the person.

A young woman living at home in upstate New York near Canandaigua in 1864 who described the teacher's life as "weary" and "thankless" commented to her diary upon an offer of marriage: "I can't see him on it. If I should marry unsuitably, I should be unhappy for I could not be contented away from home with one I do not love."[9] Teaching, even though she had few skills to become accomplished at it, gave her some freedom.

Teaching absorbed the energies of Mary Atkins Lynch. She apologized to her brother and sister in 1843 for her two-year silence, attributing it to her work: "School, *school, school* takes my entire mind, morning, noon and night from one week to another. Only two weeks have past for more than a year without finding me engaged in school . . . " This twenty-four-year-old did not know what the future would bring, but presumed she would "get married and have a home" of her own "some day." But, she reiterated, she must have love: "I shall not marry a person I do not love; for unless I loved a person I could not be happy in his society." We may assume she never did find love, for when she died in 1882, she had developed a solid teaching and administrative career, but had never married.[10]

Abigail Smith Tuck left New England to teach in the South because of her health. Her sisters and brothers frequently questioned her in their letters about her marriage plans. She interpreted their questions as pressure, but wrote frequently of her refusal to compromise: "I do not think much of getting married for the sake not being an *old maid*. I think it is best to wait until you can find some one that you can love." She would not make do with someone she did not admire (mistakes are in the original):

> I think you will be mistaken abaout my getting married though I presume I might if I would take up with such as I might have but if I cannot have such as I want I waont have any one. I expect there is as much as one smitten allready but he cannot come in for he is not tall enough for me but he is very good and pios but that is not all thought [though] it is much. Not [Now] you will say what a fool you are. I knew you would be an *old maid*. So be it if it is to be so.[11]

Abigail did marry, in 1851.

Whether or not a woman wanted to marry, teaching often provided her with some space to make that decision. It clearly served those women who found success at it, even benefiting those who showed little skill, if only by providing a salary for a short time.

Another facet of women's independence was the status that good teachers earned. When Abigail Smith Tuck wrote home in 1846, she shared the pleasure her renown brought:

> I have had no trouble in teaching nor do I fear any, for they think I know about every thing. [Y]ou might have thought that I had been

of considerable importance if you had been here at the party for they had to ask Miss Tuck how every thing should be done for they think she has so much taste and if she came from the north she must know how every thing should be done in the most fashionable manner. [Y]ou might think this poor ignoramous was something if you did not know.[12]

Her occupation contributed to her valued place in the community.

HOW TEACHERS EVALUATED THEIR POSITIONS

Fanny Kingman Holmes liked her new position at the New Bedford Grammar School because it was a "good" situation. That is, work was not too demanding, she had good colleagues, and her living arrangements suited her. "We have but 66 pupils in the whole school & the labor is so well divided that it is ever a pleasure to instruct the school. . . . I am no less happily situated at my boarding house than I am at school. . . . I have a very pleasant front chamber & Mr. & Mrs. Beane are very pleasant people."[13]

Elizabeth Payton Prentiss taught in Virginia at a private school of about 125 students. Sometimes she got sick of the girls' behavior, their "chattering forever and ever about lovers" and occupying their minds too much "reading novels, love-stories and poetry." But generally she expressed happiness in her work, as entries for June 1 and 9, 1840, suggest:

> My life is a nice little life just now, as regular as clockwork. We walk and we keep school, and our scholars kiss and love us, and we kiss and love them, and we read Lamartine and I worship Leighton, good, wise, holy Leighton, and we discourse about everything together and dispute and argue and argue and dispute, and I'm quite happy, so I am! (Prentiss, 1882)

Clearly, teachers measured their particular situations against certain general standards or criteria. Those that appeared prominently in their diaries included the conditions of work, their relationship with their students, and their living arrangements. Teachers' views of their work depended on how they measured their actual situations against their expectations and standards.

Even women who enjoyed teaching as a way of earning a living or who wanted to serve God through teaching disliked situations they found disagreeable. Similarly, teachers who evidenced little commitment to teaching as an occupation of choice expressed enjoyment of their work when it was amenable. They compared positions, pointing out the qualities that made particular situations favorable. Because teaching positions were organized during the early part of the century in two- or three-month blocks, they had frequent opportunity to compare one job to the other, and they took advantage of it.

Conditions of Work

Like any workers, teachers wanted working conditions that were as pleasant and functional as possible. Teachers evaluated some aspects of their working conditions, such as the physical environment, by comparing their circumstances with other possible ones. Sometimes letters from other teachers spoke of more or less favorable schoolrooms. Sometimes teachers would peek in the windows of other schoolrooms when they traveled. In 1876, for example, Clara Burt visited Ada, a friend and also a teacher. After school, they went to Lockeford, another northern California town. "We peeped into the schoolhouse. It looked very pleasant through the windows."[14] In addition to the physical environment, the size of the school and the teacher's relationship to administrators, school board members, and parents (particularly as these relationships were expressed through public examinations of the teachers' students) also constituted working conditions.

Physical conditions. Educational historians have described the variety of physical conditions of nineteenth-century schoolrooms (e.g., Fuller, 1982; Gulliford, 1984; Tyack, 1974). Teachers evaluated their situations positively if they had supplies, furniture, a functioning stove, light, and enough room for their students. Malfunctioning, smoking stoves that forced cancellation of school, not enough slates for all children, and worn, outdated, or inadequate books all caused teachers to complain. Cold drafts that fostered colds and flu made teachers wonder if they had strength enough to teach.

Anna Webber, born in 1860 in Kansas, passed the teachers' examinations in the spring of 1881 and was hired to teach at a district school in Mitchell County. A three-month school running from May through July, it contained 17 students between the ages of 8 and 13 (Webber, 1972). This was Anna's first teaching experience, and though her "anticipations" were "great," her schoolhouse was, at best, meagerly supplied. Her first reactions: "There is no benches, seats, black board or writing desks. . . . For seats we have two boards placed on rocks. I think if I had more scholars, and things more convenient I should like teaching very much." Anna could distinguish between her particular situation, which was unsatisfactory, and the occupation in general, which attracted her. Her diary entries continued to note problems caused by the lack of furniture and conveniences in the schoolroom, as well as the low number of scholars.

School size. Size of the school was a major issue for two primary reasons, financial and personal. Before the regulation of school systems, teachers' salaries depended on how many students they could attract to a school and keep in attendance over the course of a term. If teachers were paid by the number of pupils, they prospered when their schools were large.

Since pupil attendance affected their salaries, many teachers felt depressed when attendance was low. In fact, in all geographic locations, teachers who worked in privately funded schools complained when attendance was small. When Caroline Poole started teaching in Monroe, Louisiana, in 1835, for example, her small class worried her: "Commenced school with 5 scholars, prospect dark but brighter." Caroline reported to her diary on many occasions how dispirited she was when attendance was low, but finally could report the gratifying news, about halfway through her two-year stay in the South, that "I have now 33 scholars & my time is entirely occupied" (Padgett, 1937, pp. 654, 674). Caroline Hentz (Ellison, 1951), teaching in Alabama during the 1830s; Mary Mudge, teaching in Lynn, Massachusetts, during the 1850s; Elizabeth Hatheway, teaching in Tennessee towns and in Philadelphia during the 1850s; Dema Higbee, teaching in Wisconsin during the 1860s; Mary Ann Nearing, teaching in upstate New York during the 1860s; and Anna Webber (1972), teaching in Kansas during the 1880s: All were concerned with the size of their classes and the financial remuneration it implied. [15]

Size often related to the challenge and diversity of the classroom as well. Charlotte Forten, for example, confided to her diary: "Had a perfectly *immense* school to-day. 147., of whom I had 58, at least two thirds of whom were tiny A.B.C. people. Hardly knew what to do with them at first. But I like a large school. It is inspiriting" (Forten, 1961, p. 165). Lillian Wester, born in 1872 in Kansas, taught for several years during the 1890s in and around Taylor, Texas. She found her country school particularly "interesting" because there were so many students at such different levels (Wester, 1952, p. 21). Anna Webber, teaching in Kansas in 1881, commented, "I have quite a large school now, And I tell you it keeps me busy, but I like it better than haveing so few" (Webber, 1972, p. 326).

Later in the century, at least in New England, where the public education bureaucracy was the most developed, teachers did not always look at big classes in such a favorable light. Charlotte Conant (1931), who taught in Massachusetts during the 1880s, had to choose between two teaching positions, one at a public high school in North Adams and the other at the private Northfield School for Girls. She wrote to her mother, explaining how she measured the different positions against each other. In North Adams she would "have charge of a room, and have all the High School mathematics classes in Algebra, Geometry and Trig., classes in Botany, Physics, History and possibly Greek or Latin, though the principal prefers to take these himself." The salary was $580. Charlotte remarked:

> It is a hard place. I do not want to shirk work or refuse a place because it is hard, but it seems to me there is such a thing as trying to do too much. To have the charge of a roomful, say fifty students to put it at a low estimate, to keep them in order, and at the *same time* and in the same place hear recitations all day long, keeping your classes interested and lively, is some work. (p. 167)

Planning and preparation would take all her time out of school because she would have to prepare well. She "cannot teach carelessly" if she is "able to help it." She might be able to handle this if it were her second year because she would have preparations to fall back on (Conant, 1931, pp. 166–167). Charlotte chose Northfield because she "should have a class of pupils more anxious to learn than those in a high school and therefore easier to teach" (p. 167). And she would be almost as close to home.

Student examinations. Relationships with persons in a position to evaluate and hence affect rehiring were central to teachers' assessments of their jobs. They did not want too much interference on the part of superintendents, school commissioners, school board members, and parents. But on the other hand, they definitely wanted their praise.

Negative evaluations would cause teachers to have to look for new situations. Mary Atkins Lynch, for example, wrote to her siblings that she did not know how much longer she would last in her particular school, as "one of the Trustees is rather opposed to my teaching." And unhappy parents could cause so many students to be withdrawn that the school would collapse.

A major aspect of teachers' evaluations were student examinations (which should not be confused with the examinations that teachers had to pass to get licensed). During parts of the nineteenth century, examinations of student achievement were organized as public displays (and entertainment). It was as much the teacher as the student who was examined. In fact, these were sometimes called "teachers' examinations." The examination would be scheduled and publicly announced for a certain day. Townspeople, friends, and even other teachers would come to the program, these crowds sometimes numbering as many as 70 or 80 people. Mary Nearing, a Pompey, New York, teacher, for example, wrote in her diary on April 8, 1862, that she and her friend Libbie planned to go to the examination of the other teachers in her town. [16] The examiners, usually members of the school board or other elected officials, but outsiders always, would hear the students recite, read out loud, sing, or do arithmetic problems, the particular performance depending on the subject area. Women teachers worried about and dreaded these times. Edna, a New York teacher, wrote to her friend Lizzie Ives, also a teacher, that she sympathized with her during those three days of her "dreaded examinations." But, she continued, "they have passed and I suppose you lived through them as I did." [17] Charlotte Forten called them a "horrid nuisance" (Forten, 1961, p. 114).

As dreaded as it was, a successful examination offered compensation for hard work. Mary Mudge, a teacher in Lynn, Massachusetts, in 1854, had her examination scheduled for February 7. On February 1 she complained: "This morning had the worst lessons that ever were. [D]on't know what kind of an examination I shall have if the scholars go on at this rate." On the 4th, she worried, "Don't know what kind of an examination I shall have. Live in hopes of having a good one. Yet scarcely dare to hope." Two days later she reported that "Miss Neall had her examination and it was a terrible one. Boys talked out loud, whispered, laughed &c and the recitations were not very good. I longed to get hold of some of the boys to punish them; Miss Newhall had hers this A.M. Mother went and says it was very good."

On the morning of February 7, Mary confided to her diary before going to school, "today is to be my examination O dear! how I hope & fear . . . " She wrote again in the middle of the day that the arithmetic classes had done well in the morning and she hoped that all would go well in the afternoon, too. She had about 75 visitors in to view the examinations. After the students performed in arithmetic, geography, reading, singing, and recitations, the examining committee reported their reactions:

> Abba West . . . said he had been pleased with the examination. Mr. Bullfinch followed him, said they had improved, commended the reading. The other members of the committee did not favor us with their opinion of the school. Mr. West (Abba's father) said he had been much pleased with the exercises. Thought they might have spoken a little louder. Isaac Brown "Esq." said it was not well to spoke in praise too much and pointed out one or two faults—[?] and laughing at mistakes. Then we sang "Lord dismiss us" and then the Company left. The com seemed to be well satisfied.

She left school that afternoon "feeling as though a load had rolled off my shoulders." She was happy that her students had performed well in school: "This has been a very pleasant day to me. I feel as though I had been paid for my trouble and pains through the year."[18]

Good examinations publicly attended also served as advertisements for future students. Julia Tevis taught her first school in Virginia in 1819 or 1820. In spite of her distaste for public examinations, which she had never before experienced, she benefited from them:

> This examination closed my first half-year, and, of course the material was somewhat raw; but with the assistance of my sister and some of the older and more intelligent pupils, matters were so arranged as to give entire satisfaction to the community and infinite delight to my patrons. Owing to our success, the fame of which was spread abroad through the country, our next term opened with increased numbers, and the school became much more profitable. (Tevis, 1878, p. 186)

Some teachers who performed well publically and who could get their students to perform put examinations in a positive light.

Finally, public examinations could overturn social stereotypes. Fanny Jackson-Coppin, "given the delightful task of teaching [her] own people" at the Institute for Colored Youth in Philadelphia, used the examination to reinforce the idea that black youth were capable of "higher learning." At one examination, when she "asked a titled Englishman to take the class and examine it, he said: 'They are more capable of examining me, their proficiency is simply wonderful'" (Jackson-Coppin, 1913, p. 20). Most competent teachers, though they developed high anxiety before examinations, got great pleasure from positive evaluations.

Relationships with Students

Examinations revealed not only the nature of student learning, but the nature of the student-teacher relationship as well. And the quality of this relationship played an integral part in a teacher's determination of her success, both pedagogically and financially. Good relationships brought happiness, poor ones despair. The quality of teachers' relationships to their students were central to their evaluation of their enjoyment of teaching, and affected whether they were rehired the next year. Hence, in diaries and letters teachers monitored how their classes progressed and what their relationships to students were like.

Mary Mudge valued doing a job well and liking it. Mary began a new term on February 27, 1854. For two months her diary entries marked difficulties she faced with her students: They were slow to learn, they were difficult to discipline. Mary seemed alienated from her work, certainly lacking in control over her situation. By April 24, however, Mary sounded more hopeful. The class must already have been improving, but Mary now saw a pattern: "Had real good lessons and no whispering. [I]t begins to seem a little like my school. [I]t has not before. [T]he scholars seem more ambitious than they have. [H]ope it will so continue." The next day, she remarked, "Every scholar at school today. Every thing pleasant—I believe it does us good to get discouraged sometimes; I begin to love my school again. Had beautiful lessons today." Mary's words point to a cycle of feeling, a series of responses to new situations. [19]

Teachers' careers depended on good relationships with their students. Not only would parents hear of difficulties, but so would supervisors who came to observe teaching behavior. In the case of Mary Mudge, school commission members visited her classroom during the course of the term. On April 3, for example, she remarked: "Mr. Nath'l Ingalls into school a little while this P.M. He said he was much pleased with what he saw & heard." But when Mr. Ambler attended her classroom two weeks later for two days, things did not go so well. On the first day a pupil nearly fell over the stove and her first reading class read poorly. On the second day: "The 1st class had a miserable lesson in Geog. today. Lowest class did well. Mr. Ambler says I must punish if they do not do as I want them to." So the following morning when Mary went to school, she was "determined to stop the noise with the lips. Have punished several. Had quite a quiet school." Mary did not like to punish students and always took pains to avoid doing so. The week before Mr. Ambler's visit, for example, she confided her hope of getting through a week without punishing the children, but "this P.M. I had to punish several."[20] The class continued to improve, and by the next week Mary's fears about her reputation seemed at rest.

Teachers became more specific in their descriptions of their relationships as the century progressed. But teachers always commented on how things were going, what their scholars were like, and how this affected their sense of themselves as teachers. Electa Snow Bramer wrote to her family in the 1820s about her class of 60 or 70 students: "I have a class in geography, two classes in grammar, and more than twenty studying arithmetic, and a fine lot of little ones to attend to besides. I find it fatiguing but get along without any difficulty, and I think that my scholars are doing very well."[21]

Seeing progress on the part of their students made teachers feel successful and contributed to their enjoyment of teaching. In 1875 Clara Burt wrote in her diary about her first teaching experience: "I am enjoying teaching very much for my pupils are good and seem to be improving rapidly." She commented frequently over the years on how much some of her pupils liked her: "Rosie Ray says that she likes to go to school because she likes the teacher. Little Gerry Thompson says that if he went to school to Miss Burt he would go out and gather flowers for her *all* day."

Part of this response included putting their imprint on the setting. Teachers wanted to have control for the ease it brought, but they also wanted it because class control provided an indicator of their own capabilities and worth. If they could shape a class to reflect their values, then they had some power. Managing difficult students discouraged teachers, as it distanced them from the classroom. Lizzie Ives received a letter from her friend Edna describing her attitudes about her new occupation: "I have been three days a *schoolmarm*. [S]ome of the time I like it first rate and some of the time (grammatical isn't it) I am almost discouraged when I have unruly ones to manage."[22]

Some teachers complained of their students' ignorance but had difficulty strategizing to overcome these problems. Others, more skillful and resourceful, worked hard to help their students develop. A young, anonymous upstate New York teacher had a terrible time: "What a weary thankless life a teacher has. . . . Why don't they learn easier. I could lay my head on my desk and cry for my heart is full of tears. . . . I must leave the old school house and lock up my cares but they will be sure to greet me the first thing in the morning."[23] Perhaps she would have appreciated visits by Mary Mudge's Mr. Ambler.

Clara Burt also had difficult students, and although she found strategizing hard work, she did it: "I worked real hard in school today.

If some of the young ones don't know anything it will be no fault of mine if I am able to do anything by trying for I am using all my powers to get some of them started."[24] Clara did not see her students as static personalities whose abilities, unshaped and unformed, reflected on her. Rather, she saw students as people who came to learning in different ways, some of which amused her:

> I am getting along nicely in school. Little Pidgie Thompson says all the word I teach her to spell is "boy". She says I never say anything about spelling *girl*. Its so funny she said that for I have never told her how to spell either word.
>
> The other day I was teaching Carrie Stayton how to spell some words. I came to the word "Kit" and I wanted her to tell me what she *thought* it spelled. She did not know. There was a picture of a kitten on the page. I asked her what it was. She said that it was a cat. I told her that words did not spell cat. What is a little cat called? "A little mouse" said she. She said it so cunning that I could not get over laughing for a good while.[25]

Clara was skilled and energetic with children. Teachers' relationships with students affected their financial security, their self-esteem, and their happiness with work.

The structure of schooling could interfere in the development of good relationships. Short school terms often meant that a teacher would just get a feel for her school, for the parents' expectations, and for the children's personalities and then it would end. The teachers needed to continually readjust. If teachers disliked their situations, they felt relief when the term ended; if the class was progressing well, teachers regretted the end. Overall, however, since teachers usually worked to develop a class, they usually faced disappointment. The term would come to a close just when the atmosphere the teacher had promoted developed.

Living Situations

Living conditions entered into teachers' evaluations of their work. A good situation improved their attitude toward teaching. If they did not live at home or at a boarding school, teachers boarded out while they taught. A good place to board provided either a private room or one shared with a single roommate (hence, some space for solitude), good food, and interesting company. People of interest could be other boarders or the landlords themselves. Elizabeth Hatheway, teaching in the South during the 1850s, tried to convince a friend teaching in

Philadelphia to join her. The friend replied that she had been "abundantly successful" in Philadelphia, earning $70 per month, though her "expenses curtail that amount considerably for I board comfortably." She had moved from the Dronin household, where they expected four to a room, to the Maroteau household. Even though she had to do extra work tutoring the Maroteau daughters, a good boarding situation was worth it.[26]

Not everyone, however, could attain such an agreeable situation. When Jennie Lines took a position at the Southern Female Masonic College, a secondary school, in September 1858, she went to the town to "choose a boarding place." She knew what kind of place she wanted: "I wish to get in a family of good standing, have a room to myself, or room with some of the teachers. I do not wish to be with the school girls; they will be no society for me." Unfortunately, the place she obtained planned to take schoolgirls as well as Jennie. Jennie would not "much object to having one in my room, but I do not much like the idea of having more than one with me." Her first roommate was a "young thoughtless frolicksome school girl. I can neither read, write, or think where she is. How I long to have a room to myself or a room-mate, more congenial, one with sympathies in common with me." When more girls moved into the house, Jennie remained for a few months, but on January 1, 1859, she changed her boarding place, moving to Mr. Henderson's to get away from the confusion and noise to peace and quiet (Lines, 1982, pp. 107, 111–113, 125–126).

Lucia Downing's first teaching job in Vermont in the 1880s brought her a very different boarding life. Lucia taught at School Number 9 in the Keeler District when she was 14 years old, boarding at the Nichols farm. Nichols was a "wealthy farmer"; there were:

> menservants and maidservants galore, and we all sat down to most marvelous meals. . . . [W]e had delicious home-smoked ham and tender roasts, and milk-fed chickens and honey with biscuits rich with cream, and then all the fruits and vegetables that early fall makes possible on a rich "interval" farm, besides plenty of eggs and cream and butter. (Downing, 1951, p. 237)

Lucia liked the Nicholses for more than the food: "I was treated like an honored guest, and given the 'spare room' with blue walls and curtains, and was always addressed as 'Teacher'—much to my satisfaction."

When Lucia Downing taught in Vermont in the 1880s they had halted the process of "boarding around," but 25 years earlier, Midwesterner Molly Dorsey was supposed to board around at her first school. It was in "a kind of Mormon settlement," and she stood the boarding around "just two weeks" until she refused to do so any longer "and . . . moved into permanent quarters." The first place she boarded served food she could not bear to eat. She slept on the floor, where "festive bedbugs held high carnival over my weary frame the night through." Her second family was nice, but her stomach was still upset from the first situation. When that week was up and she found out that she had "to either go back to 'beverage' and greens, or into a Mormon family with four children and two small rooms, I utterly refused to teach. Mr. Cole, one of the directors, came to the rescue and brought me to his house, where I have a nice room and everything comfortable" (Sanford, 1959, p. 87). Molly, who was not sponsored by any group, had similar criticisms as those women who went West to teach for the National Board of Popular Education who refused to board around (Kaufman, 1984, p. 25).

Many teachers who traveled West to teach during the nineteenth century complained about rough conditions in their boarding experiences. Without her "keen" sense of humor, remarked Esther Selover, who began teaching in Ohio in 1841, she might have been "quite unhappy at times" because of bad experiences "boarding round" (Gulliford, 1984; Sengstacken, 1942). Ironically, when they told their stories, many teachers seemed to realize the effect their stories would have on their readers and listeners, and appeared almost proud to have lived through these situations (for a good example, see Sneller, 1964).

Teachers included loneliness as a problem when they evaluated their living conditions. We can easily imagine that women who traveled far to their teaching positions might well have felt lonely. The literature richly portrays these situations. If a New England woman traveled South, she hungered to meet other Yankees. When a New Yorker traveled West, she compared Indiana preachers to those in Glens Falls. When Agnes Sengstacken's mother traveled to Oregon, she contrasted the cooking with what she remembered in Ohio and New York. And for everyone, letters from family, friends, and lovers shaped moods. A letter raised the spirits, a lack of mail depressed them. Especially for those teachers who were unhappy in their work, letters seemed to provide some cushion or support that enabled them to overcome their loneliness and stick with their jobs (Gulliford, 1984; Husband, 1974; Kaufman, 1984; Lines, 1982; Padgett, 1937; Richards, 1984; Sengstacken, 1942).

Teachers experienced loneliness as well at even shorter distances from family. Though their views may reflect the nature of travel and distance as they experienced them, many women boarded but a wagon ride from home. They wanted not only letters, but weekend respite from their boarding situations. They wanted connection with family and community.

Eleanor Gordon, born in Illinois in 1852, was the oldest of six children. An invalid mother and very little money meant that she had to contribute to the family's income. When she was about 20 she went to teach at a country school, not her first. She was isolated, and hence lonely:

> I shall never forget the late afternoon of that November day when I found myself standing by a small frame house surrounded by a muddy yard watching a one-horse wagon vanishing down the road. Brother John and a neighbor's boy had brought me and my truck to this desolate place where I was to teach a three month's term of school. Never again in my life have I been so tempted to play the coward as then.
>
> I started once or twice to call them back, to say I could not stand it, could not live there three months. (Gordon, 1934)

The 12 weeks turned out to be as dreary as they first appeared. She described the community as "poor and ignorant" and the conditions for living and working as "poverty-stricken." Thrown on her own during the long nights and longer weekends, she learned to entertain herself, discovering George Eliot.

Ann Stoddard was a schoolteacher in North Ridge, Vermont, whose family lived nearby in Lyndon. Ann boarded around near her school in North Ridge during the week, and liked going home during the weekends. On Friday, January 5, 1866, Ann noted that she wanted to go home for the weekend but her father did not arrive to get her. She complained that if they did not want to see her badly enough to come after her, "let them stay away."[27]

Dema Higbee also taught during the 1860s, though far from New England. Born in 1843, she lived in Dellton, Sauk County, Wisconsin, with her parents. While working, she would travel to other towns to teach, boarding there. She lived with her Uncle Joe and Aunt Dema, for example, while she taught in Holland, Sheboygan County. Dema disliked the school there, commenting on February 13, 1864, "Only six more weeks of *bondage* + then I am *free*." She appeared very lonely, even at her relatives' house, remarking so on several occasions. On January 2, 1864, for example, she could not teach because of cold weather, commenting, "Oh! have been so lonesome, would give almost anything if I was at home today." The next day's entry read similarly: "Was so lonesome I hardly knew what to do. Will spring ever come?" On January 23, she again complained, " . . . am so lonesome I hardly know what to do with myself." Many other entries portray a lonely young woman isolated in a cold, "humdrum" existence. A lack of mail made things worse: "Every thing goes wrong with me. [D]id not get any mail at all" (February 5, 1864). During the week Dema looked forward to a "long rest" on Sunday, but when Sunday came, she would always complain of loneliness. March 10, two weeks before the start of her vacation, found her at a very low ebb: "It has rained nearly all day. I am homesick lonesome and discouraged. It seems as though my school dragged hard this week. The going is miserable." Entries in her diary suggest that receiving mail was the primary event in her life, with school a secondary necessity to earn money.

A new school on the prairie, which began on May 9, seemed to put her in a new frame of mind. She had taken teachers' exams and received her teaching certificate during her vacation, commenting on April 6, "Good for me." On her second morning she predicted: "I think I shall like my school very much." She reported several times how much she liked the school and how "pleasantly" things were going for her. At this prairie school she went home on the weekends, walking back to her school on Monday mornings. Perhaps this arrangement suited her better. Even so, by the middle of June, teaching began to get her down again: "Still very warm and dusty. I feel about jagged out —, after school. I wish I was rich so that I need not teach school for a living." So even when school went pleasantly for her, Dema felt negatively about her work.

By the end of 1865, letters from family no longer blunted Dema's loneliness. Now she wanted letters from "the boy I love." When she received one, for example on November 23, she was "raised from the depths of despair." She remarked on her 22nd birthday, on December 12 of that year: "22 and an old maid yet. Wonder what I shall be doing my next birthday? [N]ot teaching school I'll bet a cookie."[28]

Anna Webber, on the other hand, came to like teaching in spite of the horrendous working conditions she first encountered. Once Mattie — another young adult who boarded at the McPeake family with her — arrived, her loneliness disappeared: "It does not seem near as lonesome, or dull since she has come." At the end she was sorry to see the school over: "I believe I hate to leave this place, yes I do . . . " (Webber, 1972, pp. 321, 326, 330, 334, 336).

CONCLUSION

Teaching brought rewards of some kind to many nineteenth-century women. These rewards included financial remuneration, intellectual stimulation, an occasion for service, and the opportunity to gain some independence. This independence came not only from one's actual position in the world of wage work, but also from one's heightened status in the community.

Teaching provided both a position in the public world of work, where one had to interact with children, supervisors, and parents, and a series of experiences broader than actual classroom interaction. Think even of Charlotte Forten, whose struggles with children tested her abilities throughout her tenure in this role; teaching enabled her to participate in working with freedmen on the South Carolina Sea Islands, an experience she cherished. The Harriet Cookes could enact their spiritual devotion through pedagogical practice. The Clara Burts could learn about child development when they saw teaching as an intellectual challenge. The Mary Mudges could center a full life of social and cultural activities around the flexible occupational hub of teaching. These were the women who stayed in teaching.

Not all stayed. The lonely Dema Higbees could not wait for marriage to extract them from distasteful work. Others disliked children and the domestic nature of the teaching experience. Emily Blackwell felt constricted while teaching because she wanted to go into medicine.

Today we understand Emily Blackwell's chafing at her occupational bonds. We sympathize with Charlotte Forten's forced attention to controlling small scholars when she would rather have been a scholar herself. Structural constraints on women limited their occupational horizons, but teaching provided many women with opportunities that were both intellectual and widening.

The very structure of teaching enabled women to participate in public life. They made choices about particular situations (whether to stay or leave), they negotiated with parents and other teachers, they devised strategies when faced with predicaments. When their choices, negotiations, and strategies succeeded, women's confidence increased. These decisions gave them at least more public presence, at best some public power.

NOTES

1. Fanny Kingman Holmes, *Diary*, January 18, March 10, March 14, and April 10, 1836, Schlesinger Library, Radcliffe College (hereafter SL).

2. Fanny Kingman Holmes, *Diary*, May 20, 1838, and June 23, 1839, SL; letter to Anna, June 21, 1839, Fannie Kingman Holmes Papers, SL.

3. Mary Mudge, *Diary*, 1854, SL.

4. Clara Burt, *Journal*, February 10, 1877, Bancroft Library, University of California at Berkeley (hereafter BL).

5. Elizabeth Hatheway, letters to her sister, September 26 and October 11, 1852, Hatheway Family Papers, Olin Library, Cornell University (hereafter OL).

6. Clara Burt, *Journal*, May 24, 1880, BL.

7. Frances Jane McCulloh Bartlett, letter to family, September 20, 1891, McCulloh Family Papers, BL.

8. Harriet W., letter to Elizabeth Hatheway, September 19, 1852, Hatheway Family Papers, OL.

9. Anonymous, *Diary*, 1864, BL.

10. Mary Atkins Lynch, letter to brother and sister, April 8, 1843, Atkins Family Papers; obituary, *The Cleveland Leader*, October 24, 1882, BL.

11. Abigail Smith Tuck Marsh, letters, July 13, 1845, August 14, 1846, and July 14, 1851, Marsh Family Papers, BL.

12. Abigail Smith Tuck Marsh, letter to Reverend Z. P. Wild, August 14, 1846, Marsh Family Papers, BL.

13. Fanny Kingman Holmes, letter to Anna, June 21, 1839, Fannie Kingman Holmes Papers, SL.

14. Clara Burt, *Journal*, October 12, 1876, BL.

15. Mary Mudge, *Diary*, SL; Elizabeth Hatheway, letters (September 26, 1852; October 11, 1852; January 20, 1853), Hatheway Family Papers, OL; Dema Higbee, *Diary*, SL; Mary Ann Nearing Berry, *Diary*, Berry Family Papers, OL.

16. Mary Ann Nearing Berry, *Diary*, OL. See also Mary Mudge, *Diary*, SL.

17. Edna to Lizzie, December 6, 1866, Lizzie Ives Collection, OL.

18. Mary Mudge, *Diary*, February 1 and February 3–7, 1854, SL.

19. Mary Mudge, *Diary*, SL.

20. Mary Mudge, *Diary*, April 14, 1854, SL.

21. Achsa Snow Parker, "A Pioneer School-Mistress," Electa Snow Bramer Papers, p. 7, BL.

22. Edna, letter to Lizzie Ives, November 2, 1866, Lizzie Ives Papers, OL.

23. Anonymous, *Diary*, August 23, 1864, BL.

24. Clara Burt, *Journal*, June 17, 1875, BL.

25. Clara Burt, *Journal*, July 26, 1875, BL.

26. Annie Devlin, letter to Elizabeth Hatheway, January 20, 1853, Hatheway Family Papers, OL.

27. Ann J. Stoddard, *Diary*, SL.

28. Dema Higbee, *Diary*, SL.

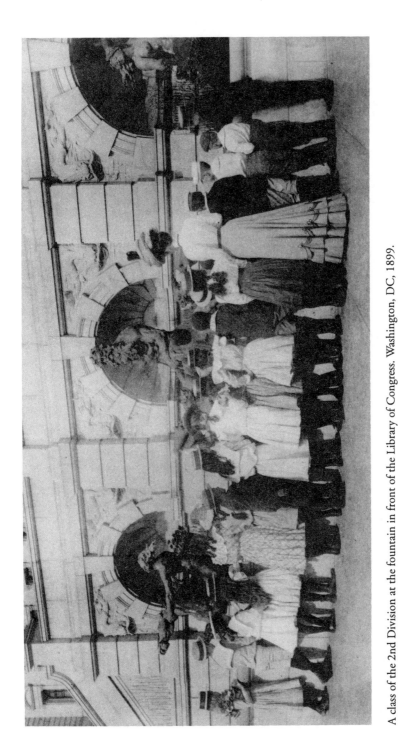

A class of the 2nd Division at the fountain in front of the Library of Congress. Washington, DC, 1899.

Photo by Frances Benjamin Johnston

Frances Benjamin Johnston Collection, Prints and Photographs Division, Library of Congress

A Seed Lesson: Primary class studying plants. Whittier School, Hampton Institute.
Photo by Frances Benjamin Johnston
Frances Benjamin Johnston Collection, Prints and Photographs Division, Library of Congress

Ozark School Teacher in Arkansas: This 1935 photograph of the smoking teacher contra-
dicted stereotypes of the straitlaced schoolma'arm. September, 1935.
Photo by Ben Shahn
Prints and Photographs Division, Library of Congress

Education in the Rural School. William County, ND. October, 1937.
Photo by Russell Lee
U.S. Farm Security Administration Collection, Prints and Photographs Division, Library of Congress

"One room school in an isolated mountainous Spanish-American community, which has eight grades and two teachers. Most of the teaching is in Spanish, the language spoken in the children's homes, and as a result they rarely speak English fluently." Ojo Sorco, NM. January, 1943.
Office of War Information Collection, Prints and Photographs Division, Library of Congress

Room in the Primary School. San Augustine, TX. April, 1943.
Photo by John Vachon
Office of War Information Collection, Prints and Photographs Division, Library of Congress

CHAPTER 4

Autonomy in the Texts of Teachers' Lives

Emily Blackwell chose teaching in the 1850s, even though she detested the occupation, to support herself and to save money for medical school tuition. In addition to lacking talent for it, she hated its smallness, its limitations, and its boundedness, and frequently complained about it in letters to her older sister, the medical pioneer Elizabeth. "O for a truly noble life—to be—to do great works for humanity" (January 6, 1852). Teaching, Emily Blackwell made very clear, had nothing to do with noble action or great human endeavor. Emily Blackwell's view of teaching related directly to constrictions on women's occupational choices. She wanted a life different from the one she had, she wrote on August 31, 1853, enclosed with children in a room all day: "I long with such an intense longing for freedom, action, for life and truth" (in Chambers-Schiller, 1984, p. 141). Emily Blackwell depicted teaching as a form of containment.

If teaching constricted rather than expanded Emily Blackwell's horizons, it did just the opposite for Mary Mudge, Lucia Downing, Mary Bradford, Fanny Kingman Holmes, Clara Burt, and many other nineteenth-century women for whom the occupation provided not only economic remuneration, but also challenging daily experiences (Bradford, 1932; Burt, 1875–1889; Downing, 1951; Holmes, 1836–1839; Mudge, 1854). Arozina Perkins, a pioneer teacher sponsored by the National Board of Popular Education, had to overcome her image as an "adventurer" before she was accepted into an Iowa community (Kaufman, 1984, p. 140). Eulalia "Sister" Bourne, teaching in rural Arizona during the 1910s, emphasized the challenges and demands that making oneself into a teacher demanded: "My responsibility was great. Could I measure up? It was a wit-challenging ordeal. Without training, without the moral backing of a principal or colleague, without self-assurance, I had to self-make a teacher" (Bourne, 1974, p. 23). She was on her own.

As I argued in Chapter 3, the occupation of teaching contributed toward increasing women's independence in the nineteenth century. Tyack and Hansot suggested that "teaching provided a secret passageway to greater autonomy for many young women committed to the gospel of the common school" (1982, p. 66). Many women made more out of teaching than many educational reformers, with their construction of the occupation as feminine and domestic, may have wanted them to make out of it. At the same time, limited opportunity for women pushed the talented and untalented into teaching. A Nevada county superintendent, for example, wished in 1877 that teaching was not "the only respectable occupation which a young lady can follow," so that those who would make "good clerks or waitresses" but not good teachers would go elsewhere (Goldman, 1981, p. 29). If the image of teaching we have today is more like Emily Blackwell's and less like the adventurer's, it is because we must contend not only with its social valuation and occupational character, but also with cultural images of teaching.

Those social images are reflected in, shaped by, and swirl around the stories that are told about teachers' lives and in the stories they tell others about themselves. Teachers draw on these discourses to tell their own stories. These shared cultural texts, in other words, become part of commonsense understandings about teachers and teaching as an occupation. People develop these understandings in different ways. We may read novels, short stories, magazine articles, or biographies about teachers. We may listen to teachers' stories told about their own experiences as students, or their experiences of teaching. And children in school talk about their teachers, prospective teachers, and past teachers continually.

A central theme in stories about women teachers, as well as an important ingredient in the current cultural construction of teaching as an occupation for women, is the question of how much autonomy is available for women who are teachers. Do teachers have freedom? Independence? This chapter explores that question through the examination of both selected writings by and about teachers and stories teachers told in interviews about their own entrance into teaching.

The opportunities offered to teachers, the way teaching is understood as an occupation, what being a teacher means in American culture(s): All these issues relate not only to the organization of teaching as work but also to the commonsense notions of "being a teacher." Dorinne Kondo has written: "The process of making sense of each other involves efforts to force others into preconceived categories" (Kondo, 1990, p. 25). In this chapter I want to examine these preconceived categories and how they influence how teachers are made sense of. I will argue that women sought autonomy and transformed it at the same time.

INDEPENDENCE AND WOMEN'S IDENTITY

Feminist theory has sometimes constructed autonomy and connectedness oppositionally. Jane Flax suggests that this construction is fraudulent:

> Sometimes feminist theorists also tend to oppose "autonomy" and "being in relations." These theorists do not see that, for adults, forms of being in relation can be claustrophobic without autonomy, and autonomy without being in relations can easily degenerate into mastery. (Flax, 1990, p. 181)

When these positions are idealized their value is exaggerated and their complexity read out of them.

It is easier to see how these positions can shift if a woman's identity is understood not as a single, unified entity that can be summed up with adjectives like "strong," "domestic," or "ambitious":

> Identity is not a fixed "thing," it is negotiated, open, shifting, ambiguous, the result of culturally available meanings and the open-ended, power-laden enactments of those meanings in everyday situations. (Kondo, 1990, p. 24)

Kondo's representation of fluid identities emphasizes that particular contexts highlight different parts of one's identity. At the same time, identities are the "result" of "culturally available meanings." The culturally available meanings of teaching have, at least for women, always been represented in their connection to safety and domesticity.

To talk about Blackwell's freedom and action in relation to teaching is to explore characteristics of agency and independence. Do we think of teachers as able to make independent decisions? How much agency do they have when they carry out their work on a daily basis or when they plan their goals? While I am not interested in its deeper philosophical meanings, the word that I will use to represent these concerns is *autonomy*.

Freedom and action accompany the life of the autonomous person, the person free to travel or to initiate activities of choice. For most people, men and women, this sort of autonomy is more ideal than reality, since conditions of birth, class, ethnicity, and race, as well as gender, play such a major part in shaping one's opportunities. In fact, metaphors of the autonomous person seem linked to travel rather than to staying at home. This image of traveling is significant because autonomy as we have known it is characterized by distance rather than by connection.

During the nineteenth century, women associated autonomy with adventurers who were free to travel far and wide, experiencing the out of the ordinary. Dependent images run counter to the autonomous adventurer; they are more domestic, perhaps because mothers, probably the ultimate symbol of the unautonomous person, are so tied to others. Where nineteenth-century images are more out of the ordinary, today autonomy is represented in more ordinary ways. One does not have to travel to the Arctic, that is, to be autonomous. Work that is not imagined as autonomous, however, is elementary schoolteaching, because the image is of women enclosed all day with children in small rooms.

One of the guideposts that marks the cultural position of women schoolteachers is their relationship to autonomy. It does not matter whether the writers want the teacher to be autonomous or not. Rather, what is key is the central importance of autonomy as a factor in these women's lives, no matter what stand on it the author takes. Autonomy is directly confronted in the texts of nineteenth- and early-twentieth-century works as women struggle to legitimately have it as well as talk about it. In later works, autonomy becomes the subtext; that is, authors do not confront it directly in the texts, but the assumption of its importance, its existence embedded in the subtext, enables the reader to make sense of the text.

Autonomy refers, in the sense individuals use, to personal freedom, to the "freely operating 'individual'" (Kondo, 1990, p. 26). Some philosophers define autonomy as a characteristic of people who identify with their "desires, goals, and values" (Christman, 1989, p. 7). These people must have "critically reflected on these goals and desires and decided they are their own."

If we understand the world to be a place where discourses are central in fostering and limiting people's choices, it is difficult to imagine that someone can be autonomous. We are connected to one another by the discourses of our institutions, and by discourses of, among others, gender, race, and class. Yet we make use of these discourses in uneven and unequal ways; some become particularly important when groups are marginalized.

DISCOURSE AND AGENCY

Discourses are institutionalized ways of understanding relationships, activities, and meanings that emerge through language (talk, rules, thoughts, writing) and influence what people in specific institutions take to be true. Discourses shape how people understand the world and therefore how they act in it. In fact, they are aimed at producing certain effects (Benveniste, 1971, in Cherryholmes, 1988; Eagleton, 1991). It is knowledge, like child development, educational psychology, or school administration, that is inscribed in a particular vocabulary (Belsey, 1980).

While discourses may be said to facilitate certain ways of understanding daily life (in the institution of the school), they also proscribe what will be seen. Kress argues that a discourse will "produce a set of statements about that area that will define, describe, delimit, and circumscribe what it is possible and impossible to say with respect to it, and how it is to be talked about" (Kress, 1985, p. 28). A discourse provides a way to understand the life of a school, family, or university, but rather than functioning in terms of providing and facilitating, discourses are usually seen as restraining. As Popkewitz (1992) notes: "Discourse practices have the potential for disciplining the individual to the sets of rules, norms, and relations that are implied" (p. 145). People working in an institution can be disciplined by the discourse without directly intending to be, and without having the rules of practice directly articulated to them.

Discourses are central in producing shared meanings in institutions, but people negotiate the meanings they make. People are not automatons who are simply obedient to the perceived shared rules that guide the institutions in which they work and live. Discourses must be continually shaped and are renegotiated by how people live and act in their daily lives. Social agents, as Pierre Bourdieu (1990) says, "are not automata regulated like clocks, in accordance with laws they do not understand" (p. 9). Bourdieu argues that to understand social life, sociologists need to look both at the structures that shape human actions, and at the ways in which these structures are interpreted, negotiated, and represented:

> On the one hand, the objective structures which the sociologist constructs in the objectivist moment, by setting aside the subjective representations of the agents, are the basis of subjective representations and they constitute the structural constraints which influence interactions; but, on the other hand, these representations also have

to be remembered if one wants to account above all for the daily individual and collective struggles which aim at transforming or preserving these structures. (pp. 125–126)

Here I am considering the structures to be the discourses that shape what is normative at school, and upon which the teachers draw for their understanding, and the representations to be the perspectives teachers had on school life.

These discourses are not neutral ways of understanding the forces that shape school life. As Foucault (1984) argued, discourses rest on power relations. Discourses are "produced" by power. This power, however, Foucault argues, is not simply negative and repressive, but also productive:

> It doesn't only weigh on us as a force that says no, but . . . it traverses and produces things, it induces pleasure, forms knowledge, produces discourse. It needs to be considered as a productive network which runs through the whole social body, much more than as a negative instance whose function is repression. (p. 61)

Power is produced through people's daily actions and interactions. Its textual construction and social enactment are open to analysis.

Questions of power are important to an analysis of autonomy because autonomy becomes important when one is restrained. The demand for it "arises from the strained relations between subordinate and dominant groups" (Boehm, 1947, p. 332). Hence it is a relational characteristic. One does not think to emphasize autonomy when one's liberty or personal freedom does not seem constrained.

THE TEXTS

The major texts for this discussion are published and unpublished work concerning the lives of nineteenth- and early-twentieth-century women, and the stories of contemporary teachers based on interviews. The materials represent letters and unpublished diaries, as well as published autobiographies and fiction. The fiction includes Augusta Evans' *Beulah*, first published in 1859; short stories by Kate Chopin (1969), Anna Fuller (1892), and George Marion McClellan (1906/1975); and *The Revolt of Sarah Perkins* (1965) by Marion Cockrell. The autobiographies are Harriet Cooke's *Memories of My Life Work*, published in 1861, and *Tisha* (Specht, 1976), a memoir about teacher Anne Hobb's work in the 1920s published in 1976. The diaries and letters represent the work of teachers during the second half of the nineteenth century. Each sort of work comes at the life of the teacher differently, emphasizing certain aspects of the experience.

Twentieth-century readers and writers have come to expect more direct consideration of women's autonomy than nineteenth-century writers offered. Historian Mary Johnson advises the reader not to look for an autonomous character in Antoinette Brevost, an early-nineteenth-century schoolmistress: "Neither the spirit of adventure nor the quest for independence impelled her to withstand the physical and psychological hardships concomitant with teaching in the unpolished society and unhealthy atmosphere of early nineteenth-century Pittsburgh." She suggests that readers who expect the frontier pioneer woman to be adventurous will be disappointed (Johnson, 1980, p. 151).

Nineteenth-Century Letters and Diaries

Diaries do not represent unproblematic transfers of personal experience to paper. Their writers shaped and selected in order to represent themselves, their intimates, and the events in their lives in ways they desired. Lensink's (1989) reading of the diary of Emily Hawley Gillespie, for example, reveals a certain construction of characters and way of portraying self. Lensink contrasts the reporting of events in Emily's and her daughter Sarah's journals. Emily portrays herself as a superior person and her children as good. She leaves out details of her children's misbehavior (entered in Sarah's journal) that would challenge that picture. When her husband Henry is insensitive to her she leaves out his thoughtless remarks (pp. 390–393).

This idea of the constructed self of the author is apparent in other examples as well. Elizabeth Fox-Genovese (1988) portrays Sarah Gayle's journal as "self-representation . . . in a crafted idiom" (p. 16). The idea of the constructed self does not suggest that women lied or covered up (though it can suggest this—and they sometimes did), but rather that like other people, women in the nineteenth century developed ways of looking at themselves that are reflected in their diaries (Biklen, 1990).

In nineteenth-century letters and diaries, travel represented one expression of autonomy. Travel from the relationships and ties of close family life or of friends represented bravery. Women did not always have the courage for it. Electa Snow was teaching in Seneca Castle, New York, six miles west of Geneva, in 1831 and wanted to visit her stepmother and sisters in Ohio, but was too afraid to make the trip alone. She wrote to them on September 20:

> With regard to my visiting you I am necessitated to tell you that I have relinquished the idea of visiting you this fall or of ever saying any more about visiting you. I did think when I wrote before I should go, but as the time drew near, my resolution began to stagger. To start alone, to find my way into the wilderness, and that Lake! (Parker, n.d., p. 9)

The trip was more than she wanted to undertake.

Whether travel called up fear or excitement, it took women away from contacts with others and known patterns of their daily lives, and pitted them against physical environments they did not know, conditions different from those they were accustomed to, and real and/or imagined physical dangers. Women often described standing in desolation as the wagon or vehicle that had transported them to their place of work went on its return journey, or running sobbing after it. Homesickness was common.

As important as family members were to the traveler, female friends were essential. Mrs. Harriet B. Cooke, who traveled alone to many places and was financially independent for much of her life, had incredible adventures. Like many other early-nineteenth-century women who taught for financial remuneration, and like most other women who wrote about it, Harriet's father had died—in her case, when she was 12. She got her first teaching position at 16, in 1802, leaving Connecticut and moving to Vermont, motivated, she says, as much by a desire to see the world as by finances. In 1819 she traveled South. Her husband, whom she married in 1808, had gotten into debt, and moved South in 1813 to find work. She had remained in Vermont with their four children working as a teacher "to remove from my husband during his absence the burden of supporting his family from his slender means" until he could support them. In the summer of 1820 her husband died during the yellow fever epidemic. Harriet mourned: "I was, literally, *alone*, with no female friend to comfort me in this time of trial" (Cooke, 1861, pp. 14, 41, 61). Harriet had supported her husband and children, traveled for pleasure as well as for financial necessity, and wanted to make new connections when she traveled. She wanted to reconstitute autonomy.

Harriet Cooke represented herself as free to travel because her father had died. Images and metaphors of the orphan framed the necessity for women's autonomy in nineteenth-century teachers' texts. Orphans of "middling" class origins were justified in gaining greater autonomy and independence. This greater autonomy was not necessarily welcomed, but it is a textual justification for liberty.

The mother of Elizabeth Hatheway (1823–1908) died when she

was young; it fell to Elizabeth to take care of the house. When her father planned to remarry, she left her home because he indicated to her that the young age of his new bride made it difficult for Elizabeth to remain in the house, and went to a private school in Philadelphia to train for teaching. Elizabeth was offered a position in Tennessee in 1852, which she accepted. She left her friends, traveling alone to a new position in a new community. Harriet W., a friend, wrote to her, on September 19, 1852, of her courage:

> I have thought of you often of late and of what firmness and resolute-ness of character you must be possessed to leave your home and friends and become a teacher. I feel a vivid emotion of pride and pleasure when one of my own sex thus proves themselves possessed of great and noble sentiments.

The friend saw Elizabeth's actions as a bursting of the bonds that con-stricted women's lives. She continued: "There is so much that is tri-fling in the daily avocations of woman, that generally we become tri-fling, and fall far below our natural rank among God's creatures." To her friend, Elizabeth's adventure symbolized meaningful rather than trifling activity, and hence elevated women's standing (Hatheway, 1853).

Elizabeth could, during this part of the nineteenth century, repre-sent her experience as an adventure, rather than as a misfortune, be-cause she had been pressured to leave home. It was as if being a kind of orphan enabled Elizabeth to leave. If women had to look for excuses to travel, then being an orphan was a good means to justify the decision.

These private writings suggest women confiding to themselves or to one another. In public writings, becoming orphaned is license to travel. It is as if the writer asks for the reader's sympathy, pursuading her that her heroine was forced into this situation, so it is not her fault. Elizabeth Winston (1980) supports this view when she argues that before 1920 women who wrote autobiographies had to defend any "un-traditional" decisions that they made about their own lives, and that they would do this by working to develop the reader's sympathy for their plight (p. 93). Winston called the relationship that the autobiog-rapher attempted to establish with her readers a "conciliatory" one. Then the reader would not, presumably, be judgmental.

Nineteenth-Century Fiction

In nineteenth- (and early-twentieth-) century fiction, women en-tered teaching because of financial reasons. Fathers died, crops failed. In some cases the characters were happy about their choice; in other cases, they were not. Those who were happy received pleasure from teaching, became persons of note in the community, and enjoyed feelings of independence (Chesnutt, 1899/1967; Chopin, 1969; Fuller, 1892; McClellan, 1906/1975).

Fiction during this period constructed European-American women in teaching as resisters against social constraints on women. Teaching represented an avenue to independence, and hence was slightly unrespectable. Three nineteenth-century fictional texts suggest this representation. Melitte, in "Aunt Lympy's Interference" (1969) by Kate Chopin, could have been supported by her relatives, but she preferred her independence and was attracted to teaching, a job which gave her pleasure. Mary William, in Anna Fuller's "The Schoolmarm" (1892), planned to make a "declaration of independence" when she was 21 to become a teacher. In August Evans' *Beulah* (1870), Beulah could have depended on Dr. Hartwell, her guardian, for financial support, but chose instead to maintain her independence and support herself as a teacher. The necessity of financial difficulty provided the "excuse" to explain their attraction to teaching.

Family members and friends of these three female characters reacted negatively to their teaching. Aunt Lympy, "an old family servant," returned for a visit to her former place of residence and searched for Melitte. She told the 18-year-old that she had heard a rumor in town that she could not believe was true. When Melitte questioned her, Aunt Lympy replied: "I don' wan' to spick about befo' de chillun." After the children were sent away, the dialogue continued:

> "I yeard you was turn school-titcher! Dat ant true?" The question in her eyes was almost pathetic. "Oh!" exclaimed Melitte; an utterance that expressed relief, surprise, amusement, commiseration, affirmation.
>
> "Den it's true," Aunt Lympy almost whispered; "a De Broussard turn school-titcher!" The shame of it crushed her into silence.
>
> Melitte felt the inutility of trying to dislodge the old family servant's deep-rooted prejudices. All her effort was directed toward convincing Aunt Lympy of her complete self-satisfaction in this new undertaking. (Chopin, 1969, p. 13)

Melitte turned down the money Aunt Lympy offered her as well as the later offer from the rich uncle to live with him.

Mary William's grandmother, in *The Schoolmarm* (Fuller, 1892), objected to her teaching not only because she did not "approve of young women gettin' dissatisfied with the sphere to which they've been called," but also because it was not respectable for ladies to work for a living. Additionally, the grandmother suggested that being a teacher raised the woman's expectations for a husband's qualifications. She worried that Mary William would become Eliza Pelham: "She got so set in her ways and so high-flyin' in her notions that the Gov'nor himself wouldn't have suited her." But Mary loved teaching: "She had never been so happy in her life as she was the day on which she stepped upon the platform at school and assumed the responsibilities of 'schoolmarm'" (p. 183).

When Beulah, living in an orphanage, expressed her wish to become a teacher, one of the managers on the orphanage's board of directors told her that it would require too much education, and that she would have to settle for less. Once her status rose through her adoption by a doctor, her continued desire to teach still met with hostility. She was told that were she to teach she would be "lowering herself" in the eyes of their (upper-class) community, who would look upon her with "contempt" (Evans, 1870, p. 227). Once she began teaching, another friend challenged her:

> "Shut up all day with a parcel of rude stupid children, and released, only to be caged again in a small room in a second-rate boarding house. Really, I should fancy [your sources of enjoyment] were limited, indeed." (p. 242)

Beulah argued that she was no prisoner:

> "No, I enjoy my brisk walk to school, in the morning; the children are neither so dull, nor so bearish as you seem to imagine. I am attached to many of them, and do not feel the day to be very long." (pp. 242–243)

No one understood her desire to be independent. The novel linked teaching with that independence. Beulah resisted pressure in order to become a teacher. She was forced to leave the house of her guardian in order to teach.

In her boardinghouse lived Clara, another orphaned teacher. Clara, in contrast to Beulah, despised teaching, so the two friends often argued about their situations. Clara told Beulah she should stop resisting; she would not have to be a teacher if she would admit she had a guardian, and let her guardian provide for her: "Would you leave summer sunshine for the icebergs of Arctic night? Silly girl, appreciate your good fortune" (p. 140). Clara questioned whether a woman would choose to leave the safety of the home (known) for the insecurity of the distant and unknown spot to which one must travel. Beulah responded, "Would you be willing to change places with me, and indolently wait for others to maintain you? . . . You are less a woman than I thought you, if you would be willing to live on the bounty of others when a little activity would enable you to support yourself" (p. 140). Clara disagreed: "Woman was intended as a pet plant, to be guarded and cherished; isolated and uncared for, she droops, languishes and dies" (pp. 140–141). Beulah rejected this perspective:

> Don't talk to me about woman's clinging, dependent nature. . . . You can wind, and lean, and hang on somebody else if you like; but I feel more like one of those old pine-trees yonder. I can stand up. Very slim, if you will, but straight and high. Stand by myself; battle with wind and rain, and tempest roar; be swayed and bent, perhaps, in the storm, but stand unaided, nevertheless. I feel humbled when I hear a woman bemoaning the weakness of her sex, instead of showing that she has a soul and mind of her own, inferior to none. (p. 141)

Clara responded that these words would sound very "heroic" if they were found in a novel, but they were not in "real" life (pp. 140–141).

Clara represented traditional feminine values, disliking the necessity of supporting herself. She took a governess position on a Southern plantation and married, enabling her to stop teaching. Beulah, on the other hand, continued her independence to the last few pages of the book, even minding when, through unfortunate circumstances, she had to give up her own cottage. She accepted an invitation to live with good friends. But she missed the autonomy of living independently:

> They were all that friends could be to an orphan; still, she regretted her little cottage, and missed the home-feeling she had prized so highly. True, she had constant access to the greenhouse, and was rarely without her bouquet of choice flowers; but these could not compensate her for the loss of her own little garden. (p. 496)

Beulah married her guardian in the last few pages of the book. The author succumbed to tradition only for the sake of form.

Sources about the late-nineteenth-century fictional African-American woman teacher are limited. Charles Chesnutt wrote about teachers of African-American children, but the teachers were white. The single story I have found from this period celebrates the woman who becomes a teacher as a figure of major importance in the community. Lizzie Story, in George Marion McClellan's "A Creole from Louisiana"

(1906/1975), was a freeborn black woman from Rhode Island who went to Northern Alabama to teach school after graduating from high school. She obtained a position at the "colored free school at Mercury" and in this rural setting gained importance: "She was a born teacher and soon became a person of great note in that community." The independence she obtained also applied to her personal life. The short story represents her as socially, though not emotionally, free to develop relationships as she pleases. She can experience love and teach; she does not have to be desexualized. The restrictions that fictional European-American women had to confront did not apply. Subject to neither these controls nor the privileges, the African-American teacher in McClellan's short story had more independence in daily life. Though she could have dignity, she could not be a lady.

Twentieth-Century Autobiography

After a few decades, texts of teachers' lives no longer have to argue for autonomy, pleading and encouraging the reader to understand the unusual situation. By now, the conjunction of female persona and male adventure delights. Because women's place has changed, readers as well as characters behave differently. Characters have more freedom and readers have higher expectations. At the same time, women still have to explain themselves when they do unusual traveling. They may not have to explain traveling from Massachusetts to California, but they do to Alaska.

The main character in *Tisha* (Specht, 1976), the autobiography of a teacher who journeyed alone to Alaska to teach during the 1920s, could go to Alaska only because she was an orphan. Detached from family relationships, Tisha was free to make her own choices because she had to support herself. Her representation reflects a male adventurer pattern enacted by a woman.

One of the complications of reading *Tisha* is that the form the autobiography takes is as an "as-told-to" story. While Anne Hobbs, the teacher, is said to have told the story her way, Robert Specht was an intimate collaborator. Additionally, the story is told retrospectively from a vantage point of several decades later. The book is very useful, however, in suggesting the discourses about gender that were useful in framing and describing the choices made by a young woman with few material resources but with some strong female figures in her life.

Tisha holds readers' interest because of the adventures that Tisha experiences, the risks that she takes, and the presentation of herself as alone and independent in a strange, and in many ways fearful, place.

Anne Hobbs was born in Colorado around the turn of the century. Her
father had been a coal miner. He had cared little about his daughter or
his wife, deserting the family on many occasions. Luckily, her grandmother had always loved her deeply, often providing a home for her
when her parents were unable to care for her. In high school Anne's
family completely broke apart, and her mother could no longer support
her. Miss Ivy, a high school teacher, had "taken me in and treated me
as if I were her own daughter," providing both a place for her to live
while she completed her education and a role model for her to become
a teacher. When she completed her normal school training, she taught
in Oregon for two years. While she was in Oregon, the territorial com-
missioner of education tried to attract teachers to Alaska. To Tisha,
"he made it sound so exciting and adventurous that I made out an
application" (p. 23). At age 19 she left for the trip to Chicken, Alaska,
the town where she would teach.

Tisha associated teaching with possibility: travel, adventure, and
independence. The trip to Chicken must have fulfilled many of her
dreams, because she had many adventures. She rode an uncontrollable
horse, watched a grizzly bear attack caribou, got caught in a bad snow-
storm, and experienced the beauty of the land. About to arrive in
Chicken, Tisha reaffirmed teaching as a ticket to ride: "I'd come
to a far place, just as my Grandmother Hobbs used to tell me I
would. . . . 'You be a teacher, Annie,' [Granny] used to tell me, 'an' you
can go anywhere in the world you want'" (pp. 32, 49). Teaching expanded the horizons of women like Annie.

Tisha was poor, dependent on some occupation to earn a living.
In contrast to others, like Emily Blackwell, who felt forced by social
values and limited opportunities for women to take up an occupation which contained and alienated them, Tisha enjoyed teaching
and was intellectually stimulated by the children. She worked at developing good relationships with them and was challenged by the demands of a one-room school that served a multicultural and age-
diverse student body. She was interested in pedagogy that empowered
students.

Although Chicken, Alaska, was an isolated community, it had a
web of social relationships that Tisha had to learn. This web managed
the status of community members. Tisha had to struggle against many
community members, including influential parents and the board of
education, in order to counter racism against native peoples. This racism took the form of the exclusion of native children from the school-
room, prohibitions on interracial relationships, and economic segregation. Chicken was a colonial town.

The representation of autonomy in the novel is more complex to signify. If Tisha conforms to the community's values about whom to teach, whom to love, and whom to adopt, she can keep her position, and experience inclusion within the village's social network. Tisha does not acquiesce to pressure, but engages in resistance along with others with whom she can collaborate. Autonomy signifies independence for all peoples, particularly those who have been oppressed. Tisha's autonomy depended on other community members in two ways. First, she was free only if others like the indigenous people of the region whom she valued and had made friends with were free. Her freedom was not unaccountable because she could not be free at their expense. Second, autonomy could be attained only when she joined with allies to struggle together against racist practices. Her autonomy was limited by these racist practices, which could be overcome only by some form of collective resistance. This vocabulary does not reflect the tone of the writing, but it does suggest its message.

This form of autonomy is also represented in the autobiography of Septima Clark, an African-American woman whose representation of autonomy contradicts the usage of metaphors of travel. *Echo in My Soul* (1962) describes her development from a schoolteacher to her public renown as a well-known educator and civil rights activist. She related her early commitment to teaching as an occupation of choice not to its meaning for her independence, but to its connection to the community:

> From my early childhood I wanted to be a schoolteacher. That desire grew and strengthened through the years. And I believe it was born and nourished out of both my heredity and my environment. (Clark, 1962, p. 13)

Independence for Septima Clark did not involve leaving her community, but leading her community toward independence. When marriage leads Clark away from her community, she is lonesome and experiences homesickness; her different accent helps to displace her as a leader who can give service to her people in order to help them work toward more agency in their own lives. Clark's work suggests that the use of travel metaphors to signify autonomy may be bound up with race.

Twentieth-Century Fiction

By the mid-twentieth century, autonomy moved from the text to the subtext. The writer and the reader share certain minimal values about women's independence, and these shared values are essential for the story to make sense.

The Revolt of Sarah Perkins (Cockrell, 1965) is a historical novel that uses the reader's distance from nineteenth-century controls on women to examine women's agency. Published during the 1960s but set in the 1860s, Sarah Perkins's story tells of independence developed and character strengthened by the heroine's move West. Thirty-year-old Sarah, whose parents had both died, lived as the maiden aunt with her brother and his family, tutoring the children, receiving room and board, and having no control over her inheritance. Though outwardly calm, she chafed under these constraints. She applied for and obtained a position as a teacher in a Colorado mining town in 1869. The town was looking for a plain, and therefore unmarriageable, teacher, one easy to control; they thought Sarah was their match.

The West "made" Sarah independent, however, and less willing to compromise on her educational and humanitarian principles regarding the quality of the curriculum, the school facilities (what was good enough for all the former schoolteachers was not good enough for her), and her insistence that the daughter of a leading prostitute, the son of a former slave, and the daughter of an American Indian would all be students in her school. Challenged on all of these fronts, she insisted on the moral propriety of her views, surprising herself with her ability to be firm. In an early battle the author represented the changes in her character's perspectives: "She didn't understand it. In Medfield she didn't used to get so excited about things" (p. 63). When she insisted that a half-Indian child come to school she told the father, "You bring that child to school tomorrow, Tom Sellers, and I'll teach until they drag me out of there!" (p. 234). As clear as she was on her principles, however, she feared that her challenges to authority would force her to lose the position she cherished:

> They were going to take her school away from her . . . her school, her happiness, her wonderful feeling of purpose and accomplishment . . . her . . . future. For a moment she was tempted to surrender, to tell Redbird she would have to come after school was out, for special classes. But she knew she was literally unable to do such a thing. (p. 235)

Her resistance against the town succeeded. She transformed the town, forcing the community to face and overcome their prejudices, and her Western experience transformed her.

It also transformed her appearance from a plain spinster to an attractive single woman courted by several men. Her marriage to a member of the school board ended her teaching but confirmed her femininity. She did not remain a single woman. Her attractiveness as a woman was linked to her growing willingness to resist the town's prejudices and defend the voiceless. Sarah's experience of teaching in the West freed her from her brother's control, enabled her to earn her own living for a year, brought out her character and principles, and, by marrying, gave her back her father's inheritance, which her brother had controlled while she was single.

The author constructs Sarah's character, through most of the book, as a woman who learns, in Judith Butler's terms, to "return the gaze" (Butler, 1990, p. ix). In this text, however, this position does not equate with feminism. Teaching enables Sarah Perkins to escape nineteenth-century constraints on women (viewed through the next century's eyes), not twentieth-century ones. Her transformation from a private woman constrained by her family to an active woman who assumes her place in the public world accepts the restrictions on the nature of that public participation.

Autonomy for Tisha and Sarah Perkins is represented by travel to and settlement in the frontier. Many characters in both books commented on how relaxed social customs were compared to the East. These communities also actively preserved distinctions between settlers and native peoples through racist and oppressive practices. Who was the "other" was partially determined through control of access to the schools. In both the real town of Chicken, Alaska, in 1920 and the fictional town of Belle City, Colorado Territory, in 1869, Tisha and Sarah insisted that outsiders get an education. While nineteenth-century texts enabled women's autonomy, they do not represent this autonomy as unfettered. Fighting for themselves meant fighting for others.

HISTORICAL PERSPECTIVES

I have read these texts for their construction of women's agency and its relationship to teaching. The history of women in teaching includes a history of women's struggle for agency both in the workplace and outside it. Outside it, texts could position teaching as a vehicle for freedom. But in order to be such a vehicle the text had to be constructed so that women had no choice but to become teachers. In sional autonomy of authority such as Abraham Flexner (1915) described, but rather one of independence and/or adventure in their personal lives and one of moral conviction and pedagogical principle in their work lives. Their autonomy had to do with independence and adventure, not with distancing themselves from children. Hence, the kind of autonomy that concerned women in teaching both in the nineteenth and early twentieth centuries was of a different order than the autonomy we generally consider. The kind of autonomy these teachers sought did not distance them from the demands of their students. Categorically, teaching is a form of work that enmeshes its practitioners in a world of relationships and knowledge. If a teacher develops a respecting relationship with a particular class, exiting that relationship suddenly causes disruption in the lives of students.

Traditionally, autonomy has entailed distance from other people. Nursing mothers can only attain autonomy by giving up nursing, for their children physically depend on them. New products—baby formulas, answering machines, and so forth—are often touted for the autonomy they make possible. As the mother does not have to nurse her baby, so the answering machine enables people to screen engagement with callers.

Hence the dilemma of autonomy. Autonomy brings freedom, but it also separates or distances individuals from caring, needy, or dependent relationships with others. Personal autonomy is important. Feeling cramped in one's sense of expansiveness by oppressive household duties is generally disabling. I do not reinforce the idea of the nobility of women's self-sacrifice. Any feminist definition of autonomy must critically examine women's position in the world in relation to men and children, to the old and the sick—in other words, to the world of service. Autonomy as traditionally defined referred to the civic world, not to the personal realm of nursing babies, caring for sick relatives, and being a wife. But feminist accounts of how the personal is political disrupts a clear demarcation between public and private. The authors I have examined also represent fluid boundaries.

The women in these texts wanted both independence and community. The author of *The Revolt of Sarah Perkins*, writing in the 1960s, suggested that Sarah gained agency through her revolt from her brother's family. This resistance made her not only a good educator but also more beautiful. This is a liberal feminist position. Sarah learned to speak for herself and for others. This speaking does not indicate the importance of marginalized people speaking for themselves, because the book suggests that Sarah can advocate for them in a way they cannot do for themselves; but it did pay attention to the importance of speak for herself and for others. This speaking does not indicate the importance of marginalized people speaking for themselves, because the book suggests that Sarah can advocate for them in a way they cannot do for themselves; but it did pay attention to the importance of listening to the perspective of others. Sarah felt more a part of the community of Colorado's Belle City than she ever did back East, where she had a history of relations with others. From the perspective of the 1960s (when the book was written), Sarah's decisions seemed sensible, rather than unusually daring (especially since she does marry in the end; her behavior is not too threatening). We do not need textual justifications for Sarah's actions—these are assumed in the subtext—but rather we want the vicarious pleasure of watching her defy nineteenth-century popular opinion, confirmed in her right choices by our knowledge of historical changes that substantiate her decisions.

These historical texts suggest that the story these women told about teaching and agency is a transformative story. Women transformed autonomy as they sought it. While travel and its textual imagery enabled women to escape relations with people that proscribed their independence, their images of autonomy did not center around distance from people. The community they sought was one they helped fashion, rather than the constricting community that was imposed by birth. These teachers connected the idea of service with autonomy even as they did not deny their ambition and desire for public and financial recognition. It was not solely that women felt they had to justify their independence with a service ethic, but that the kind of independence they wanted was not outside a community.

THE INTERVIEWS

Contemporary teachers talk about the desire for "control." By this many of them mean "deciding how they're going to do their job." Teachers' representation of autonomy in interviews for this project expanded on earlier meanings. These teachers did not envision autonomy taking them away from connections to others, but they did not want to be subject to bureaucratic authority; they struggled for the freedom (and responsibility) of negotiating decisions about work. The texts of interviews contained a vocabulary of autonomy that referenced struggle. This struggle concerned a cultural construction of teaching that reflected the work of teaching as the teachers themselves experienced it.

A teacher describes "control" as "a basic fact of human life." One of this teacher's major concerns was the feeling that she did not have control over her work. The grass looked greener elsewhere: "A plumber has control over his job—he comes when he can and he leaves when he goes out, says 'Sorry, I have to get something from my truck,' and he's gone for three hours. Nobody questions about . . . somebody deciding how they're going to do their job." This teacher's frustration rested on many daily experiences in which pedagogical and occupation decisions were made for her rather than by her. Teachers read these decisions as directives about what it means to be a teacher. Though the quest for it is central, having control is not a basic fact of human life. But it is important to the ways in which professionals represent their work lives. The teachers did not object to having some decisions made for them, but particular decisions came to represent parameters on their freedom.

One type of decision teachers resented were those of a bureaucratic nature that suggested insensitivity to how much work teachers had and how they spent their time. One incident arose over children's report cards, which parents received during a conference rather than in the mail. Kate Bridges reported the example:

> Teachers have devised various forms which they use to report. In any place some form of written record [about the conference] is expected to be put in the kid's file. It was just— "you devise some system and no big deal." Well, downtown [the director of elementary education] decrees that . . . all teachers had to report what conference form they were going to be using by such and such a date and copies of these had to be put in some folder and sent downtown. And she would decide if these were going to be valid or not. And then teachers would be notified by such and such a date if these were legitimate or not. Furthermore, she didn't tell us on time so that we weren't able to get the reports written on time. It was such arrogance, such inconsideration of the teachers.

Such incidents represented to teachers "how powerless you are." The stories they told about their powerlessness were stories of critique.

The texts of their lives in teaching, particularly of how they came to be teachers, framed the critiques differently. Some described themselves as free agents, choosing teaching because they "knew" it was the job for them, or falling into it without acknowledging why it was into teaching that they fell. Others acknowledged gender relations in the telling of their stories. Still others nod to gender, but construct their stories as tales of individualized resistance. These teachers' stories tell of their understanding of autonomy because they suggest how the teachers position themselves in relation to different forms of authority (and, hence, control) and other discursive constrictions on agency such as gender and class.

Christine

Christine Bart's text narrates a free agent. She had always wanted to be a teacher because she "loved working with children." She was a "very independent little girl" who had "gone off to overnight camp since I was five years old for eight weeks at a time." The wilderness camp she had attended had been "an absolutely formative experience" in her life. It was "an expensive and wonderful" camp. There she developed a "self-confidence" that would have taken much longer to achieve without the camp experience. When she was a senior in high school she became waterfront director for the camp and continued in that job through college. This camp held such importance for her that when she became engaged in May of her senior year in college, she went back to work at the camp for the summer and "put off getting married until December."

Christine's father was a "successful" businessman in Boston; her mother, who was "trained in the law," had owned a radio station there. Her father, however, "absolutely" would not "allow" the mother to work at anything after the children were born. "So she didn't." Christine had two siblings. When Christine was two her family moved to a city in the western part of the state. For college, she chose an institution in the central part of the state, where she entered the early childhood program. She selected this program because it gave her "leeway to take all the different courses I wanted. I wanted to take as many electives as I could." She had wanted to become a physical education teacher (she had always been a talented athlete), but her parents told her that they would not pay for college if she went into physical education. They said it was "not feminine enough." She decided to "do sports on the side."

For her first student teaching experience she was placed with a teacher with whom she had serious conflict. Her years at the summer camp had given her considerable experience with children, so she said that she "*never* doubted" her abilities to relate to them. In fact, she "had a lot to offer the kids." In this placement "there was a real marriage" between she and the children. Her teacher, however, was "threatened" by her new apprentice and was unresponsive when Christine went to her with questions surrounding all of the things she wanted to learn. Christine said, "I'm structured, but this teacher was rigid." The teacher gave her a C and her university supervisor gave her an A, so she got a B in the course. She said that "all of these things were just obstacles" to her; they did not deter her at all from wanting to teach. She just had to get through them to get to her "real goal." Christine graduated from college in 1960.

Over the next few years, she had several full-time teaching positions, had four children, taught as a permanent substitute, and was an adult basic educator. The family moved from one upstate city to another, finally settling in the Vista City area. By 1974 she was determined to return to teaching full-time, realizing that if she did not make a move, she might never get back in. Times had changed since her graduation from college. Then there were many teaching positions, and she had simply walked into a school that looked promising and obtained a position. Now there were few jobs and a long list of applicants. When she went down to the school board for her interview she found 10 interview rooms. Each room contained a parent, a teacher, and a school board official, and a long line of applicants waited to get into these rooms for their interviews. Several days after her interview she received a letter informing her that she had made the list of candidates to whom positions would be offered when they arose. She said to herself, "How is anybody going to know who I am just because I'm on a list? There's no way I'm going to get to the head of this list." At the end of the summer she called the director of elementary education. The secretary asked Christine, "Is this about a job?" "No," Christine replied, "this is personal." "Of course it was about a job," she said, "but if you tell him that, he's not going to give an interview."

Christine narrated a story of personal initiative. She recalled saying to the elementary education director during her appointment:

> Look, I'm a really good teacher. If you hire me, I'll be one of the best teachers that you have. But why should you know me? I wanted you to see my face and know who I am. I want you to think of me when you think of hiring someone for a job.

She gave him a detailed description of what kind of a teacher she was and why she wanted to teach in the city rather than in the suburbs.

The director must have remembered her because Bart reported that over the next few weeks he called her to offer her several positions. She rejected two of them for different reasons. But on the third call, when a kindergarten teacher had a nervous breakdown five days after school started and the director asked her to take the position as a favor to him because he really needed her, she took it. She was then in the school system as a teacher.

Christine's story is a gendered story. Her parents refuse to finance a college education if she majors in physical education because they feel it is too unfeminine. She agrees to change majors. She chooses early childhood education because the program allows her many electives. Though the social construction of femininity shapes the narrative she tells, Christine shows little interest in the constrictions of gender, except to note that her father forbade her mother to work after they had children and the mother consented, and to tell about why she did not go into physical education. She attends much more openly to the story of her life as an assertive, strong woman who had many early independent experiences away from home, who was not deterred by an early negative experience with a cooperating teacher, and who acted inventively to stick out from the crowd when she wanted a job. In these ways, Christine represents the text of her life as one of agency and the overcoming of obstacles even as she describes examples of constriction and negotiation.

Maria

Maria Johnson, one of the few teachers who identified herself as a feminist, had been teaching for 15 years. She constructed a gendered text. She was the only daughter in an Italian family of five brothers. During high school she was interested in being a social worker. When she met with her guidance counselor, however, she was told that she was "definitely not college material." She still wanted to be a social worker, so she got a friend to go with her to the local Catholic college, where they picked up applications. They applied to go there "all by themselves," and got in. By her senior year in college she thought she still wanted to be a social worker, but she was not certain. She had always done volunteer work with children, and was clear that she wanted to work with them. Social work around the issue of adoption would be a good job. But when she looked into further training, she discovered that the master's program for social work was two years, but only one year for education. Summers off seemed a good idea, too (although she had never had children, she adopted a child a few weeks after this interview).

Maria Johnson's story tells of limited options for her as a woman and her resistance to these limitations. She had become involved in feminism through a teacher with whom she had worked closely for several years who had since gone to medical school. Her friend invited her to go to a NOW meeting. She was uncertain whether to go because she worried that her then boyfriend (now her husband) would think her unfeminine. But she went. Women spoke at the meeting about how little opportunities for women had changed since her own experiences with the guidance counselor in high school. She discovered how "stereotyped" her own thinking was about what she could do and be. Her surprise at how little conditions for women had shifted for the better since her youth convinced her to return to more meetings. She moved gradually toward greater involvement. She served on the board of NOW.

Maria Johnson drew on the discourse of liberal feminism to shape the story of her entrance into teaching. Teaching was one of the few options open to women. When, because of gender, her guidance counselor attempted to keep her from higher education, she resisted the parameters he attempted to impose and through her own efforts received a higher education. This education, however, had limited options for women. Johnson's story emphasized gender. In the text of this interview, autonomy can be obtained through struggle. Social forces that constrain women's lives can be overcome if women join together to challenge the restrictions. Autonomy means liberation.

Amelia

Amelia Dickensen attended in her story not only to gender, but to ethnicity and class as well. She was born in Mexico to a very poor family. She had liked school ever since she was five years old. She connected her pleasure in learning with work, saying that she had always known that she wanted to be a teacher.

When she was six, her family left Mexico and moved to Texas. The father, mother, and four children lived in extreme poverty. She did not think that her father "ever earned more than a dollar an hour in his whole life." He valued education for his children but never learned to speak English.

Amelia married during her sophomore year of college. A month and a half later she got pregnant with her first child. Shortly after her husband graduated, sometime in the early 1960s, they moved to Vermont. She was not able to teach right away because she was pregnant when they moved there. One day, though, while she was pregnant, "they let me" substitute in Orwell, Vermont. She had a great day. It was "crazy" not to let her teach because "these farm kids knew a lot about pregnancy and had seen many animals being born." And the district "kept me out just because I was pregnant."

After her first child was born, she got a teaching job, but found a better one shortly after in the larger town of Fairhaven, Vermont. "I was going to have a job at Fairhaven until I got pregnant. And in those days when you even thought you were pregnant, you had to go tell somebody." Amelia said that the person she was replacing had gotten pregnant. When Amelia got the job, she also found out she was pregnant. Then the person who took her place got pregnant but did not tell anyone about it. She got to teach there for a while. Amelia said, "In those days, if you didn't tell anybody and they found out about it, then you'd never get to teach again. And three months after I had my child I was teaching again full-time." At the time of the interview Amelia participated in a women's group and considered herself a politically progressive person.

Amelia's textual construction wove together her gender, her Mexican roots, and her early poverty. Her family left Mexico when they discovered that her entrance into public schooling would be postponed. Amelia had excelled in school and had been supported in her educational endeavors by her parents. She emphasized the restrictions of the educational system, which controlled her through her body. Though the body is anything but docile during pregnancy, the rules of the school system made her body docile in relation to her work by excluding her from the school (Foucault, 1977, pp. 136–138). The autonomy Amelia represented indicates its complexity: autonomy rests on economic security that can be obtained through hard work. But women face barriers to working hard because of gendered and ethnic circumstances. Restrictions can sometimes be circumnavigated in particular instances, but they must be resisted in order to change them. Autonomy is only really possible when all representatives of a group can envision it.

Jennie

Jennie McAuliffe constructed a story of individual resistance to forces trying to contain her, particularly her body. She attends directly to the religious framework of her Catholic upbringing, also representing how gender shaped her life.

Jennie was "very sheltered" as a young woman. During the Vietnam period, when she was going to college, she knew nothing about drugs. She was born in 1950 and went to a parochial elementary school, the oldest of eight children. Her Irish family had "really different expectations for the girls and the boys." In fact, she did not think that there were always expectations for her to go to college. Her father had dropped out of high school. He ran his own successful insurance company. The mother had dropped out of college after two years. They lived in a "middle-class" Irish neighborhood where "everybody had between eight and ten children." She grew up thinking that this was the norm for families. When she went away to a junior college in Vermont, she met many students who came from Protestant families with only two children.

When she first went to college she had no expectations of "doing anything" with her life because it was expected of her that she would marry and have a family. Jennie described her transformation at the junior college into a "serious student." She decided to go to a college in Boston that emphasized education. She had also been accepted to a nursing program at Boston College, but she decided that she would "have to take too many religion courses at Boston." Jennie had become a serious student, but she did not yet have much self-confidence about herself as a student. She said, "Look at me then. I was always attracted to safe, comfortable roles: nurse, teacher. But I think it would be really different now. . . . I have a lot more experience and a lot more self-confidence."

Jennie enjoyed the college in Boston partly because the students were so varied. She did some student teaching in one of the "only middle-class" schools in a wealthy community. She was "thrilled" with her experience. When the teacher left to have a baby, the school asked Jennie to teach the class as a substitute.

She graduated from college in 1972. Her friends worried about whether or not they were going to "get placed," but Jennie represented herself as unworried; she "didn't think about it at all." For one year she "bummed around," trying unsuccessfully to settle in Colorado. But the next year she obtained a position at a parochial elementary school in the Northeast. Though her relations with her students were "terrific," she "clashed" with the principal over dress. She wanted to wear pants for teaching and the administration did not approve. When called into the principal's office she said to him, "Look, I wore a navy blue and white uniform for twelve years of my schooling, and I will no longer have anyone tell me what to wear." The struggle was over her body, in this case, how it would be adorned, presented, and covered.

She left the school after one year, missing her close relationships with students who had so appreciated her liveliness. After some time, she got a job teaching at another parochial elementary school in a suburb of Vista City. Though she described the school as lacking in "diversity," she had very good experiences teaching there. After three years, however, her father said to her, "We paid so much money for your education and you are only earning $6500 a year. Don't you think it's time you got more financially independent?" She finished her master's degree at the local university and became a permanent substitute in the city for a couple of years before getting her present position at Vista City Elementary.

Jennie constructs the text of her entrance into teaching around her ethnicity and her class privilege, but she rejects framing her story from a feminist perspective even as she is attentive to gender through her descriptions of her family's low expectations for her in higher education. While she evokes the importance of her Irish Catholic heritage to her own development, she does not comment on whether her family's class position would have supported her attendance at college. She begins in a two-year college, and had she not taken some initiative she might have concluded her education there. She also describes the impact that growing up in a protected environment had on her as a woman. This attention to gender helps her to note the lack of economic constraints on her when she finished college, and her struggle with the parochial school principal over how she would clothe her body. She constructs herself as something of a resister in this incident. She resists, however, not because she objects to constraints on women's dress but because she resists the oppressive quality of parochial schools. At the same time that Jennie attends to how her life connects to the larger sociological world, she seems also to be distant from it.

CONTEMPORARY PERSPECTIVES

Opportunity and constrictions, and the individual overcoming restraints, figure centrally in the stories these teachers constructed about their careers. Elementary schoolteaching is an occupation that is overwhelmingly female, yet each teacher pointed to the specific circumstances of her own voyage. These teachers made decisions that were traditionally gendered, but they emphasized that the meanings they made of their stories were multiple. They may have entered teaching because it was an occupation for women, but it meant something different for each of them.

The texts of these teachers' lives navigated a subjectivity that unsuccessfully attempted to ignore the discursive formations influencing their tales. Social constructions of gender, class, ethnicity, and race had to be acknowledged even as the power of these discourses was abbreviated. Since the individual took center stage in their stories, concerns about autonomy were invoked not over others who were dependent on them, but in relation to those on whom they were professionally dependent. These teachers did not suggest, for example, that their connections to children inhibited their autonomy. Rather, schooling authorities (and bureaucracies) which controlled their movement, their curriculum choice, and their class composition limited their autonomy. In their worksite, they feared limitations on their autonomy in terms of their relationship with others seen as more powerful.

Their stories about becoming teachers connected autonomy to choice. Some emphasized their own agency; they entered teaching because they were, as individual people, drawn to working with children. They did not acknowledge that they are linked with many other women who also said this. Christine Bart continually emphasized her own story, and what she had accomplished to become visible to those doing the hiring. Others articulated how gendered discourses of family, school, and society shaped their choices. Their discussions of autonomy were also linked to their identification with other women. Maria Johnson, for example, gained the strength to rebel against her parents' wishes because another young woman went with her to the local Catholic college to pick up an application form.

Some of the women told stories of resistance. Amelia Dickensen's text constructed a history of one who was, as a Mexican immigrant, a marginalized outsider in the Texas of her youth. When she became a teacher, she sometimes subverted school rules that meant to forbid her to teach because she was pregnant. Amelia described how these experiences led her to feminism. Jennie McAuliffe both connected and distanced herself from a gendered text. She resisted her family's attempts to limit her educational opportunity as well as a parochial school's attempt to regulate how she covered her body. She did not, however, see these circumstances stimulating larger concerns to change women's lives.

Whether or not teachers mentioned gender critically or affirmatively, they always entered gender into their stories, whether it related to the lack of femininity in their career choices, overprotectiveness, or the control and management of their pregnant bodies.

CONCLUSION

How much autonomy teachers have at work rests on federal and state educational policies, on education law, on the particular community values in their locales, on their students, and on the colleagues and administrators present in individual schools. There are gender issues as well. How much agency women have in their lives is not constructed only in terms of separation from others. Carol Gilligan and her colleagues have done important work to make visible more than one framework for analyzing moral decisions (Brown & Gilligan, 1992; Gilligan, 1980). In addition to the economy of rights, an economy of connection is also available. But as Jane Flax (1990) suggested, these two economies of framing problems are not oppositional. Being-in-relations is not the opposite of autonomy. In this chapter I have suggested that the stories told about teachers' lives and the stories they tell about themselves relate autonomy to being-in-relations.

Teaching is in many ways a constant being-in-relations with children, even though teachers gain a certain kind of independence by teaching in rooms away from other adults. Teachers can close their doors. They can tell parents that they must meet another day. When teachers had to board around as part of their living and working arrangements, they had even less space for themselves. They had no place where their actions were not regulated. Those teachers who shared a bedroom with some of the children in their schools did not even have a door to close against the host family. In the short story "Not Eighteen" (Kellogg, 1923), the young teacher stayed in the empty schoolroom long after the children departed each day in order to have space and time for herself.

Laws that excluded women from the classroom if they were married or pregnant controlled and regulated teachers' bodies. Teachers sometimes tried to resist this management of their bodies by hiding their marriages or pregnancies for as long as they could. These regulations were also selectively enforced. Communities desperate for a teacher might hire a married woman or even a woman with children.

During the first half of the nineteenth century, schooling processes often left more up to the teacher. A teacher could end school early on a particular day if she wanted the children to attend a parade. Or she could teach longer for several days in order to prepare for exams or gain extra hours so that she might have another day free. This method worked well for those women whose dedication to the children was serious.

In earlier texts one representation of teaching was as a form of independence for women. This independence arose not specifically because of work with children, but because of what teaching as an occupation could provide women. Women in the nineteenth and early twentieth centuries represented their independence through the experience of traveling. They could travel only if they were freed from connections to family by death or by extraordinary financial pressures; much of the fiction of this earlier period therefore portrayed these traveling independent teachers as orphans. Autobiography and biography follow the same course.

The telling of stories, both contemporary and historical, is itself regulated by gendered discourses that are expected to come into the story. Harriet Cooke lived, in some ways, an incredibly independent life. Her husband was barely and rarely a financial support for her. She worked continuously, supported her children, traveled far from her home, and gained community stature. She was, like many women of her day, an entrepreneurial teacher who started numerous small schools over the years. Unregulated by bureaucratic policies, she could initiate many decisions. Some may have benefited both her and her students, while others may have benefited only her.

However, Harriet's life as a woman and the text of her life are regulated by conventions that construct her autobiography in strict ways. The deaths of her father and husband "explained" her entrepreneurialism, her travel from home, and her responsibility for decision-making. Her independence of action rested on the deaths of the significant men in her life, and was rhetorically framed around doing God's work. She was successful when religious conversions among her young female students were high.

The teachers interviewed for this study had shifted their stories from religious or other moralistic discourses to a discourse of individualism and personal choice. They emphasized their innovative and entrepreneurial movements that negotiated between the constrictions of gender, ethnicity, and class and their current positions. Some of the teachers suggested that the ways in which their lives had been shaped by their gender or class were reasonable, and they did not represent their efforts to revise their situations as resistance. Those who acknowledged how gender, ethnicity, and class were connected to the production of power relationships were more apt to frame their decisions and actions as acts of resistance.

In *Gender Trouble* (1990), Judith Butler addresses "the unanticipated agency, of a female 'object' who inexplicably returns the glance, reverses the gaze, and contests the place and authority of the masculine position" (p. ix). Elementary schoolteaching is perhaps the last place one might look for such unanticipated agency, although studies of feminist teachers get closer to what happens when women make gender trouble through their teaching (Casey, 1993; Middleton, 1993; Weiler, 1988). In our culture, teaching has been constructed as an occupation involving not daring but patience, not autonomy but nurturing. And, in fact, teaching elementary school requires both patience and nurturing. These are vital qualities. But it does not require only those. Teachers want responsibility for decisions, an intellectual investment in their work, and, in the words of bell hooks (1989), teachers need to "talk back." Central to any transformative experience is an analysis of gender and the cultural construction of teaching. A transformative analysis of this construction suggests that elementary schoolteaching is a site for studying a reconstruction of autonomy not as separation from others, but within community. These cultural constructions are not uniform across the whole population of teachers, but are influenced by class, locale, ethnicity, and race.

CHAPTER 5

Imagining Teachers: Gender, Race, and Identity in the 1950s

Participant-observers spend time with the people they study in order to understand how their informants make sense of their world and how they attribute meanings. This kind of research is interested in what people know about themselves, their situations, and their place in the world, as well as what epistemological strategies they engage to develop explanations and perspectives to account for their situations.

How schoolteachers come to be known, both to themselves and to others, depends on a number of circumstances, some of which can be accessed by ethnographic fieldwork, and some of which cannot. Fieldwork can explore, for example, how the occupation is structured, how the conditions of the particular schools where the teachers are employed shape perspectives on work, and how the teacher-informants appear to pupils and their parents. Interviews can also elicit the language teachers use to represent themselves. What is more difficult to study ethnographically are those cultural meanings that are attributed to teachers that do not arise out of the particular social context where informants are located. These attributions influence the cultural construction of teaching.

These discursive constructions of teaching are drawn upon by people who, as students, parents, and community members, see and come to know teachers from these social locations. They are also drawn upon, though differently, by the teachers themselves. Women who teach, then, negotiate the construction of their subjectivity between larger shared understandings of teaching (and *the teacher*), and their daily encounters with the specific requirements of their work. Gender is a central part of this negotiation.

These cultural constructions can be investigated in many ways, including interpretive work with social texts such as films, novels, magazines, fiction, and literature. "Thus, an author's, songwriter's, film-maker's vision of teachers and schooling becomes part of popular sensibilities and understandings" (Joseph & Burnaford, 1994, p. 8). These sensibilities guide the envisioning of teachers in particular ways, shifting understandings in one direction rather than another.

This interpretive work is complicated, however, because just as actions have no objective meanings, readings of fictional accounts can be multiple and contested. That is, what "a reading is supposed to give a correct account of" (Appiah, 1993, p. 87) depends on the opportunities for which it is used. Fiction is useful for understanding cultural constructions of teachers not because it reveals hidden truths the culture has collected, but because it suggests possible meanings that cultural groups struggle over. Lipsitz (1990) emphasizes the fluidity of these meanings:

> Although cultural products generally reflect the dominant ideology of any given period, no cultural moment exists within a hermetically sealed cultural present; all cultural expressions speak to both residual memories of the past and emergent hopes for the future. (p. 13)

These meanings are continually transforming.

This chapter offers a reading of two novels of the 1950s in an effort to get closer to some of the attributions made about women teachers. These two novels about teaching—*Good Morning, Miss Dove* by Frances Gray Patton (1954), comic and light, and *Aggie* by Lillie Muse Humphrey (1955), autobiographical and instructive—tell important stories about the cultural construction of teaching during a time of great social change and repression. Additionally, they both pay attention to the material conditions of teaching as well as to questions of pedagogy. Both popular and more literary forms of fiction, with some exceptions, show very little about the school or classroom as the actual setting of teaching and about the work of teaching itself. Therefore, in most of these narratives, readers come to know about teachers not through the representation of their labor, but rather through their actions in the social world outside the classroom. Both *Aggie* and *Good Morning, Miss Dove* significantly attend to the act of teaching, and hence can be differentiated from much other fiction on that score. In this chapter I want to examine the novels' cultural constructions of teachers.

This examination offers the opportunity to discuss how a particular period produces an understanding (Belsey, 1980) of women teachers. Its significance for this project lies specifically in neither these novels nor this period, although the period is interesting for its emergent social forces, and the novels suggest the discursive power of those forces. Rather, these novels, which each support women teachers as central characters, offer sites to investigate what larger social dramas about gender converge in the body of the woman teacher. Since these teachers share neither race nor class, these novels write the body differently. That is, they construct a sensibility about what it means to be a woman, and then each novel takes this sensibility for granted as the story is elaborated. Both novels suggest how the cultural meaning of the teacher is greater than the actual and specific work of teachers themselves.

SCHOOLWOMEN IN FICTION

Fictional narratives participate in the cultural construction of women who teach. They do so not only directly, as stories or novels read by individuals, but also indirectly, as representations that circulate among people who call forth these images when they speak, write, or think about teachers. I take culture to mean "the process through which we circulate and struggle over the meanings of our social experience, social relations, and therefore, our *selves*" (Byars, 1991, p. 2). Fiction provides another avenue for understanding what currency women teachers have in the culture, and what discourses writers draw upon as they construct portraits of such women.

How does fiction construct women who teach school? I am particularly interested in how the identity of woman and the identity of teacher intersect. As we might expect, all of the messy contradictions that position women in society also construct women in fiction. The primary markers of these identities, gender and race, are addressed in different ways in each of these novels. The vocabulary of African-American and white is mentioned in neither account. *Aggie* concerns the efforts of an African-American teacher to improve a community through educational work, but race is never directly mentioned. *Good Morning, Miss Dove* concerns a European-American community, although this is also never mentioned. Although race is central to each text in different ways, a racial vocabulary is never used. Both texts, however, directly address gender.

The contextualization of the plot and the presentation of the books when they were first published address racialization. *Aggie* is set on the rural coast of eastern Florida. The specific community is important to the story, because the novel is about a particular group of people. The author tells their story. *Good Morning, Miss Dove*, on the other hand, was written by a middle-class European-American author about people who share her ethnic heritage in small-town America. The book is represented as possibly set in any of many small towns. *Aggie* needs to be located in a particular place because being African-American was not taken for granted by readers when it was written. *Good Morning, Miss Dove* did not have the same requirements for a specific location because the author wrote as if the setting were Small Town, USA, as if white Anglo Saxon Protestants were at the culture's center. Race was pushed underground in *Aggie* in the design of the book. The original cover of *Aggie* depicted the face of a woman with European-American features. The author reported in a telephone interview that the publishers advised her that this cover would help her to sell more copies of the book.

I do not want to read these texts in opposition to each other, however, making them stand-ins for all other texts about African- and European-American women. Rather, I hope to find a way to show how race and gender intersect in each text and avoid treating race as an additive feature. Higginbotham (1992) argues that, like gender and class, "race must be seen as a social construction predicated upon the recognition of difference and signifying the simultaneous distinguishing and positioning of groups vis à vis one another" (p. 253). Higginbotham links her analysis of race to gender:

> In societies where racial demarcation is endemic to their sociocultural fabric and heritage — to their laws and economy, to their institutionalized structures and discourses, and to their epistemologies and everyday customs — gender identity is inextricably linked to and even determined by racial identity. (p. 254).

Segregated America during the 1950s (and earlier) as represented in these novels is a society that has race woven into its fabric. Very little twentieth-century fiction about teachers addresses race, although it does engage gender.

Popular fiction about women teachers depicts a world in which their lives as teachers are intricately bound up with their lives as women; what they struggle with, for, and against is portrayed as having everything to do with gender. It underscores the impossibility of discussing school reform without considering the factor of gender.

The fictional world of teaching during the first half of this century centered on gender rather than on teaching. When teaching was an adventure, the heroine traveled to get there; met interesting people; innovated around teaching processes and schooling; loved books, reading, education, and intellectual life—and being a teacher enabled her to get closer to those things. When teaching was oppressive, the heroine stayed in the same town in which she grew up, perhaps even in the same school; lived with her family—or at least with one family member—who was perhaps ill, or weak, or old, and for whom she was responsible; longed to marry in order to find true love, and/or to become socially acceptable; did not like children but was forced into teaching because she needed to earn money, and teaching was one of the few options open to women, open to her.

Themes of compromise and restraint were common in stories about teachers. Some women saw teaching as an admission of settling for less, whether it was the diminished personal goal that Ellen Webb of Mildred Walker's *Winter Wheat* (1944) experienced when she could not finish college in the 1940s because of financial hardship (she had to quit school and get a teaching job to help her farmer parents out), or an overall disappointment in what teaching means. In the words of Miss Munday, the title character in a 1940 novel that won a prize from Dial Press for the best novel about teaching: "She caught herself, a thirsting schoolteacher standing with open mouth, yearning for something beyond her own life" (Engstrand, 1940, p. 12). Another teacher in *Miss Munday* received a proposal from a man who promised her that if she married him she would not have to "wear your life away teaching!" Martha, in Agnes Turnbull's "In Such a Night," complained in similar terms about her life in New Salem: "Year after year repeating itself, in a fashion kindly enough but with a sameness that was deadly" (Turnbull, 1925, p. 29). For Sally Byrd, the title character in Ellen Glasgow's (1924/1963) "Romance and Sally Byrd," teaching represented the constraints in her life: "Drabness everywhere that she looked. Drabness and poverty and the irksome monotony of things that did not matter" (pp. 217–218). So much of twentieth-century fiction about women who teach suggests how the lives of European-American women were constrained through characters who complain about the "sameness" in their work. Autobiographies, diaries, and memoirs of women teachers during this same period disclose how varied their situations actually were. The differences among teaching situations were erased in fiction because it was gender rather than the work itself that was restrictive.

Many fictional teachers complained about the lack of adventure in their lives rather than teaching itself. Marilla Lamprey, in Cornelia Cannon's *Heirs* (1930), was an excellent teacher who graduated first in her class from the normal school but had to give up a good opportunity to teach in Manchester, New Hampshire, to live with and care for her widowed invalid father. She was forced to accept a much less interesting job, a position located in the town in which she grew up, in order to enact her gendered responsibilities. Marilla did not reject teaching, for she enjoyed the position she had to give up as well as the education that becoming a teacher offered:

> The normal school was not a great educational institution, but one or two of its teachers were unusual, and its library, larger than any to which she had ever dreamed of having access, opened to her a world for which she had been unconsciously searching from her earliest days. (p. 11)

Rather, it was the particular teaching position she rejected.

Ella Andrews, in Aldrich's (1919) story "A Long Distance Call from Jim," complained of the same situation: "Then Mother died, and from teaching in Capitol City, where she was meeting new people and having new experiences, she had come back home to keep house for Father, and to teach in the same old dingy building where she herself had studied" (p. 48). These teachers wanted adventure and/or independence in their occupational roles, but because of gendered responsibilities, their family circumstances restrained them.

When a teacher disliked her occupation, she was not represented sympathetically. Fictional teachers in these situations rise off the pages as hateful or spiteful or boring or mean-spirited or limited, or some combination of the above. The woman who chafed against her situation was not characterized as a rebel but rather as a kind of whiner. The reader is encouraged to share the author's feelings.

Authors encouraged these feelings in readers through their portrayal of a teacher's discomfort with her situation. The character did not confront conflict; rather, she complained or became unhappy. These fictional teachers embodied the outwardly compliant but inwardly distressed woman whose unhappiness ate away at her soul. Most fiction about women teachers is very uncomplimentary.

FEMINISM AND FEMININITY IN THE 1950s

Women's souls—and bodies—during the 1950s were awkwardly positioned between resistance and accommodation, and between femininity and feminism. This location resonates with Cora Kaplan's (1985) view that the "splits that characterize femininity" are those between "reason and desire, autonomy and dependent security, psychic and social identity." Yet if these were the boundaries of the splits, they were by no means centered similarly for all women.

Sociologists such as Wini Breines (1986) characterize the 1950s as a paradox:

> More than ever before women in that decade, particularly married women and mothers, were working in the labor force, continuing a trend begun early in the century and intensified by World War II. Other trends and social and cultural indicators, such as prosperity, the expansion of higher education, democratization of the family, and increased emphasis on sexual pleasure for married and single women, suggest that the trajectory of women after the war continued to include more autonomy, equality, and possibilities. Yet, and here is the central paradox, the 1950s were conservative years, not only politically but culturally as well, particularly with regard to gender and family issues. (p. 69)

Many American texts of this period emphasized domestic and family values. C. Wright Mills wrote in *The Sociological Imagination* (1959) that during this decade Americans were more interested in problems of soap operas than of economics.

This paradoxical decade emphasized American defense of what seemed to many cold warriors a fragile and insecure liberty as it attempted to control political subversives and generally promoted the status quo in race relations. Elaine Tyler May (1988) has related a sociology of the family to Cold War politics, emphasizing how European-Americans battled the insecurity of the nuclear age through the nuclear family. The words "under God" were added to the Pledge of Allegiance in 1954 to emphasize differences between American Judeo-Christian society and a godless Communism. The McCarthy trials and witch-hunts of the House Un-American Activities Committee struggled, often successfully, to frame people either as collaborators with Communism or as enlistees in the Cold War against it (Whitefield, 1991, p. 10).

This notion of sides was significant. "Literal and figurative boundaries were important in the fifties. . . . The borders of the United States became a central metaphor on the fears of invasion by communists" (Breines, 1992, p. 9). Films of the period that portrayed invaders from the skies who could destroy relationships and property suggest the insecurity. Sayre (1978) pointed to the insecurities connected to the Cold War, the:

> uncertainty about the nature or location of our enemies: the communist who operates behind the scenes, the delinquents who lurk

around the next corner, the prehistoric monsters reactivated by the atom tests of science fiction or the neighbors whose brains are manipulated by Martian technology, seem to be part of a vast mosaic of ambiguous fears. What was threatening was right in our midst—the subversive who belonged to the Parent Teacher Association or the dinosaur that reared up in one's backyard. (pp. 25–26, cited in Breines, 1992, p. 9)

The 1950s witnessed many repressive attempts to control subversives.

During a period when it was common to view social problems as rooted in psychological causes, many women still looked to Ferdinand Lundberg and Marynia Farnham's *Modern Woman: The Lost Sex* (1947) for advice about their gendered identities. They found, in this vituperative and woman-hating book, the resting of blame for social troubles on women:

The central thesis of this book is that contemporary women in very large numbers are psychologically disordered and that their disorder is having terrible social and personal effects involving men in all departments of their lives as well as women. (p. v)

Their blame-the-woman attitude was both flagrant and punitive, since it located within mothers an incredible power to shape identity:

Biographers will one day, we hope, come to understand that their true subject is hardly the man (or woman) they have chosen to scrutinize, and not his or her mistress or lover, but the mother or her substitute. Men, standing before the bar of historical judgment, might well begin their defense with the words: "I had a mother . . . " (p. 3)

If women had this kind of power, then they had to be contained. We might ask how fiction participated in promoting such containment or challenging its boundaries.

How central this construction of women was in the lives of African-American women is doubtful, for they "did not share either the complacency or the anxiety of the 1950s." During this period they continued to work as domestics, but they also obtained positions for the first time with the New York Telephone Company, and found jobs in the West as teachers. They "emerged as leaders in the renewed struggle for civil-rights legislation" (Kaledin, 1984, p. 149).

The 1950s witnessed the "expansion of the role of the federal government in education" (Spring, 1986). On December 1, 1955, the year

Aggie was published and a year after the Supreme court decision in *Brown vs. the Board of Education*, Rosa Parks sat in the white section of an Alabama bus, beginning the Montgomery bus boycott. The eventual influence of this action for students and public schooling was enormous. Aggie's world, however, was still a segregated world, and she negotiated within these boundaries.

Good Morning, Miss Dove

Frances Patton's novel, chosen as a Book-of-the-Month Club selection for October 1954, tells the story of the meaning of a geography teacher's life for a community. Miss Dove spent her whole career teaching in the racially segregated community of Liberty Hill:

> a small freshwater town—not a hill, really, but just a modest rise in the land—where streets were named for trees and heroes, and a sense of life's continuity ran in the air. It was like a hundred American towns, smug and cozy, and it put its special stamp upon its own. People born and raised there—high and low, rich and poor—were neighbors in an irrevocable way, because their imaginations had been nursed on the same sights and sounds and legends and early ordeals. (p. 1)

One of these shared (European-American) experiences was the classroom of Miss Dove, the town's elementary school geography teacher. The people of Liberty Hill "had all, for the space of a whole generation, been exposed at a tender and malleable age to the impartial justice, the adamantine regulations, and the gray, calm, neutral eyes of the same teacher—the terrible Miss Dove" (p. 1). Miss Dove's "neutrality" is central to her influence on the town. Townspeople may call her "the terrible Miss Dove," some of the townswomen may worry that her methods are not "progressive" enough, but what Miss Dove has to offer, this book suggests, is irreplaceable.

Miss Dove's ability, as Patton says, to mix children who were high and low, rich and poor, against the backdrop of neutral justice suggests the centrality of Miss Dove to maintaining democracy. Miss Dove is the kind of teacher for whom chalk never squeaks; she is a teacher who had learned from personal experience at a young age that life was not easy, that it did not "excuse mistakes" (p. 32). She was at home in a classroom, where she had enacted responsibility and enjoyed "making and keeping rules." Her students benefited from this:

> By her insistence upon even margins and correct posture and punctuality and industriousness, she told them, in effect, that though life

was not easy, neither was it puzzling. You learned its unalterable laws. You respected them. You became equal to your task. Thus, you controlled your destiny. (Patton, 1954, p. 34)

Miss Dove employs her authority to "empower" her students to follow rules and, hence, become "good" citizens.

Good Morning, Miss Dove is narrated through the perspectives of the teacher and, when she falls ill and is taken to the hospital, her former pupils. The story is told through flashbacks. Miss Dove became a teacher for the same reason that all women in fiction become teachers: financial necessity. Crops fail and fathers die. In Miss Dove's case her father not only died, but had embezzled money from the bank he directed. Hence, Miss Dove had to give up all thoughts of marriage because she had to contribute to the support of the remaining family members. She began teaching before she was 20; when she falls ill she is 54. Her work became her life and she calculates that if she can survive her illness, she will not have to retire until she is 67. She knows that the children need her.

The book portrays Miss Dove's present and former students, reveals what students were like when they were young in Miss Dove's classroom, and examines how they turned out as adults. Miss Dove has a ledger in which she marks children on their quality:

In it each child was given a single letter of the alphabet indicating what Miss Dove considered the basic trait of its character. (Miss Dove generally thought of children as "it's" instead of "he's" and "she's.") She could have guessed that trait, with fair accuracy, the day any child first came into the geography room frightened or boisterous or homesick for its mother. But, in charity, she deferred her judgment. Unpromising as any lump of humanity might be, there was always the possibility that half a dozen years of thumping and molding might work it into respectable shape. Not until Miss Dove was nearly done with a child, until it was about to escape forever from her supervision, was she willing to call its character established.

The commonest letter in the ledger was T for Tractable. That letter was appropriate for the rank and file of Miss Dove's pupils— youngsters not born for Who's Who but amenable to reason and capable, under wise leadership, of becoming decent citizens. There were a number of W's for Willing given to those children who showed more than the usual desire to be improved. There were some A's for Awkward and a sprinkling of B's—a really bad mark—which stood for Babyish and was given most frequently to the kind of pouting little girl who would become, in the future, a fattish middle-aged woman who wore frilly bathing-suits that showed her stomach and

wept when the cook failed to come. O's for Original went to unregulated children who formed ideas of their own without consulting
Miss Dove, who decorated their maps with pictures of Viking ships
off the coast of Denmark, or were disposed to argue points of philoso-
phy. (O's were not signs of Miss Dove's esteem; she gave them regret-
fully. She had given one to Geoffrey Lyons.) But beside William
Holloway's name she placed the symbol that she might, without
undue complacency or spurious modesty, have placed beside her
own. It was an S. It stood for Satisfactory. (Patton, 1954, pp. 102–
104)

The categories in Miss Dove's ledger look for and reinforce consistency
over time.

Good Morning, Miss Dove reifies the stability of identities; it casts
her as teacher in an all-knowing stance whose knowledge is timeless,
and her students as characters who remain predictably consistent.
That is, her knowledge is privileged because it is detached from a
social context and from changes people experience. Miss Dove can act
with complete certainty in and trust of her perception, gleaned from
her 30 years of teaching in the same community, that the Simpsons
are flighty, the Bakers are jokesters, and the Webbs are romantics.
When another Simpson, Baker, or Webb child comes into Miss Dove's
class, she knows what to expect because family culture and character
are consistent and unchanging.

Miss Dove's power as a teacher is her ability to connect with this
psychological nugget within each person and work to improve a child
to the best of his or her capabilities. Lying in the hospital, she "thought
of all the children she had pruned and polished and kept in line, and to
whom she had explained, by precept and example, the hard, the true,
the simple and beautiful meaning of the human adventure" (Patton,
1954, p. 216). In a world framed by the kind of erosion of liberties
represented by the House Committee on Un-American Activities, Liberty Hill and Miss Dove promise a kind of order that leans toward the
fascist even as it employs the language of democracy. Miss Dove keeps
people in line. While no social or political event of the times enters
these pages, they are present as the subtext against which Patton
writes. Miss Dove is the town's spinster teacher who is so regular, so
just, so predictable and responsible, that the townspeople can set their
clocks by her as she walks to work. In a democratic society, the author
suggests, people can be unorganized, flighty, and undirected. It takes a
Miss Dove to pull everyone back to task, and to demand the best of
them. The importance of this firm but just authoritarianism is inscribed in the *Atlantic*'s review of *Good Morning, Miss Dove*: Ms.

Patton, the reviewer declares, "describes the teacher-town relationship which is so fundamental in our democracy. The author makes us see education for the dedicated task it is. She lets us touch the strands of loyalty and tradition which we have all felt and sometimes resisted" (Weeks, 1954, p. 90). The unmarried and asexual teacher upholds this tradition and prevents a society from producing too many O's for Original.

Aggie

Unlike Liberty Hill, where matrons have cooks, Aggie Small's world is rural, poor southeastern Florida. *Aggie* is the story of the title character's career in teaching, from her inauspicious beginnings in a small, rural community, through her university and graduate school career, her marriages, and her struggles to enact an educational program that will improve the material conditions of her pupils' lives. Over the years she faces a number of conflicts with community members about the regulation of a female teacher's life. Can she contradict the boardinghouse owner? Can she meet with parents of the children she teaches in the places where they spend their time, whether these places be bars, restaurants, or village streets? Can she go for a ride with a boyfriend? Can she engage students in activities that seem part of a more progressive education curriculum than is traditional in that area?

Aggie was written by a teacher, Lillie Muse Humphrey, who hoped to become a novelist. She could not get her manuscript accepted by any commercial publisher, so she signed up with a subsidy press, Vantage Press. *Aggie* is particularly important because there are so few fictional narratives that have been published about the lives of ordinary female African-American teachers.

When Aggie Small arrived in the rural community in southeastern Florida for her first teaching position, she discovered a place where:

> houses for the most part were small. Most of them were unpainted and in a dilapidated condition. The yard and streets were littered with paper and rags. She saw that a lot of teaching would have to be done here, to better the living conditions of the people in this community. (p. 26)

Lillie Muse Humphrey represented the material conditions of the community in which Aggie taught as inspirational for her work.

The boardinghouse in which she had to live, however, was anything but inspiring. Aggie resented the domineering attitude of the

woman who owned it, an attitude represented in the speech the boardinghouse owner, Mrs. Jannie, gave to Aggie when she first arrived in
town:

> You are welcome to my home. . . . Now I am going to tell you some-
> thing for your own good. You will find the people here very lovable
> and very easy to get along with, if you don't come here feeling that
> you are better than they are just because you are a teacher. . . . Be
> very careful when you are around other women's husbands. You've
> got to speak to them, mind you, but the women don't like teachers
> flirting with their men. . . . I don't think I will need to give you a key
> to the house because I do not go to bed early. . . . You had better go
> to bed on time and play it safe because these people will surely tell
> the professor about you. Some of them will even tell the superinten-
> dent. . . . My husband is the only man who comes in that door, un-
> less some of our kin or the minister decide that they want to come.
> You will have to buy your own food and cook it. You will have to
> scrub the kitchen, the dining room, the living room, and the back
> porch every week. You will have to pay me six dollars a week for
> your room rent. When there is an extra week in the month, you will
> have to pay six dollars extra. . . . You will have to pay one dollar for
> kerosene, for the use of my stove, one dollar per week to wash your
> clothes—that's for the use of my tubs; you do the washing—and one
> dollar per week for the use of my iron and for part of the electric bill.
> (pp. 24–25)

After this exchange, "Aggie went to her room and sobbed bitterly,"
worrying that if "other people in this community [were] like Mrs.
Jannie . . . I shall be dead of heart disease before the Christmas holidays" (p. 26).

Aggie Small, a southern rural African-American teacher, envisioned social change in the community as intrinsic to teaching, but
she needed to live in the community as well as teach in it. As a woman
she was subject to constrictions on bodily display, friendship, and residence. Lillie Muse Humphrey represented African-American teachers
as figures who, motivated by concerns of racial uplift, transported cultural and intellectual ways from their college or university teacher
training programs to poor rural communities. Humphrey characterizes
teachers as facing resistance to change—in the behavior and actions,
for example, of the conservative, elite women of the community who
dominate their husbands—as well as accommodation to change—for
example, in the engagement with learning and personal betterment
reflected in students and their parents. Gender and race intersect.

Aggie emphasizes the importance of education for the uplift of her people. The people themselves are portrayed in large part as inadequate citizens of their community. They do not spend enough time with their children, they do not discipline them enough, they do not emphasize school adequately, and they do not keep their community in decent enough shape. After attempts to visit the families of the children in her class fail because of absent or drunken parents, Aggie comes to the conclusion that:

> for the most part the children in her class were being neglected, either because their parents were working or because the children were allowed to romp the streets at will, with the parents going in one direction at night and the children the other. She found that most of the children went to bed after eleven o'clock at night for one reason or the other. She also found that one of her sixteen-year-olds was expecting a child. (Humphrey, 1955, p. 42)

Aggie wants to expand the people's opportunities through attention to the community culture.

She develops a plan of action to remedy the wrongs she sees and can address. She attends to the material conditions of people's lives in tandem with their intellectual and educational lives. She connects the pregnant student with a county health nurse so that she can get decent medical attention. She develops projects that students can work on "to keep these children off the streets." She develops a plan to encourage parents to paint their houses without making them overstretch their finances. Aggie's evaluation of her success in the community rests on her actions as a force for social good.

The author locates barriers and problems not only within a resistant community (e.g., the garden club members who are so antagonistic to change), but within inadequate pedagogy. The book opens, in fact, when Aggie has been a successful teacher for many years. She worries that the methods she has been using to teach children were not successful because many of them did not grasp ideas as quickly as she thought they should. She wondered:

> if it were possible for a teacher to love her work if she was not able to find a way to bring out the very best performance from each of her pupils each day. She thought, "How can I say that I love a child if I am depriving him of his right to develop to his fullest capacity at this level or at this stage in his young life?" (p. 8)

Within the segregated communities in which she learns and works, race is central to how her life is constructed. The book is coded, however, so that the problems originate in rural poverty. Themes of uplift sit next to critiques of poor teachers and spiteful community mothers. When Aggie is first approached by the director of the education division at her university to take the position in the rural community, he says:

> "The teachers complain that the people are backward, and they were unable to do a good job under the conditions in which they had to work. This principal needs someone to assist him—a teacher who will stay and try to help these people and encourage the other teachers to stay. . . . Aggie . . . Will you give it a try?" (p. 19)

Aggie's attention centers on overturning the people's "backwardness" through efforts including self-improvement. At the end of one school year, for example, she and her students develop a list of "Things We Are Going to Do to Improve Ourselves This Summer." The list includes, besides reading and talking in complete sentences, Item 7: "We are going to help our parents to keep clean the house, the yard, and the streets in front of our houses" (pp. 11-12). Aggie had identified the conditions which made people poor and wanted them to change not only those conditions but also their presentation. Humphrey identifies education as the most significant means of social change, combating what she portrays as the conservatism of the church and the hostility of community social leaders.

READING GENDER, READING RACE

Both *Aggie* and *Good Morning, Miss Dove* engage with communities whose living conditions and social realities are significantly marked by race. For different reasons neither mentions race. Patton's novel rests on the construction of the European-American experience as normative. When race is not mentioned, whiteness is assumed. *Aggie* describes the difficulties faced by a rural, poor community. The community members are African-American, but the author constructs their circumstances nonracially as poor and "backward." Humphrey writes as if being poor and rural were the only problems the community faced and that these circumstances might be encountered by any poor and rural community unexposed to new educational ideas. Humphrey was looking for a wide readership and thought her book had a greater chance of reaching the public if race were not emphasized.

Gender is directly addressed though differently conceived in each novel. How gender emerges is tied up with race as well as with the orientation of the text. While earning money the summer before she starts her job as a teacher, Aggie is sexually harassed by men on the way to work, and once forcibly imprisoned in an automobile by a strange man until a policeman rescues her. In her community her behavior is monitored by a group of narrow-minded women whose lives are threatened by the young women who come into the town to teach. Interestingly, these negatively portrayed women are the elite of the town. Her clothes (e.g., short skirts) are criticized as too representative of loose women, her behavior questioned when she goes into a bar to meet the parents of a child in her class (who own the bar) or when she in any way acts independently.

Humphrey connected women's autonomy with educational and professional advancement. Potential restrictions on their independence are represented through views of church members and the elite community wives as regressive for women. Aggie experiences few second thoughts about her personal deportment.

She is committed to improving the lives of the rural community where she lives, and resists attempts to move her up the professional ladder into easier, more comfortable, urban positions. She criticizes those who would get her to move because they "did not understand the position in which a teacher finds herself, the responsibilities she feels for the development and welfare of people, and the joy she experiences when the people improve themselves" (pp. 59–60).

While Aggie never mentions any movement around civil rights, she continuously acts to improve people's lives. She attends both to the material conditions of their lives and to the importance of education as an instrumental force for change. Not only will the community be better off, but the position of women will improve as well. Gender and race intersect.

Unlike Aggie's situation, where she can be married several times and still work professionally, Miss Dove must lose her femininity in order to teach. She is introduced in the novel as a young woman who was not pretty but who was elegant. She came from the town's first family: Her father was the bank president; her mother "was a fragile woman who smelled of violets and had the kind of gentle beauty that 'trembles over children sleeping'"; and her two little sisters were like the mother (p. 22). Miss Dove learned geography and many languages from her father, who also taught her to play chess and to ride: "No girls in town . . . could sit a horse the way Miss Dove could" (p. 24). These characteristics distinguish Miss Dove from other females who do not have such intensity. Miss Dove determines to pay back the money her father had embezzled to buy the rare travel books from which she had learned geography. She uses all of her salary as a geography teacher to support her mother, educate her sisters, and repay the money her father had stolen. To do this she had to become self-sacrificing: "Miss Dove had denied herself much. She had ignored fashion. (Hair styles came and went—the spit curls, the overblown ear-puffs, the boyish bob, the page-boy, and the pony tail)" (p. 34). Miss Dove was able to show fortitude because she relinquished what femininity she possessed. Aggie wanted to be able to wear shorter skirts and still claim her authority as a teacher. Gaining authority did not require rejecting herself as a woman. Miss Dove, on the other hand, associates femininity with the dissolution of her authority, which can be sustained only if she is desexualized.

CONCLUSION

Separated by their representations of race, gender, and class, these two novels share other textual similarities. Both are squarely situated in the midst of popular culture, bounded by the decade in which they were published. Neither are books that would hold much interest today. Miss Dove epitomizes the stereotype of the spinster schoolteacher drawn so wickedly in Waller's (1932) *The Sociology of Teaching*— although where Waller saw her as "abnormal," Patton perceived her as a stabilizing force. The ignorance of community members in the rural community where Aggie teaches suggests another stereotype: that knowledge is borne of formal education. The knowledge that women in the community might have of midwifery or that men or women might have of agriculture is never explored. Also, race is coded in this novel because skin color is never mentioned.

Both texts also draw on discourses of individuality. *Aggie* counsels that racial uplift rests on a person's hard work, discipline, and education. Miss Dove relies on psychological insight into her students even as she resists "newfangled" ideas from the progressives in education. Her personal authority is represented as strengthening a democratic society—a democratic society that was then seen to be under attack. Seen this way, Aggie and Miss Dove represent conserving forces in society. Both teachers work to pass on a certain social organization of society, even though they represent different aspects of that society.

This conservatism, however, does not quite capture all of the texts. Both books also narrate resistance. Aggie, unlike some of the other young teachers fresh out of the university, is not subject to the repression of the women in the garden club who are trying to act white and who separate themselves from the working people. She resists identifying with those who act white and aligns herself with those who need the most. She does not chastise the student who is pregnant, but gets her medical help. Miss Dove manages to resist maternal and many feminine discourses and remain an independent woman who enjoys her power (justly enacted and restrained) and who feels comfortable in the world. Lying in her hospital bed, in the dreamy state between anesthetized sleep and awareness, she toys with the possibility that she might toss it all to the wind for a more free-spirited and less independent mode, but rejects this thought.

Taken together, readings of these fictional teachers as conserving and resisting suggest the contradictory ways in which teachers were socially constructed. At the time these books were published, Miss Dove, like other European-American teachers, was regulated by social and sexual repression. To resist this repression her fictional representation distanced her from ordinary, everyday life. This distancing demeaned femininity by stereotyping it.

The African-American teacher was controlled by segregation. Aggie was educated and worked in communities that were completely African-American. Segregation loomed so large that the author did not even challenge it even as she poked holes at ideas on the place of women.

The contradictions suggest that the social constructions of these teachers were attempts to discursively manage her power. As a force for social change in the southeastern, rural Florida community, she is invested with the power to raise up the people's standard of living. As a force for boundary maintenance and stability in Cold War middle America, she has the power to shore up a faltering democracy. Contained and regulated on some fronts, she keeps breaking through.

The cultural meanings attributed to teachers are complex. Teachers and others draw on these meanings, along with their specific experiences of particular teachers and the told experiences of their friends and families, to socially construct the teacher. Women who teach must always negotiate their direct experience of working as a teacher with the representations of teachers others have.

CHAPTER 6

Teachers' Perspectives on the Mother's Gaze

When white middle-class mothers and their children's female elementary schoolteachers come into conflict, they both grapple with the same concern, though it plays out in contrasting ways in their lives. Both mothers and elementary schoolteachers share social and gendered positions because of their relationship to children. They also share the desire, even though both groups often feel great hostility toward each other, to increase social recognition for paid or unpaid work with children. They both attempt to resist the devaluation of work labeled "domestic." Within the construct of school–family relations, however, they resist the image of domesticity through conflict with each other, the teachers by resisting mothers' demands and the mothers by attempting to insert their knowledge into the pedagogical arena.

While each group can give the other headaches, while each can behave in outrageous ways in relation to the other, the same social problem, the devaluation of work with children (traditional women's work), underlies their conflict. This chapter examines, from teachers' point of view, how teachers and middle-class white mothers negotiate their relationship, focusing particularly on tensions and conflict. I look at what teachers choose to tell as well as how they structure their stories. What are the effects of these narrative structures? What assumptions undergird their relationship? What are the politics of this discourse?

A GENDERED CONFLICT

There is nothing new about conflict between parents and teachers. Researchers have long recognized its presence and have named it to reflect the considerable hostility that exists between the parties. In the 1930s, Willard Waller called teachers and parents "natural enemies," though he suggested that the conflict benefits rather than harms children; Howard Becker argued that teachers labeled parents' entrance into schools as "potentially dangerous"; Seymour Sarason referred to parent-teacher relations as a "cold war"; and Gertrude McPherson attended to the "hostility" between parents and teachers (Becker, 1970, p. 155; McPherson, 1972; Sarason, 1982; Waller, 1932, p. 68).

Many other writers examine the sources and nature of this troubled relationship, though some focus on mothers and some on parents. What to call the participants lacks agreement. References to "parents" could mean interchangeable talk about either mother or father. My research at Vista City suggests that when teachers talk about parents, they generally mean mothers. This view is revealed in many examples throughout this chapter. Most comments began with the word "parents," but then focused on mothers. For example:

> The parents of the downtown kids and the black parents are
> just fine. The parents in this neighborhood are very social.
> They're wives of university professors, and they're just so sure
> that their kids have to be bright and do well because of the
> families they come from.

I do not mean to suggest that teachers do not have conflicts with fathers. But encounters are gendered. Fathers, in the case study data I report, tended to get more involved in schoolwide problems, such as building renovations, leaving the classroom concerns to mothers. This was not always the case, however; teachers came to fear fathers with degrees in psychology who carried a repertoire of IQ measuring skills to chart their children's progress.

Others have remarked on these issues. Miriam David (1989) critiques researchers for their use of this problematic term: "*Parent* is used for both mothers and fathers where their roles might not be interchangeable. It is also used as if it were a social category" (p. 51). In a discussion of parent-teacher relations, Ray Rist (1987) also describes conflicts using the word "parents." The teacher he directly quoted, however, said, "This damn group of meddling mothers has gotten me so mad, I feel like leaving this school" (pp. 60–61; see also Levin, 1987, p. 275). In this chapter my vocabulary follows that of the teachers in their interviews as to how they reference mothers and parents. I do this in order to attend to the complexity of their perspectives on mothers. When teachers refer to parents rather than to mothers, they sometimes attempt to avoid the gender issues that connect them. The gendered positions of both mothers and teachers lurk as the subtext to each encounter.

The history of the relationship between middle-class white mothers and teachers reflects the lack of partnership between these two groups and the lines of argument each group employs with the other. William Reese argues that during the Progressive era, earlier in this century, middle-class mothers thought that schools should be extensions of "ideal" middle-class American homes. Schoolpeople were not any less drawn to middle-class norms than the mothers, but wanted parents to be well aware that teachers and parents could not be equal partners. Parents had to respect the teacher as expert professional. When parents organized around an issue, educators attacked them as "meddlers, malcontents, and the worst enemies of the public schools." When schoolpeople espoused a vocabulary of "cooperation," they generally meant "parent submission"; then parents and teachers could get along. An anecdote Reese (1978) tells reflects parents' refusal to accept the limits of teachers' professional authority with their children: "A Chicago principal who regularly interacted with parent groups stated that they simply never understood that the world was run by professionals" (p. 4). Teachers' desire to have parents recognize them as professionals and parents' resistance to their wish has a long history.

What started as the National Congress of Mothers in 1897, was transformed in 1908 to the National Congress of Mothers and Parent–Teacher Associations to the National Congress of Parents and Teachers in 1924. While the mothers who started the National Congress of Mothers had taken a charity perspective to help educate schools and families to reflect a more middle-class orientation, the new name developed because relations between schools and the community outflanked parent education (Schlossman, 1976).

Much of the research on relationships between mothers and teachers focuses on the detrimental effects of a "discontinuity" between family and schools. Hence, studies of relationships between schools and less powerful groups such as working-class families, poor families, and traditionally underrepresented families have examined the negative effects on children's performance of the lack of parental involvement, on the one hand, and on the racist, Eurocentric, and classist characterizations teachers can have of parents (David, 1989; Davies, 1988; Henderson, 1985; Lareau, 1987; Lightfoot, 1978). These characterizations are interactive.

The tensions between middle-class white mothers and teachers have been characterized as more subtle than the direct racism or paternalism in the relationships between teachers and working-class or poor parents. Teachers see working-class parents as not providing a good "foundation" at home for the children. Working-class parents see teachers as not expecting anything of their children. White middle-class parents, on the other hand, criticize teachers as too "rigid and uncreative," while teachers criticize these parents as too "pushy" (Levin, 1987, p. 274). The relationship between teachers and mothers of poor, working-class, and African-American children has been characterized as "worlds apart" (Lightfoot, 1978).

Some explanations of the conflict apparent in the mother–teacher relationship include gender, while others do not. One explanation suggests conflicting emphases. Teachers, that is, have universal expectations of their students, needing to spread their attention over a group. Mothers, on the other hand, have a particular focus on their own children. McPherson (1972) and Lightfoot (1978) both draw upon the functionalist views of Parsons (1959) to argue that the mother's relationship to her child is primary, while the teacher's is secondary. Social class, ethnicity, race, and language also provide important sources for the conflicts between mothers and teachers (Lareau, 1987; Levin, 1987).

Neither have scholars ignored the gendered aspects of the relationship. Madeleine Grumet (1988) suggests that:

> gender contradictions, the simultaneous assertion and denial of femininity, have served to estrange teachers of children from the mothers of those children. Instead of being allies, mothers and teachers distrust each other. (p. 56)

The social construction of gender puts women, as teachers and as mothers, at odds with one another. Lightfoot (1977) reflects this concern when she argues that "mothers and teachers are caught in a struggle that reflects the devaluation of both roles in this society" (p. 404). One might wish that mothers and teachers would collaborate over children's interests, and in many cases, they do. The literature on parent–teacher relations offers many examples of how mothers and teachers cooperate (Epstein, 1986).

In studying the structure of women's everyday worlds, Dorothy Smith (1987) looks at "how the organizational practices of the school penetrate and organize the experience of different individual women as mothers" (p. 187). Using interviews with both mothers and the women who teach their children, Smith shows how mothers attempt to read the desires and expectations of teachers in order to work with their children. The work of the teachers, on the other hand, rests on the work mothers have already done with their children. Smith avoids pitting woman against woman because she embeds her discussion in the structure of school days and school practices. Her examples, however, reflect discord.

INTERPRETING TEACHERS' STORIES

The theme of parent–teacher conflict came up in most conversations I had with Vista City teachers. It took me a while, however, to understand how the conflict was gendered. I was cued by a teacher who started talking about "parents" and concluded that she was not like those "mothers who sit around the kitchen table with a coffee cup in their hands criticizing teachers." A review of the data revealed that although examples of teacher annoyance or anger with parents consistently began with the more gender-neutral term of "parent," each example that teachers gave specified mothers.

The relationship between women who taught at Vista City Elementary School and the mothers of children in their classes reflected interdependence as well as the hostility they most frequently voiced. Many teachers depended on volunteer help from parents in order to structure their classes in ways that fit their educational goals. Teachers made statements such as, "I can't run the kind of program that I want without a lot of hands." Mothers, particularly, helped in classrooms by bringing their own talents and expertise to improve what might be offered to their own and other children. They helped in this way by running weekly mathematics groups, by doing science lessons—activities that enriched and advanced the curriculum. Whatever the subject matter, be it reading or mathematics or science, mothers could be counted on to volunteer their help. These mothers valued schooling and had expertise to offer. The pool of mothers was such that some mothers could be counted on for education or experience in all these areas. Mothers also volunteered to tutor groups who were behind, to accompany classes on trips, and to organize parties for the class. They helped outside the classrooms in the school at large as well as through such activities as running the RIF (Reading Is Fundamental) program, by organizing fundraising activities including an annual carnival, and by helping in the large musical productions that different grades sponsored several times a year. Some teachers complained that they could not depend on parents in quite the same way as they had even several years before. A third-grade teacher said, "I've been fortunate in the past to have parents come in, three or four parents on a regular basis for an hour or two a day so that I have a lot of extra help in the classroom." The teacher attributed declining parental help to "more and more working parents. And I put out these pleas to my kids. 'Somebody come in and help us do this, that or the other thing.' And kids look at me sadly and say, 'My mom's working.'" The kids knew how to interpret the teacher's call for parental help. They read it as mother's help, and they read it correctly. Teachers liked the help that mothers provided.

The Content: Good and Bad Mothers

Teachers developed ways of thinking about how mothers and teachers are connected to each other. They called on their common interests to do this. Both are interested in the child's welfare. Both believe in the value of education for the child's future. Both need each other's help to develop an educated child. They have to work as a team.

Teachers also developed ways of thinking about how mothers and teachers were in conflict with each other. For this purpose, they called upon how they were oppositionally positioned in relation to classroom needs. The conflict was over the power to define; mothers could not refuse to accept the authority of the teacher. Put another way, even though mothers and teachers had to team, teachers had to be the team leaders.

Teachers not only valued mothers, then, they also strongly criticized mothers. The mothers they particularly disliked were the neighborhood mothers, to whom they referred as "pushy parents" and "professional parents." They were sometimes called "the intellectual or pseudointellectual ones." One teacher remarked that "the parents of the downtown kids and the black parents are just fine." It was the "parents in this neighborhood" that she found difficult. Teachers ardently criticized mothers' intensity and determination around their children's achievement. Many teachers described the "pressure" this achievement orientation created. They felt like mothers were "on our backs." One teacher described this orientation of mothers as "self-centered interest" because they were "only concerned" with the achievement of their own child, but not the welfare of the class as a whole or, for that matter, the teacher's. As one fifth-grade teacher admitted, "It's boring to talk about some kid's math for a whole hour. Some of these parents are too concerned about how their kids do." Teachers criticized parents for an overemphasis on their children's accelerated achievement.

Some teachers suggested that too often many parents ignored the close relationship between the situation of the class as a whole and the position of their child. If mothers thought more expansively about others, about the whole class, teachers suggested, the mother's child would benefit. Interestingly enough, some parents who volunteered in classrooms did so with this very goal in mind; improving the class as a whole improved their own child's prospects for a valuable educational experience.

Another kind of complaint teachers made about parents centered on mothers' challenges to their professional identity, and reflected teachers' insecure status regarding their roles. Teachers often felt that mothers did not trust their abilities to teach: to diagnose, to develop curriculum, to stimulate their children. This lack of trust, teachers felt, reflected mothers' diminished respect for their abilities as individuals and for the occupation of teaching generally. Teachers complained when mothers wanted to look over their lesson plans, when they stopped in to talk after school without making an appointment, saying, "It will only take five minutes," and then "proceeding to talk for an hour." When mothers did not make appointments or value teachers' time, they showed, from teachers' perspective, that they did not respect teachers. A common refrain was, "Don't they know we're professionals!"

Teachers had to face parents who wielded impressive educational vocabularies. Some mothers commonly used phrases like "instruction time" and "large-muscle activities" in their discussions of teachers' strengths and weaknesses. Teachers were right when they complained that neighborhood parents spent a lot of time talking about individual teachers. Teachers could say about mothers that they either took the education of their children seriously, or that they were "busybodies." Teachers said both, but were critical of what they saw as maternal "overinvolvement" in their children's education.

Middle-class white parents made two kinds of objections to teacher practices. *Principled objections* centered around the morality or justice of particular practices. Some mothers, for example, strongly criticized a musical production that a novice teacher had spent many hours preparing as "sexist." The teacher and her coproducers had taken Richard Rodgers's songs and strung them into a play for kids. The mothers were particularly upset that the song "There is Nothin' Like a Dame" was included. The teacher reacted angrily: "Can't everybody realize that it's just Richard Rodgers? That's just how it was then, and that's how we're using it." She threatened to quit if anyone tampered with the play. The teacher had looked at the material in one way and wanted others to see it in the same way, refusing to recognize any broader dimensions. At the same time, teachers felt that when parents made principled objections, unfair outside concerns were often dragged in and provided parents with ammunition that teachers had difficulty challenging.

Individual objections, on the other hand, centered around actual teacher practices with mothers' own children. If principled objections were made in the name of the good of all children, individual objections could (but did not always) separate the needs of particular children from others in the class. These were the most frequent kinds of objections mothers made to teachers. In these kinds of objections mothers wanted to make sure that the teacher did not treat all children in the class the same. One mother described a point in a difficult year with a teacher when she went in to talk to the teacher about her daughter's unhappiness in the classroom: "She [the teacher] really didn't know the kids individually at all. She talked about the whole group. It was very hard to get Heather to focus in on Margaret." Teachers often worried that too many demands by mothers would multiply; hence, they read this sort of objection as greatly increasing their workload in the face of diminishing resources.

Not all teachers were equally critical of parents. Some had only praise for mothers' involvement in the school: "They're very concerned about their kids' education and very involved in it." Many teachers who withheld criticism had either had worse experiences with parents in other schools or had young children of their own and were personally familiar with the parental role in schools. These teachers, however, were in the minority. Most teachers wanted parents to help in the classroom at activities and in ways that teachers determined or of which they approved, and at the same time criticized them for "pounding down our doors."

The Narrative Structure

The content of the stories teachers told about mothers was also informed by their narrative construction. Although what teachers said about mothers varied, although some were more or less critical than others, two lodestars guided the stories. I will describe the forms, try to account for these constructions, and discuss their effects.

One way teachers organized their stories of parents employed what I have come to call the *juvenile delinquent approach* ("it's only a few 'bad apples'"). That is, after describing difficulties they have had

with particular parents, or talking in general about parent–teacher relationships at Vista City Elementary, teachers would say, "It's really just
a few parents." Here are some more examples of this construction:

> There might have been five parents who were absolutely diffi-
> cult, just impossible.
>
> It's really only a few parents who cause problems, but these
> parents make life miserable for the teachers.
>
> In fact it is only very few parents who are so intrusive and
> busybodyish.
>
> Actually, just a few parents give the parents a bad name.
> Only a few of them make trouble.

The behavior of some parents came to represent the possible behavior
of and potential threat posed by all middle-class parents.

These comments about parents (read mothers) never came at the
beginning of a story about parent–teacher relationships. They came
after some negative comments: a particularly vehement criticism, or a
depiction of a series of incidents that described run-ins with mothers,
or some sweeping statement that generalized parent behaviors. The
teachers seemed to regulate their critical stance toward the mothers
by these statements. They also showed that they could differentiate
between kinds of middle-class parents with whom they came into
contact. But by suggesting that parents came to be represented by
those who behaved inappropriately, they insisted that parents were the
problem.

The juvenile delinquent approach also provided a way to categorize parents into good parents and bad parents. Both good and bad
parents had a classroom presence. Good parents volunteered in the
classroom under teachers' structure. Bad parents intruded in the classroom to observe and monitor the teachers' competence. Both good and
bad parents privileged the teacher's position in the classroom. Good
parents at best respected the teacher's abilities, and at worst understood how the difficulties of a particular class interfered with good
teaching. Bad parents questioned or challenged the teacher's authority,
competence, and abilities, perhaps blaming the teacher for a child's
unhappy school year. Both good and bad parents communicated information and feelings about family life to the teacher, although in different amounts. Good parents shared with the teacher family difficulties
(such as divorce) that might be occurring, or problems a child might
be having outside of school. Good mothers, in other words, were will-

ing to be vulnerable. Bad parents, on the other hand, postured the ideal world of family, and behaved in a closed fashion. They covered up. Bad parents revealed little, and teachers had a hard time believing what they did tell.

When teachers took the juvenile delinquent approach, they were also communicating to me that I was not one of *those* parents. By differentiating the majority good parents from the minority bad parents, teachers were permitted to criticize all parents to the parents they liked, and then qualify their remarks as only applying to certain "bad" parents. It also meant that "horror stories," rather than cooperative alliances, came to represent normative relationships.

The juvenile delinquent approach also had an essentializing effect on teachers' vision of the mother–teacher relationship. Teachers could develop a characterization, that is, of what neighborhood mothers were "essentially" like. If mothers in the neighborhood were reflected and came to be known by the rotten apples, then teachers acted as if mothers were "essentially" pushy and demanding. Mothers who cooperated, volunteered, and made few demands were distinguished as different, even though they were in the majority. Hence, teachers were on the defensive with mothers and unable to articulate the class issues around work, child rearing, and style that existed.

A second construction of teacher narratives about neighborhood parents distanced the individual teacher from other teachers in the building, at the same time revealing teachers' vulnerability. The outline of this construction followed a basic pattern: "Others have problems with difficult parents, though I do not. But their difficulties show me that it could be me." Another feature of this narrative included a discussion of the teacher's strength or self-confidence, which prevented her from having difficulties. At the same time, narrators would contradict these statements by presenting situations where their interpretations of parents' words or behaviors caused them to feel like objects rather than subjects. Or observations of the teacher's "shaking voice" in front of parents suggested fear rather than self-confidence.

Some examples of this kind of narrative structure reveal teachers differentiating themselves from other teachers as they position themselves in opposition to mothers. One teacher distanced herself from other teachers because she depended on daily parental help, while "most teachers do not want parents around in the classroom." While other teachers might feel self-conscious around a mother's gaze, in other words, she did not. She also did not have personal problems with parents: "Just by being strong, I don't usually get friction, like the parents bothering me. I don't feel any problem with them." Yet before and after this statement, this teacher had described conflicts with parents that made her feel that she had no control, that she was an object to them. Before this statement, she criticized parents for "pounding on our doors," and not making appointments to see teachers but "just" stopping by to talk: "The parent feels no need to stop at the office and say, 'Would it be all right if I went down to the classroom?' or to call the teacher the night before or send a note: 'I would like to come'; 'Can I come in?' 'When can I talk to you?' or whatever. Just feeling they have complete open entrance."

After her statement that she did not have friction with parents, she described an incident that made her feel like an "object." A mother took a child out of her mathematics class without even talking to her about it because the child, another teacher told her, was afraid of her. The teacher had no opportunity to negotiate the incident. To make matters worse, she only heard the reasons secondhand.

Another teacher said that what made teaching most difficult for her, and made her feel most pressure, were parents. As examples of this pressure, she said that parents sometimes came in and wanted to see her lesson plans or wanted to observe in her class. The teacher pulled out a letter she was carrying with her and proudly showed it off. The text told how much the mother appreciated the teacher, how wonderful the daughter thought her as well. The mother had written, "As you know, we've had many ups and downs with Ginger this year and being in your class has been a wonderful experience for her." The teacher said that she actually got quite a few letters like this, and personally had very few problems with parents. Yet earlier she had described parents as "really pressuring," a population that came in and made her life difficult. The exaggerated importance of parent praise was the flip side of parent criticism.

A teacher in the primary grades with a reputation for leadership and strength talked for many interview sessions about parents. At the same time she said that she never had any difficulty with parents, but a lot of other teachers had. She did not like it when parents challenged her competence. She said a number of times, "I'm a professional. I'm trained [in my area] and I make judgments on this basis." When parents come in and argue with her, she wants to make it clear that she has the files, that she sees the child daily, that she knows the score. She noted many cases where parents have given "absolute grief" to the teacher by demanding things of them. Many of the teachers, however, do not have her self-assurance and "give in." She then told a story of a difficult mother who criticized her reading methods, and of another who challenged the quality of her relationships with children. In this latter instance, the parent had said to someone, and this comment had gotten back to the teacher, "I hear she makes them march." The principal reported that the teacher had been "devastated." The teacher, however, said only: "Many of the parents are surprised because I am a very structured person and structured in the class, but I have a very warm, wonderful relationship with the kids." At a recent roller-skating party, the kids were "hanging all over" her and prevented her from skating.

She also told a "horror story" of a mother who came in to observe the class. During the instructional time the parent rifled through lesson plans and papers on the teacher's desk. Her self-confidence helps her to handle situations like this, but these conflicts with parents devastate teachers with less confidence. Her narrative construction positioned her as capable of overcoming any difficulties a parent might pose.

Another teacher of the upper elementary grades said that she had never had problems with parents, perhaps because she has made a point of having an open classroom and because she does not want to be "either on the offensive or the defensive with parents." Yet an observation of this teacher in a meeting with parents had revealed her "shaking voice." She had sworn to a "good" parent before the meeting: "These goddamned parents. I'm not going to go in there." The good parent, who had set up the meeting, reported that she literally held the teacher up, supporting her body, as she said to the teacher: "You can do it, Ellen. If you don't want to say anything, that's all right. I'll sit next to you or you can sit next to one of the other teachers and someone else can say something for you." The teacher did not like that idea. She decided she would say something.

The contrast between this teacher's comments to me about not having any problems with mothers and her high level of anxiety before the meeting (which went well) not only reflects the power that middle-class white parents have in teachers' eyes, but also the shame involved in perceiving it as a problem. Novice teachers might be allowed problems with women who were mothers, but not expert, professional, experienced teachers. Hence, Ellen could not refuse to speak with parents and have someone else speak for her; the shame would be too great. Mothers might make life difficult, but not being able to handle them meant you were not a professional.

Teachers agreed that one needed to be strong and have self-confidence to manage parents. A second-grade teacher said, "Confidence helps me deal with the parents because I don't doubt myself when they come in." In addition to confidence, experience provided leverage. "When I had all these highly skilled kids in my class, the parents would come to the door. I would see them standing there with worried looks on their faces. When they found out this was my eighth year teaching, their faces visibly relaxed."

A sixth-grade teacher had said to me in the teachers' room, "You're interested in what concerns us. I guess one thing is parents." The afternoon before she had had a conference with a child's parents and the child's psychiatrist that had greatly upset her. She also reported an incident in which a mother whose daughter said that the teacher had lost her homework had pressured her terribly (and the daughter had not done the homework). Yet in an interview with this teacher several weeks later, she reported that she had very few problems with parents "herself." She has a way of "dealing" with them; she shapes the relationship. She cannot blame parents for advocating for their children because "we all want the best for our children."

The Underlying Conflict

Teachers tell their stories of parents in these ways because they read their situation as a conflict between parties with different interests rather than as a problem of gender that both parties share. Hence, contradictions arose. They distanced themselves from "problems" with mothers and then gave examples from their own experiences that contradicted the assertion, showing examples of conflict. They argued that they were professionals who made good clinical judgments about children, but felt humiliated that mothers' activities, viewpoints, and words had the power to affect them so deeply. They did not want to continually have to prove themselves to each new group of parents when the school year started.

Vista City teachers see good teachers as moving through stages. As a novice, one has parent problems, but as an experienced teacher, one does not. Most teachers structured their narratives to reveal that they were no longer novices. The one novice teacher who reported parent problems identified herself as a new teacher. She expected to have parent problems. It was not that problems went away, but teacher narratives did not make room for vulnerability.

Teachers have internalized the negative value accorded their occupation. Many teachers said that if they had to do it again, they would go into management in order to gain more status and more financial security. Hence they call on professionalism to defend their decisions about children, and to separate their relationship with children, which rests on professional training, from mothers' relationships and advice, which rest on the purely personal. Complicating matters at this school were the educational credentials of some of the mothers.

The effects of structuring their narratives about parents as they did led to the mystification of the parent–teacher relationship. Parents' image as unpredictable and demanding meant that teachers could never really know what parents wanted. As one teacher said, "Some mothers say, 'You're giving my kid too much homework; my kid's up till ten o'clock doing your homework,' and other parents say, 'Gee, why doesn't my kid get any homework from you?' These conflicting demands are hard to take." If some parents want one thing (an open classroom) and other parents want something else (a fast-paced class), the teacher cannot please them all. Hence she can solve the problem by following the curriculum. The teacher presents herself as caught in a world that makes no logical sense. If some want this and some want that, what can she do? She can do what serves her interests. The school principal participated in the mystification of middle-class white parents in her assertion that one could not predict how mothers would respond to changes in a classroom. The same incident will please some and anger others.

Teachers resist mothers' interference in the classroom because they see it as a challenge to their professionalism. Rightly perceiving their flimsy status in the occupational world, they envision an old-fashioned professionalism, as I discussed in Chapter 4, untouched by consumer movements, as the potential rescuer from this situation. They resist mothers' interference because they want their work taken seriously and they see mothers' activities not as a parallel effort, but as a challenge to this desire.

Both teachers and white middle-class mothers call upon traditional ideologies of professionalism. These assumptions about what a profession is interfere with their collaboration because, ironically, both understand what professionalism is similarly. The mothers want teachers to have more of the training and abilities of doctors. The teachers want the mothers to act more like patients, making appointments and respecting their expertise with children. So they share the same definition of professionalism even as they lament each other's participation.

Teachers' relationships are embedded in a web of other relationships and material conditions of school life, including teachers' relationships with the principal and with each other, parents' relationships with other parents, the amount of the school budget, the attitudes and behaviors of the central administration, and the curriculum. Class differences were significant as well. Some teachers understood differently from the upwardly mobile middle-class neighborhood parents what knowledge was necessary to develop curriculum.

How teachers thought about the curriculum influenced how they evaluated parental demands. Reactions varied. Those who took the curriculum for granted as an expert-developed measure of how much their students should accomplish for the year fussed when parents wanted more and more challenging assignments. They saw the students as "two years ahead of themselves" or as "way beyond grade level" already. Hence, they could not understand why parents were "so worried" about how their children did in class. Teachers also pressured teachers of lower grades to make sure they did not tread on the higher grade's turf by teaching beyond a certain level. Kindergarten and first-grade teachers engaged in heated dialogue over reading levels. First-grade teachers did not want children in kindergarten to go beyond reading-readiness levels. So it was an issue of workload as well. A first-grader reading above grade level forces the teacher to find extra work to challenge that child. Teachers who saw the curriculum as a guideline did not object to mothers' concern for their children's achievement if mothers were, at the same time, cooperative and available.

When they thought about mothers, in general, teachers worried that they would not think of teachers sympathetically, that they would not understand what was "legitimately" difficult about their work. Teachers needed confirmation from others that when they faced difficulties in the classroom, it was not necessarily because their class management skills were deficient in some way (say, not enough large-group instruction), but because the constitution of the class was challenging.

How parents were categorized was also not always the result of single, individual encounters. The school culture supported a warning system for self-protection so that teachers could advise each other about particularly troublesome parents. Parents had developed city-wide reputations at Vista City Elementary that magnified what they did. When Mrs. DeFransisco demanded more homework, everyone knew about it. When Sally Martin made "outrageous" comments to a teacher, the others commiserated. The teacher who had the children of one of these parents in her class could depend on the support of other teachers to criticize and, in a way, dismiss these parents' concerns.

CONCLUSION

This examination of the conflicts between mothers and teachers sets up the classroom as a site where women seem to struggle with each other for status and control. I emphasized conflict rather than cooperation because teachers highlighted conflict with parents as a major problem for them. The difficulties in their relationship center on a socially devalued domesticity associated with the education and care of young children. How teachers construct and structure their stories reveals the tenuous hold teachers have, if they have it, on respectable work when read against middle-class rather than working-class social mobility.

As the opening of this chapter suggested, mothers and teachers are in the same predicament: Society devalues the work they do with young children. Teachers and mothers, then, struggle against the same obstacles even though it appears as if they vie with each other for status and control. They need, however, to name these obstacles and to recognize the similarities of their positions.

I take the risk of holding a kind of essentialist position. This position would describe teachers as if they were all alike, rather than examining their class, race, and ideological differences. Teachers are not alike. We must continually emphasize this point. They do, however, have a standpoint shaped by their particular social contexts from which they view mothers. At Vista City the commonality of position among teachers in relation to parents was noticeable. Teachers who called themselves feminists as well as others who were progressive joined with more conservative teachers in their criticisms of mothers' behaviors in the school. At schools in the city where staff struggled to involve parents, teachers shared the concerns of those at Vista City Elementary. This view was not particular to the school.

Teachers' position of vulnerability in traditionally hierarchical schools leads them to what we might also call an essentialist view of parents. But their daily experience challenged this approach; teachers depended on parents, teachers liked many parents, teachers had good relationships with many parents. So to avoid this position, teachers developed a way of talking about parents that categorized them as good or bad. Talking as if most parents were "bad" when they were really "good" or fitting parents into only one (or the other) category was a form of needed self-protection that was ultimately self-damaging. In daily life they easily negotiated and distinguished mothers individually, though they recognized that class issues were involved. They were caught in a contradiction.

Social class shaped teachers' reading of middle-class white mothers. Teachers' discussion of pressure suggests that they saw mothers' demands as the desire for preference. The stronger the working-class background of the teacher, the more clearly she read it this way.

Teachers from middle-class backgrounds could understand this view even if they fought it. Connell and his colleagues (1985) noted similar emphases in their Australian sample. Upper-middle-class mothers showed their "class fear" when asserting that an education could not be taken away from their children, therefore implying that other family possessions could be.

Teachers' lack of control over the conditions of their work made them vulnerable to the demands of white middle-class mothers. At Vista City they recognized their vulnerability, but their way of thinking about their positions pushed this recognition to the background, and thence underground.

Both mothers and teachers wanted to change the social configuration of their work. Teachers wanted to be considered full-fledged professionals with all of the privileges entailed by that status, while middle-class white mothers wanted recognition that the bearing and nurturing of children does not render them vacuous. At the same time, valuing the domestic as a complementary sphere leaves women powerless. Many of the women who taught felt that distancing themselves (and their professional credentials) from the mothers (with their commonsense understandings of child development) would enhance their own professional credibility. But this view did not recognize the gender link. Calling the problem "parents" rather than "mothers" might mystify the question, might detract from centering gender, but its consequences were that the analysis always missed the mark. Teachers need a model that allies them with rather than separates them from mothers and fathers.

CHAPTER 7

Teachers' Talk: Community and Conflict

The cultural construction of teachers gets accomplished not only by the attribution of meanings *to* teachers, but also *by* teachers themselves. Through their talk, teachers continually interpret what it means to be a teacher, both calling on and producing certain gender arrangements as they do so. How people talk and the forms of talk employed "are strategic actions, created as responses to cultural and institutional contexts" (Gal, 1991, p. 176). When women who teach elementary school negotiate with each other about how they will or will not work together in a school, they articulate cultural constructions of gender to do so. Gal (1991) emphasizes the importance of talk to gender relations: "Patterns of talk and interaction play an important role in maintaining, legitimating, and often hiding the gendered aspect of these institutional arrangements" (p. 185). This camouflaging can occur because, as Orner (1992) argues, drawing on Foucault's notion of disciplinary power, "we internalize systems of surveillance to the point that we become our own overseer" (p. 83). And we also chip away at the walls that contain us. The teacher's identity is a complex site.

I studied the women who taught at Vista City Elementary School not to explore how feminists worked to subvert their gendered lives, but to examine how gender worked in a group of ordinary teachers, a group that included some who were active feminists, some who were fellow travelers, and some who were not. The negotiation of gender relationships through talk is particularly interesting at an elementary school, where women so predominate, because these arrangements are constructed through talk with other women.

Talk was central to the women teachers at Vista City Elementary. They did more of it than almost any other activity. They had conflicts with the principal when they did not get enough of the kind of talking they wanted. Resolving conflicts with each other when they disagreed with a particular method of pedagogy or control was made difficult without an atmosphere promoting deep talk.

143

Exploring how teachers talk to each other, however, engages more than language. Teachers make decisions about what they can talk about and what they cannot. What influences these decisions? Why do teachers retreat from some conflicts and not others? How do teachers support each other through talk? What institutional resources do they draw on? What cultural understandings? This chapter addresses talk, not linguistic practices.

INSTITUTIONAL TALK

Studying talk illuminates not only relationships but also boundaries. What teachers do and how they talk about what they do are partially constructed by what schools do to teachers as teachers spend time there. Schools as institutions provide certain boundaries to construct acceptable or unacceptable behavior, to promote one kind of acting over another. These boundaries also frame the teachers' choices. Within these boundaries, teachers can make certain decisions and still stay within the framework of the acceptable. Teachers disciplined and regulated each other through talk just as they increased their agency when they talked with each other about the subversive. They also nourished and engaged each other through talk.

Talk is also central to understanding the intellectual meaning elementary schoolteachers make of their work with children. Elementary schoolteaching is both a nurturing act and an intellectual one. Teachers need community to make it an intellectual one and to draw upon reserves when needed for nurturing. Talk is central to this community. Nurturing children could be done within the confines of a classroom. Teachers needed to be outside the classroom to be nurtured by other teachers. At the same time, much of the intellectual part of teaching could not be accomplished in the classroom. Teachers could be intellectually stimulated by their work with children, but needed interchange with other adults in order to do it. Because teaching elementary school is considered such gendered work, what is intellectual is not always recognized, either by teachers or by researchers.

Central to school work are the relationships that teachers form with one another. These relationships mark the kind of institution a particular school is. Just as the facilities within which one works help to define the employment, so do the ways in which the teachers interact with one another. In the first part of this chapter I explore the context of the school to which teachers responded in their talk. The context is constructed through the principal's articulation of it (the structure of leadership), and through the teachers' perspectives on leadership. The teachers' perspectives are important because they explain their actions. When conflicts arose between teachers or between teachers and the school district, for example, teachers might hide the conflict from their own administrator in order to do what they wanted. On certain occasions teachers ignored the boundaries to act as agents. How is it that teachers learn what the boundaries are?

The Principal's Perspectives

The principal categorized teachers as people who were uncomfortable with other adults. As she saw it, teachers preferred children to adults: "Teachers are very scared to talk and interact with adults. Look at the kinds of people who go into education. I think that they basically feel more comfortable with kids than with adults." In her efforts to support teachers, she called few faculty meetings so as not to burden the teachers. Her many efforts to support teachers' getting together included organizing an after-school aerobics class two afternoons a week in which she participated.

Principal June Robinson's difficulties facing conflict head-on with adults collided with her views on the range of children's needs. June's pedagogical values led her to place teachers with different teaching styles and beliefs on each grade-level team so that she could put students with distinct needs with teachers who might be sensitive to these needs. When she placed fourth-grade students in a classroom for a year, for example, she might put children who "needed structure" with a very structured teacher like Jeanette Johnson. And she might put the students who seemed more like what she called "free spirits" with a "looser" teacher. These placements, of course, were only approximate; classes also had to be balanced for race, gender, and "troublemakers."

Several of the teams, then, found themselves in a difficult situation. Team members had to make decisions together about discipline and other policy matters with a group of colleagues with whom they had very different teaching styles and values but without any structure in place to work through these pedagogical differences. The principal did not retreat from conflicts with children, but she did not initiate many actions to mediate conflicts that emerged for teachers.

Another site where the principal's views on talking emerged were the faculty council meetings, held monthly. Each grade-level team sent a representative to the council meetings. These seven teachers were joined by the instructional specialist and the vice principal. The principal chaired the meeting. The faculty council meetings (and the faculty meetings) operated as the teachers described them in interviews: The principal was somewhat businesslike, did not attempt to stimulate dialogue, and gave no appearance of enjoying the sessions. I commented in my notes after leaving the first faculty council meeting I attended that the principal used words like "share" that appeared to be part of a facilitator mode, but that her tone and style suggested an opposite approach.

The February council meeting started in June Robinson's office ten minutes after school let out. Representatives sat on chairs in a large circle. June started the meeting by announcing the first agenda item and beginning to talk about it. She held a typed agenda on her lap. She had the only copy, and she did not read through it before starting to discuss the first item. Teachers did not have the opportunity, in other words, to comment on the agenda, to prioritize items, or to add to it. Bob Jackson, the vice principal, sat a little behind her and took notes.

The first item concerned substitute teachers. June announced that every teacher needed to have an extra key made to their rooms and to keep a key hanging somewhere so that substitutes would be able to get in and out of their rooms without the children being locked out. Substitutes needed to be prepared by teachers to know which children needed to go to the bathroom frequently, and whether there were any "medical problems." There was little discussion.

Other business items followed. June said that she wanted to "advise" everyone present that the purpose of the faculty council was for the representatives to go back to their teams with notes from these meetings to discuss policy. She criticized the representatives for slacking off in their meetings with team members—representatives needed to talk more with their teams about topics covered at faculty council meetings. She also reviewed school closing policy because of inclement weather conditions occurring after the school day had started, and remonstrated with teachers to stay in the building until they got official word to leave. The first several items, in other words, were informational, but they also included criticisms of teacher behavior.

Council members then talked about the ordering of supplies: how to do it, the deadlines for orders, what should be ordered. Barbara Timmitts, the instructional specialist, spoke frequently, since she did the ordering. Some council members engaged around this issue, while others remained silent.

The next item on the agenda was the superintendent's meeting that June Robinson and Christine Bart had attended. After speaking a sentence or two June said, "Christine, would you like to tell what happened?" Christine declined, saying, "No, you do it, June. I'll interrupt when I want to say something." June did most of the telling, but Christine interrupted now and then.

June told the group about two proposals she had submitted that she hoped would be funded, one on mainstreaming and one on a resource center for gifted and talented children. There was no discussion, except for an informational query from one teacher about whether students in the gifted and talented program would leave their classes for a whole day or a half-day.

June announced that she wanted to meet with any teacher in the primary grades interested in having a class like Dana Barrett's that was integrated with typical kids and kids with severe disabilities. More talk arose around this issue than about any other item on the agenda. Teachers discussed the pros and cons of having such a class. June enthusiastically described the progress students in this class had made, using words such as "fabulous" and "tremendous." Although the first year had been "very challenging" for the teachers, there were some compensations, like very small classes. Christine Bart commented that "the kids are doing well and making great strides, but the teachers are a wreck." June and a couple of teachers described success stories of children in the classes. The principal supported a policy of inclusion. Some teachers resisted this view. The principal did not attempt to build support for a *shared* understanding for the values of this educational perspective. Rather, she created an atmosphere in which you could choose to teach in an inclusive classroom or not. Hence, there was never any deep discussion of the issues.

The meeting appeared to be going over the allotted time, because June began to look at the clock frequently. But the vice principal had a few comments to make to the teachers about disciplinary policies. General laughter surrounded issues like girls wearing clogs on their feet and bells in their hair (noisy items that were potentially disruptive), and African-American pupils wearing stocking caps for hair processing (did they count as regular hats, which were forbidden to be worn inside). The meeting ended.

The principal conceptualized the council meeting as a place to announce policy to teachers, who would then announce it to their teams—the megaphone approach. Even around the issue of integration, where ideological conflict between teachers clearly existed, there was no space for exploring the conflict, challenging stereotypes, or explaining strategies. The meeting did not reflect the possibilities of talk for building democracy, but rather the uses of talk as a kind of management strategy that permitted different views but did not work to engage them with each other.

Teachers' Perspectives

Although teachers disagreed with each other about whether or not the principal was "supportive" of them, they all agreed that she "gave" teachers freedom, but little direction. One of the primary criticisms was how little talking the principal did with her staff. Teachers criticized the lack of different kinds of talk.

Sandra Miller wanted more *intellectual and pedagogical talk*. She had been hired as an "alternative" teacher on the first-grade team to represent the English infant school model, an informal, more open, language-centered pedagogy. June Robinson had also used this approach as a first-grade teacher, so Sandra expected to talk about it:

> I had a chance to look at her bookshelf in some detail. Because of the fire [set by students one night the previous year] it was moved out of her office and I helped to move it back into her room slowly but surely. I had a chance to see what her books are—they're all good books. You wouldn't find them on Christine Bart's shelf. June's very intellectual about it and I know she understands what I'm trying to do. But she should have helped me a little bit.

Their shared intellectual and pedagogical values did not lead to discussions about the problems Sandra had with others on her team who did not support her methods. Sandra asserted that freedom did not mean disengagement:

> I would always like to give the children as much leeway as I could. So if I were thinking about what a principal should do, it would be the same, I would think. That's my way of doing it. That's her way of approaching people, too. She'd like to give you as much leeway as you possibly can have. But I'm not talking about her telling you what to do. I'm just saying it would have been nice if I had had someone to talk to.

Although she turned elsewhere to find colleagues with whom she could talk, no other person besides June had similar training:

> She's the only person who's read some of the same books. She's the only person who knows how I was trained to teach

reading. But she's also read some different books, so she could say, "Sandra, why don't you read such-and-such a book. It will help you out." It was disappointing to me that she didn't have time to talk to me.

Talking to the principal would have helped this teacher to teach better and explain to her colleagues what she wanted to do.

Another sort of talk teachers wanted from the principal concerned *process*. This kind of talk centered on how to structure dialogue. What processes would be useful for people to use to engage one another? Some examples of these processes included how meetings were organized and how criticism should be voiced either to the principal, to parents, or to each other. Many teachers wanted June to show leadership in how to talk as well as what should be taught.

The teachers' major criticism concerned the lack of meetings for teachers to talk together. Amelia Dickenson wanted more faculty meetings but did not mention it to the principal because "she would take it as criticism." Kate Bridges said that faculty council representatives often enter meetings with "burning concerns" and issues that are "weighing heavily on their minds." These concerns may or may not find room for expression during the last five or ten minutes of the meeting, and "it is never enough time." Additionally, she said:

I am very upset about the policy of teachers' meetings, which is basically not to have them. To me, a teachers' meeting is a bonding; it is a time for teachers to get together and talk about the issues that are crucial to them.

Her view was echoed in similar language by many others. Sandra Miller said that the content of most of the year's meetings could have been handled through memos. Christine Bart reported having to convince June to hold a meeting to discuss upcoming building renovations with the whole faculty. June had planned to make a few announcements about this at a council meeting. The faculty meeting that was finally held about the renovations was extremely lively. Christine had been right—everybody did want to talk about it.

The principal considered herself supportive because she did not hold many meetings. She based this policy decision on her understanding that teachers prefer talking to children than to adults. The faculty felt unsupported by the principal because she did not foster enough deep talk in the building. Neither party voiced their perspectives on this to the other. And yet they all talked considerably.

RELATIONAL TALK

Certain institutionalized features of school life provided sites and opportunities for teachers to engage in talk with one another. The teachers' room was a particular place where teachers could go to be with one another. At the time this study was conducted there was only one teachers' room, so teachers who did not like the smoke avoided the place. Faculty meetings were occasions where talk about issues could have occurred. That it did not continually disappointed faculty. Grade-level teams were part of the organizational structure; they were supposed to meet at least two Monday afternoons per month. Some teams were close, met very frequently, and supported each other; others were conflict-ridden and met infrequently. Teachers often described years on a particularly good team as "the best years of my working life."

The rest of this chapter will attend to talk about community and conflict. Teachers drew upon discourses of gender to figure out how to build supportive relationships with one another and to handle the conflicts that arose. These two specific kinds of talk were central to producing gender arrangements at the school. I artificially separate these two kinds of talk. One has conflicts in the process of collaboration, and one collaborates through conflicts. Both are intertwined and connected to the ways teachers evaluate their workplace.

COMMUNITY

In my first interview with a teacher, I asked Kate Bridges what made a good atmosphere in a school. She did not hesitate a moment to reply, "One of the central things is the fact of colleagueship in working together as a teaching community." Kate's views were echoed by many other teachers. At the same time that the teachers wanted some autonomy in their work, they also desired a sense of community, by which they meant a psychological sense of community: "The sense that one [is] part of a readily available mutually supportive network of relationships upon which one [can] depend and as a result of which one [does] not experience sustained feelings of loneliness" (Sarason, 1974, p. 1). In an elementary school the mutual support applied to pedagogical, organizational, ethical, and personal concerns. This psychological sense of community supplied to people a sense of belonging ("I am a part of this school"); supportiveness ("others will support me if I am in trouble or am unsure about what to do"); sharing ("I will share materials; I will help and be helped"); and validation ("my views and values are important").

Teachers used different kinds of talk to develop community at Vista City Elementary. This talk occurred in team meetings, privately, or in the teachers' room. I categorize four kinds of talk that teachers employed to strengthen community: solicited advice, clinical talk, social talk, and defending. Social talk and defending were always part of the informal ways teachers related to each other. Advice, depending on who gave it, and clinical talk could be either formal or informal.

Solicited Advice

Heather Samuels came to Vista City when she had completed one year of teaching. She described the earlier class and school as bucolic: "I never had to raise my voice the whole first year." Heather's arrival at Vista City, however, coincided with what everyone referred to as its "transition year." The closing of another city school meant that Vista City Elementary had to absorb most of its students. It was the former principal's last year, and because of doubts that she could manage the change, she shared the principalship with June Robinson.

Race informed a number of conflicts in the school. The city had stationed guards in the hallway outside the fifth- and sixth-grade classrooms. Heather described her experience:

> When I came here I was, as you can imagine, a very naive and protected person. I found myself right in the middle of this incredible atmosphere and I didn't know what to do. Imagine me having come from a great year where I never had to raise my voice once. I'm suddenly in the middle of all these kids who are hitting each other and beating on each other, getting after me, and calling me all kinds of names that I'd never heard before like "fucking this" and "fucking that" and I didn't know what to do.

It was not, I imagine, that Heather, a European-American woman, had never before heard the word "fuck." Rather, she may never have heard it used before to challenge her authority. And when she heard it used by African-American students, she connected it with danger and a lack of control. Heather described her difficulties in terms of challenges to authority, but she came up against racism in the classroom and did not know what to do. Her analysis of teaching was not informed by race.

Heather said that she would not have remained in teaching without the advice and support of two teachers on her team.

Solicited advice is the kind of talk that results when one faculty member asks a colleague for help. The colleague may give more than verbal advice—that is, material support as well—but the advice is seen as supportive rather than directive. The advice may be either specific or a general expression of support in response to a comment like, "I don't know what to do." At one fourth-grade team meeting, for example, the teachers talked about how to organize their teaching for a grant they were working on. The purpose of the grant, a special life-skills curriculum project, was to take different forms of art expression and relate them to the subject areas of the curriculum. Jennie McAuliffe, the teacher who was supposed to begin, was not sure that she knew how to translate the idea into the practice. Did any of the teachers have any advice for her? In response, Sarah Jacobs said, "Oh, I know you'll be just wonderful. You don't have to plan every little thing, Jennie. Just get the idea of what you want to do and you'll go in there and do it wonderfully. You're just wonderful with the kids!" The teacher embedded her advice, that Jennie did not have to completely structure the curriculum in advance, in a supportive commentary that clearly articulated Jennie's teaching abilities. We might think of her commentary as another way of saying, "Don't be uptight."

Sandra Miller sought advice from Barbara Timmitts, the instructional specialist. Sandra had worried because she was the last person on her team giving levels tests, and had felt threatened when another teacher said to her, "Aren't you finished with your testing yet?" Barbara Timmitts offered her advice:

> Barbara said to me, "Sandra, don't worry about that. I was the same. If you're teaching and instructing to the very last minute, you don't do those levels tests till the very last minute, then people whose levels tests are finished three weeks before the end of the year look very organized. They're looking after themselves, don't forget, and not necessarily the children." And I just breathed a sigh of relief.

It was part of Barbara's role as the school's instructional specialist to consult on instructional issues with individual teachers. She could comfort Sandra, however, because they shared important values. As Sandra said, "And I have Barbara, who just always understands what I'm talking about." The way advice was given connected these teachers to each other and to their work.

Clinical Talk

Clinical talk concerned individual children. Teachers employed it to figure out why a child had behaved in a particular way or why an interaction occurred in a specific way. They also used it when they needed to vent about a child.

The sixth-grade team, for example, who met together every day, engaged in clinical talk as a way of relaxing, to check out interpretations of children and behavior, and to reify their interpretations. Sylvia Richardson emphasized the relaxation. The sixth-grade team usually had lunch together:

> We relax with each other and our way of relaxing is to talk about what happened during the morning. And sometimes we need to just get angry and explode about a kid. If we can get it off our chests, we won't hold it against the kid all afternoon.

The team members, who described themselves as different from each other but experienced teachers, took the opportunity every day to develop consensus about how to make sense of events and personalities in the sixth grade.

Other teachers also employed this kind of talk to work through their strategies with those children teachers referred to as "difficult." Lisa Novak, who was critical of her current second-grade team, called a previous team "wonderful" because of how they talked about the students. The team members "really talked" to each other about "difficult" kids. Dana Barrett described her "fantastic" team experiences with Maria Johnson and Barbara Timmitts. She said that their team had talked over all the difficult and "impossible" children. Clinical talk referred to talk about problems rather than to doing more with kids who were achieving.

Social Talk

Another kind of connecting talk was the social talking that friends did with one another. Some of the teachers went to a local bar every Friday afternoon. When marriages, the arrival of children, or other responsibilities halted this habit, the teacher would often complain that she missed going. Amy Michaels, for instance, said that before she had her baby, she "never even thought about going home on Friday afternoon." Jennie McAuliffe had also cut down on the number of Fridays she joined the group at O'Flaherty's, since she had gotten married. Her husband was a law student and was often home on Friday afternoons.

Group friendships were only one kind of socializing that occurred at Vista City. Many friendships between individual people strengthened the feelings teachers had for the school. Heather Samuels and Jennie McAuliffe were close, spending time together after school each day. Maria Johnson and Dana Barrett were also personal friends; they shared an interest in feminist issues. Dana could talk to Maria about her divorce. Carrie Amundsen was friendly with the principal, June Robinson. She said that June felt free to discuss her work problems openly because she knew that Carrie would not share what she knew. Lisa Novak counted on the friendship of Kate Bridges, and missed what the friendship provided her when Kate was on leave.

The friendships people experienced at the school heightened their sense of connection to the school. Teachers were buoyed by friends who understood their problems. These friendships were emotionally nourishing to the people who experienced them. A teacher experienced great relief if she was able to go to the room of another teacher who was a good friend after school and say, "You wouldn't believe what happened to me today!"

The content of the friendship sometimes bridged the gap between personal and work-related concerns. Some friendships, like Sandra Miller's and Jessica Bonwit's, remained on the level of school-centered issues. Others, like Heather Samuels's and Jennie McAuliffe's, included personal matters as well. Social talk and clinical talk sometimes ran into each other.

Defending

Another kind of talk reinforced loyalties that individual teachers felt for each other. When a teacher verbally defended another teacher whose style others were criticizing, she effectively kept the criticized teacher within the circle of the school. The effect of criticism was to ostracize the offending teacher. Whoever chose to defend the offender refused to allow a successful resolution to this attempt. "Defending" provides a good example of the interweaving of community and conflict. Defending another rested on a conflict but strengthened relationships.

The case of Sandra Miller was particularly noticeable. She was often criticized by other teachers for the "openness" of her style. Some other teachers thought that her classroom was too noisy and that the activities occurring there were too disorganized. Lisa Novak referred to her as "a space cadet." She commented, "She lets them do too much playing at the beginning of the year."

Jessica Bonwit always came to Sandra's defense. She reported getting "very upset" when other faculty members could not see Sandra's strengths: "I always defend Sandra, and I always will." She also wanted to make certain that Sandra did not feel too isolated, so every morning, and often at the end of the day, she went to Sandra's room to say hello. She liked and appreciated Sandra, she said, because they "shared educational values." She described Sandra as

> a very humane teacher. There's always the hum of noise in her class because she individualizes reading for each of her children. When I go to look for a class for my own kids, I look for humanity in the classroom, and I think you'll really find that in Sandra's class.

Defending is a responsive talk.

Sandra was not the only teacher who had a colleague who would come to her defense. Lisa Novak commented that some teachers criticized Christine Bart for her style:

> There's a lot of backbiting around Christine because people think she always manages to wangle her way to getting the good kids in her class. But that is not what really happens. Christine is a really good teacher and the reason good kids end up coming out of Christine's class is that she teaches them well.

Lisa defended Christine when she heard other teachers criticize her because she believed the criticism was unjustified.

I separated "defending" from other ways of talking because it was so consciously executed at Vista City. A teacher had to be willing to contradict her peers in order to defend a teacher of whom others disapproved. For teachers who often had difficulty expressing disagreement with a group, to engage in defense sometimes appeared as such a risk that they had to "brave the elements," as it were, to undertake the task.

Defending was a significant form of talk in a context that positioned on the same team teachers with varied pedagogies but did not provide processes for talking through the differences. Sandra Miller, for example, had been hired by the principal expressly for the alternative style she employed. Within this atmosphere one could not criticize her style to the principal if one disagreed with it. Rather, one had to criticize her execution of the style. McPherson (1972) also noted the difficulties teachers face when they choose teaching styles considered nonconforming. While difficulties like Sandra Miller had were not specific to this elementary school, they were inflated by the contradictions present in discourses of change and stability.

Teachers utilized solicited advice, talking clinically and socially, and defending one another to enhance their relationships. Talk that constructed community responded to a larger concern than the particular issue at hand. Teachers may have talked about the specifics of a project, but the words also reassured.

The Professional Mystique: An Obstacle to Community

Teachers drew on particular discourses in their talk in order to make sense of their experiences. A discourse of professionalism provided firm guidelines and boundaries to what choices were possible and what interpretations were acceptable. The professional mystique, as a discourse, is a way of thinking and talking that will "define, describe, delimit, and circumscribe what it is possible and impossible to say with respect to it, and how it is to be talked about" (Kress, 1985, p. 28). In Chapter 6 I showed how the traditional professional model interfered with teachers' relationships with parents. The discourse of professionalism also interrupted the development of a sense of community among the teachers.

The teachers wanted to be considered professionals. They were motivated partly by the desire to be recognized for their work. A professional acted and spoke differently from a nonprofessional. Teachers particularly concerned with their status used the language of professionalism to refer to each other. In interviews they referred to other teachers in the school as "colleagues." They frequently avoided the use of "friend" to describe other teachers they liked and with whom they spent time.

There is another aspect to the colleague–friend issue as well. All women have friends; only professional women have colleagues. The teachers needed to emphasize their status. This need is revealed not so much in their use of "colleague," but more in the discomfort some teachers felt with the word "friend." Their focus on professionalism was a defense against their situations. The teachers needed to continually reassert to the community, particularly to the professional community surrounding Vista City Elementary, that their work was difficult and important.

An additional factor is the status of the researcher. The teachers knew that I had connections to the university and was a professional myself. It was important to them, therefore, that I understand their social conception of themselves. Had my social status differed, some of the teachers might also have presented themselves to me differently.

As an interviewer it took me a while to understand the responses I often received to questions I continually asked about whether a teacher had "friends" on the staff. Christine Bart, for example, said that she did not "mix business with pleasure." She had colleagues at school, but friends at home. Laurie Hallock did not describe the teachers with whom she spent time as friends, either. In fact, she reported that she could only call teachers "friends" if she saw them socially outside work, and she did not: "I really like to separate work and home and when I go home I don't like to see people that I work with. I don't like to see people outside of work."

Kate Bridges talked about her decision to cut her hours on the job because she felt torn between work and family. Then she described how "renewing" a particular relationship had been with a student teacher because they communicated so well. She said: "One of the reasons I was staying so late was I had a student teacher and we'd stay for an hour or so after school every day and talk. That was colleague-ship!"

As the interview continued, I asked her about her relationships to other teachers in the school in addition to the student teacher. I transposed her word, however, from "colleagues" to "friends." I did not differentiate so clearly between a colleague and a friend, and so the next time I asked her about her staying late to talk to the student teacher, I called her "your friend." The change in language registered with the respondent. She immediately asserted that although she had friends at school, she was so busy she did not get to see them. After going around a bit, we sorted this out. "Colleagues" indicated a professional, work-related situation. When one had interactions with colleagues, it was part of the job. "Friends," however, are part of our personal lives as well as our work lives. For a woman who experienced conflict over the time she gave to her family, it was difficult to justify staying after school for an hour to talk with a friend. It was much easier to explain talking with a colleague.

The professional mystique intervened in other ways as well. One of the more apparent ways was its effect on teachers' willingness to ask each other for advice (see Little, 1990). The fear of appearing unprofessional hampered teachers' queries of one another. Heather Samuels, for example, had a child in her class with a high IQ whom she considered gifted. She found it troublesome teaching this child and "dealing" with his mother. She "knew" she was not as bright as the child. Sometimes when he made a comment she did not understand, she would say, "That's a good point, Ron. I'm glad you said that," as a strategy to remain in control. I asked Heather whether she had thought of speaking with Amelia Dickenson, a sixth-grade teacher who had wide-ranging experience working with "gifted" children. Heather replied that she did not know Amelia and did not want to ask her for advice because she did not want Amelia to think that she did not know much. As she put it, "I don't want to be in the situation of the professional giving advice to the amateur." If she knew Amelia better, she said, she would consider asking, but since she did not know her, she could not predict her reaction.

Teachers sometimes wondered what professional ethics meant in relation to solving problems they had with another colleague. Could professionals get outside help or solace for a problem with a coworker? Dana Barrett considered giving up her mainstreamed class of typical and autistic children in order to avoid working with Jeff Kearnes. "It's just terribly hard for me because I don't work well with Jeff. I don't get along with him and I don't like working in a close relationship with him and this all makes it very difficult."

I asked her whether she had spoken with the principal about her problem. "No, I haven't," she said. "I worry that it's not professional of me to do this. I don't know whether I should tell about Jeff that way." Had she shared her discouragement with Maria Johnson, her close friend? "Well, there again," she answered, "I feel that it's not professional to talk about another colleague like that." Dana felt that she was left with the choice of staying in the program and consequently having to work with Jeff, or leaving the program in order to create distance between Jeff and herself, even though she enjoyed working with the parents of the children with autism. Her understanding of the professional ethic offered her few means to negotiate, work through, or seek help to resolve her conflicts.

Dana's representation of professionalism depended on a gendered definition. She read opportunities to talk about problems with a colleague as gossip. Gossip was unprofessional behavior. Women might gossip together but, in her analysis, professionals would (or should) not. Gossip is a powerful form of talk, but it is culturally condemned:

Gossip itself is women's most powerful verbal tool, but it is two edged. It tends to subvert male authority, by judging people in terms of values the male-dominant system rejects. But partly as a result of this subversion, it is condemned and decried by the dominant culture. (Gal, 1991, p. 183)

A strategy for connecting with the dominant culture, represented in professionalism, would be to gain distance from such unprofessional forms of talk as gossip (whether or not other professionals actually gossip).

CONFLICT

Teachers at Vista City engaged in conflict with one another, with parents, with the school district, with the principal. Conflicts ranged in intensity from mild discord in the group to antagonisms of ideas or interests that resulted in open hostility or divisiveness. Conflict suggests a lack of harmony, although when groups engage in conflict with other groups, the conflict may intensify feelings of group identification and promote vitality. The conflicts of teachers at Vista City Elementary ranged from friendly disagreements to outright rebellion. Their conflicts with parents were discussed in Chapter 6, so I will not refer to them here.

Teachers articulated their conflicts in many ways, but they developed practices of talking about them according to how the conflicts were resolved. I have placed the resolutions in four categories: unhappy compliance; the standoff; covert resistance; and open resistance. Each form of resolution suggests different understandings of how power functioned in the school, what power teachers could draw upon to act, and how their relationships with others influenced their position.

Unhappy Compliance

Teachers sometimes critiqued policies at the school or district level that they did little to change. Rather than bring the conflict into the open by challenging the authority or colleague with whom they disagreed, they complied with the opposing side of the conflict. Rather than strategize toward change, they went along with the conditions they disliked. In each of these situations, the teacher felt that to win the conflict, she would have to challenge the authority, whether it was administrative, collegial, or parental. Compliance meant that teachers had to continue to work with conditions they opposed, perhaps negating their own values or concerns through their lack of action. Unhappy compliance with conflictual situations represented to teachers how devalued their occupation was. Some examples of unhappy compliance suggest the range of issues that were not resolved.

No teacher I interviewed at Vista City Elementary had good words for those in-service sessions run by the district offices. At one particularly bad session, some teachers signaled their discontent by doing more than grumbling. Sylvia Richardson was not among them. The previous fall, she said, the superintendent's office had hired a woman to speak for a substantial fee. "She was telling us all these things that were just silly. All of us knew you just couldn't do them at our school." It must have been a difficult audience for the speaker:

> A lot of people sat back in their seats, crossed their arms, and literally laughed out loud at her. Others got up and walked out on her in groups. If the superintendent and the board hadn't been there, a lot of the rest of us would have left, too, but I figured we were paid to go there so we had to sit.

Sylvia opposed the session, was insulted as were others, but did not resist. She continued to complain about this session long after it had ended; the psychic irresolution prolonged her anger. Sylvia experienced conflict with the superintendent's office over values, that is, what the in-service experience should be like. But because she had been unable to act on her values and challenge the conflict, she found herself in a position of unhappy compliance. Sylvia's talk reflected her construction of authority, her interpretation of being an employee, and her unwillingness to confront sanctions.

Kate Bridges experienced a conflict of values related to the transference of a child from her classroom without first informing her. She was "extremely upset" with the principal for removing the child, but she had not spoken with her because she felt "it was hopeless. Nothing would change." When word got back to the principal through the grapevine, she called Kate to her office. "Why," June asked Kate, "are you upset about this?" Kate reported giving "an amorphous answer," not wanting to say, "June, why didn't you deal with *me*?" Nothing changed, Kate reported. Kate continued to resent the principal and her own situation, and continued to complain. She described herself as "burned out." Again, the teacher opposed an action but lived with it because she did not want to engage in a direct conflict (which might have resolved the situation to her satisfaction).

Instances of unhappy compliance were numerous. A teacher had a conflict with the principal over her policy of calling as few meetings as possible, but did nothing more than complain to colleagues. The fourth-grade team disagreed with the central office on how a project was administered. They complained to each other about how they had not been consulted, about how they were treated as automatons, and about how the central office would "get all the glory in the end," but they took the position that "we must work it out; we have no choice." They drew upon social discourses about workers that constructed them as powerless.

Conflicts that were not resolved tended to occur between teachers and an authority they represented as unmovable. When in this position, many teachers turned their frustration inward, criticizing themselves for their inability to accomplish change. The talk of unhappy compliance was complaint. It was not a form of talk that led to compromise because it so diminished teachers' agency as it enhanced the regulatory power of those in authority.

The Standoff

The standoff was another kind of unresolved conflict that resembled unhappy compliance in certain ways, but had distinctive features. Standoffs occurred not between administrators and teachers, parties whose levels of power and status were clearly unequal, but between colleagues. Although the status of colleagues was similar, how powerfully situated they were differed. Power differentials depended mainly on their clout in the district (their appointment to districtwide committees) and on their reputations among parents and faculty as good teachers. If the parties in a conflict perceived that no honorable solution existed that could resolve the conflict to the satisfaction of both parties, a standoff occurred. The conflicting parties stayed at arm's length from each other around the particular issue (although they might maintain friendly, talkative relationships over other issues).

A school policy that promoted standoffs was the placement of teachers with conflicting teaching styles and philosophies at each grade level, combined with the principal's avoidance of conflict, which produced conflicts that were not directly addressed. While some teams envisioned the differences as strengths, other teams did not. Some team members held each other at arm's length.

Lisa Novak described Charlotte Royce, another member of her team, as "a really nice person. I talk to her a lot as a friend." They had very different philosophies of education, however, and "you can't team when you have conflicting philosophies." For example:

> Charlotte doesn't do things on schedule the way I do, and I feel that you need to have a schedule. And I don't want a kid from her class in my room for reading for just twenty minutes, because I do reading, language arts, spelling, writing, and English all as part of one thing. I need a kid for all of that so I can check on his seatwork.

Charlotte's refusal to rearrange her schedule "that way" meant that they did not exchange children. They remained friends, and they planned and undertook joint activities in other areas. But they did not discuss their differences around the teaching of language arts and they did not do joint teaching in this significant arena. The conflict between them about how to organize the day and how to teach reading distanced them intellectually from each other.

The strategy of the standoff for handling their conflict, however, rested upon the basic good feelings and respect these two teachers had for each other. Lisa felt differently about a third team member whom she (and most of the other staff and principal) described as "incompetent." Lisa refused to trust one of her children to attend a math group in the room of a "professionally incompetent" woman. "You've got to trust a colleague in order to put your child in with her and I just don't trust her. After all, I'm in charge of these kids for the day and I need to feel comfortable when they're not in my room." She thought the teacher should have been fired. She would not engage with her at all. In this situation, a standoff could not occur.

Standoffs resulted in other situations in which teaching styles or values differed but teachers needed to work together. Sandra Miller and Christine Bart were both first-grade teachers, but their teaching styles differed dramatically. Christine played a major role on the district reading committee, and tended to be a firm believer in the reading curriculum. She referred to herself as a "structured but warm" teacher. Sandra, on the other hand, had been trained in England, and ran much more of an open classroom. Other teachers spoke critically of the high noise level in her room. Sandra and Christine were on one team, full of conflicting feelings about the "best" way to teach in a school where the dominant perspective was that there was no one best way.

Sandra Miller had closely analyzed the unspoken tension in their relationship. "Mrs. Bart said to me recently, 'I don't teach reading, I teach decoding,' and she does." Critical as she felt of this method, she admitted that Christine was very successful at what she did. She noted that Christine generally finished her planned work ahead of schedule and had time for creative projects at the end of the year, creative projects Sandra admired. When Sandra was hired, in fact, Christine, as chair of the first-grade team, had interviewed her for the position. Sandra reported that Christine said to her, "I teach reading as it has to be and must be taught. How are you going to come in and teach it without knowing what I know, because obviously you don't like my view of reading at all?" Sandra said that she did not have a very good response to that question, but they have "gotten on fine" since she was hired by not talking about pedagogical issues. It is difficult to imagine that the hiring discussion really went as Sandra represented it. But before they were colleagues their status was unequal enough that a more direct probing of pedagogical beliefs might occur.

Any substantive dialogue they had occurred through veiled comments. Christine invited Sandra and her class to come on the first-grade picnic. Afterward, they were searching for something to talk about that they could agree on. They wanted to avoid conflict. Sandra said, "Gee, Christine, I should have organized some cute activities for the children to do on the playground [like you did]." Christine responded, "My kids have been working so hard they need a day to do nothing." Then Christine added, "My kids do what I tell them to do all year." Sandra interpreted Christine's talk to mean, "Maybe my kids could use a little structure. But she never said that to me directly." Sandra summed up their relationship as one of "grudging respect" from a distance. "She knows that everybody's entitled to her own way."

The standoff, as a strategy of managing conflict, looks similar from the perspective of the person who is critical of another, for example Lisa Novak, and from that of the person who is criticized, for example Sandra Miller. Both perspectives suggest the desire to maintain the relationship, whether because of friendship or proximity. In both cases the teachers point to serious disagreements about teaching as they emphasize a similar respect for their concern with what is good for students. The standoff is a management strategy that teachers employed to suppress hostility, to maintain relationships among disagreeing parties, and to coexist in a context where the principal hired teachers with different teaching styles and beliefs but did not create opportunities for these differences to be openly discussed. The teachers had decided that in such an atmosphere, certain conflicts were too costly to be addressed.

Covert Resistance

Teachers did not choose to compromise around all conflicts they faced. They sometimes insisted on resolutions to conflicts favorable to their perspectives. They talked about those occasions on which they resisted openly, as well as those on which they acted covertly. This section describes their talk about covert resistance. They refused to cooperate with the rule, policy, or activity with which they conflicted. They did so not to change an institutionalized mandate with which they disagreed, but in order to act on their beliefs.

The sixth-grade team had gotten word from the district social studies curriculum committee that the state had dropped "world communities" from the social studies curriculum. In its place had been substituted "economic geography." The sixth-grade team was extremely unhappy with this decision. Not only did the social studies teachers like teaching world communities (partly because of their own extensive travel and work experiences in Africa), but they wanted to emphasize cultural aspects of African and Asian life. In their view, sixth-grade students were ripe for the study of world communities. They disagreed with the state because they believed economic geography was a more difficult framework than world communities for sixth graders. One social studies teacher described her response to the new policy: "I'm just going to go ahead and do what I want to anyway. They'll come around to my way of looking at it one of these days." She described her plan as "doing my own thing." In this case covert resistance individualized conflict. It did not change state policy, which the teacher felt she could never do, but it enabled her to "fit in" world communities.

Conflicts of this type occurred not only with administration, but also with teachers perceived as authoritative. Kindergarten and first-grade teachers disagreed about what should be taught and what materials should be used to teach. Kindergarten teachers opposed the first-grade team's insistence that kindergarten teachers not teach math. Students in some of the kindergarten rooms excelled in mathematics. Kindergarten teachers wanted to begin first-grade math with those students who were able. The first-grade team, however, did not want to have to "group" for math. Ungrouped math lessons meant that no student should be very "far ahead." One kindergarten teacher commented that Christine Bart "has everybody start from page one." The conflict over how the first-grade teachers wanted kindergarten students prepared came down to math book ordering. Christine Bart, chair of the first-grade team, told the kindergarten teachers not to order any first-grade math books for their use. The kindergarten teachers wanted to do just that.

The two teams met to discuss this conflict. Jessica Bonwit, an untenured kindergarten teacher, reported on the meeting from her perspective:

> Christine was so strong and domineering that all of us sort
> of gave in on it. I was very upset, though, so I called Jack
> Williams, who is head of elementary math, and asked him
> whether we didn't have the right to use a first-grade math
> book. He said, "Yes, you do. Just go ahead and order it." So
> we did.

In this representation of the conflict, the kindergarten team argued for their view and lost. They covertly resisted what they perceived as the domination of the first-grade team.

They ordered the book, but they did not tell Christine Bart about it. They would tell her at the end of the year. Jessica explained why they had not consulted the principal, June Robinson, to help mediate the conflict. "You have to go around June because Christine and June are tight." She held up her right hand and intertwined her second and third fingers. "They're tight like this." The kindergarten strategy did not change first-grade policy, but it provided a space for individualized mathematics teaching.

Talk about the circumstances that influenced how they confronted differences suggests that teachers' knowledge of the relationship between the principal and particular teachers varied dramatically. Observations and comments from other teachers, including Christine Bart, suggested that she was not "tight" with the principal. The assumption of Jessica Bonwit and the kindergarten team that she was, however, influenced their choice of covert resistance.

Covert resistance was an important strategy when open challenges failed. The Vista City Elementary building was about to undergo extensive renovations. A renovation committee was formed, including the principal, teachers, and community parents. Conflict developed between the principal and the staff over the makeup of the committee. Teachers wanted more representation on the committee.

Charlotte Royce expressed her interest to Christine Bart, a member, in joining the committee. Christine advised: "Don't go in and ask June if you can be on the committee. Tell her you plan to be on it." Charlotte followed Christine's advice, but was turned down. She reported her "devastation" to Christine. When the night of the meeting drew near, Christine said to Charlotte, "Look, I'm going to pick you up and bring you to that meeting anyway." They both went, and Christine reported that the principal was "gracious and lovely" to Charlotte. Covert resistance had worked.

While this action may seem indistinguishable from open resistance, there are some important differences. Charlotte kept secret her plans to attend the meeting. In open resistance, there is no attempt to be secretive, although strategic discussions may call for secrecy at certain stages. Additionally, the differences in principles were not articulated. Covert resistance helped get more people on the renovation committee, but it did not bring to the surface the debate about teachers' place in democratic governance.

Open Resistance

When teachers talked about handling conflicts through open resistance, they described challenging an institutionalized or official procedure or policy in order to change it because of principles. Open resistance referred to collective as well as individual concerns. It was not that other forms of conflict resolution did not pertain to the collectivity, rather, the teachers did not justify or explain their actions with any reference to it. When open resistance was the strategy, collectivity was central.

Open resistance took different forms. Teachers sometimes attempted to resolve conflicts through direct and open negotiations. At other times they openly resisted some plan through direct confrontation. They said, "We cannot cooperate."

Direct negotiations occurred when teachers stated their own opposition to a policy directly to the person implementing that policy, and accounted for their perspectives with reasons. Sandra Miller, for example, "had certain objections to the Distar Program": Distar was incomplete as a method of teaching reading even though it had useful aspects for "children having a tough time reading."

The district's appointee to administer the system's Distar Program had "a reputation for coming in like a sergeant major and saying, 'You can't do this; you must do that.'" Sandra wrote a paper describing her criticisms and outlining her own method of using Distar. She wrote it to give to the woman on her upcoming visit to the school. The woman's reputation made her feel like she was "taking the bull by the horns." She was apprehensive about the specialist's reaction. After the woman read the paper, however, she told Sandra, "You're doing all the right things." Sandra Miller's resistance to teaching Distar by the book took the form of direct negotiations with the city specialist. It gave her the space to teach as she wanted and to discuss her changes with other teachers who might be interested in doing the same.

Many other examples of teachers' resistance through direct and open negotiations occurred around the renovation committee. Who, for example, got to decide at a meeting whether an issue teachers were concerned about was "insignificant" or "important"? Teachers often challenged parents about this. Was the teacher who was appointed head of the committee one of the cochairs of the committee or just a figurehead, with the principal really the chair? The teacher who was cochair had to interrupt the principal at a faculty meeting to give her perspective on how the renovation committee meetings were going.

Direct and open negotiations may not seem like a form of resistance if we understand negotiations to be a form of mediation. When a teacher initiates negotiations, open discussions, or even mediation when the context is hierarchically organized, however, it requires significant agency. It disrupts the taken-for-granted flow of events, and hence is a form of resistance to the status quo. This disruption is quite visible when it fails. The case of Sandra Miller and her Distar specialist had no audience. An audience created more risk.

Lisa Novak had started to speak out a year earlier on some issues where the teachers and the principal had conflict. She reported that "nobody" spoke up to support her in public meetings. It upset her. One of these issues was the spring production. Teachers had come to her and agreed with her sentiments against such an elaborate performance, but when it came time to vote for it in the public meeting, she was the only one who voted against it. She earned the hostility of the fifth-grade teacher who was in charge of the show. In Lisa's words, "most people seem to be yes-people in front of [the principal]." Lisa had retreated from her assertive stance because she found the consequences too painful when she could not rally the support of other teachers.

Christine Bart talked similarly about her (successful) attempts to rally teacher support. She had spoken up at a faculty meeting, criticizing the deadline for reporting test scores to parents. Christine said to the other faculty and the staff at the faculty meeting that the teachers just could "not cooperate" with the principal's plan. They had never given this test at the school before, and it came right when they were doing report cards. "We just can't do it." Christine recounted that she turned around to the other teachers and said, "Come on, everybody. Am I the only one who feels this way, or are there other people who feel this way, too?" Many people spoke up in favor of her view, and the deadline was postponed. Christine worried that if she had not spoken up, no one would have, because "you have really got to know your mind and feel confident." What she did not say was that teachers agreed with each other about the critique.

Teachers also used talk to nourish resistance. In the following example teachers as a group refused to participate in a new school policy about substitute teachers that would affect their own teaching. Because of the principal's absence, the faculty council meeting was led by the vice principal. He said that the city elementary schools faced a crisis because they could not find substitutes to handle classes when teachers were absent. One of the reasons the number of substitutes had diminished was because the district had revised their substitute system payment plan. They did not want to have to pay unemployment compensation over the summer to permanent substitutes. Hence, they could not as easily attract substitute teachers. The previous week at their school had been "disastrous." An emergency had occurred on the Friday when four teachers were absent and no subs had been available. For the principal, vice principal, and the "special teachers" who had helped out, the school day had been frenetic and wild. The vice principal reported that he and the principal had developed a plan to handle such crises and were "interested" in the "feedback" of council members.

Their plan required teachers, in emergency situations in which teachers were absent and no substitutes were available, to take over these classes during their breaks each day. That is, if a teacher had a break while her students went to art, music, or gym, she would take over the class of the absent teacher for that time. Teachers would get paid extra for this work, so there would be compensation, and Vista City Elementary would manage to get through these crises.

Council members recognized the terrible plan for what it was. Geraldine Forester, the first to speak, said it would be a better idea to have the art, music, or gym teachers take over the day and to cancel the special classes. Jean Webster objected to the compensation: "You don't get paid very much for thirty minutes. I'd rather have the time to myself." Both speakers accepted the parameters of the problem as the administrator had outlined them, noting their particular takes.

Other speakers challenged the very conception of the problem as one for the teachers at the faculty council meeting to handle. Christine Bart argued that "the substitute problem" was not a problem of the school. It was a problem of the district. If Vista City Elementary brought its special teachers out of their classes to act as substitutes, then the city would "not be forced to solve its substitute problem." Meg Tinker worried that the teachers were even discussing the issue. "It's not our problem. It's an administrative problem, not a teachers' problem." Lisa Novak echoed her: "Let the superintendent come down here and teach when we can't get substitutes!" They refused to continue the discussion and told the vice principal that they would refuse to take over classes of absent teachers.

Their analysis was clear. If they handled this problem, the district would not have to manage it. The district was at fault for its shoddy policies with substitutes. In the end, the teachers would get hurt along with the students, who suffered already with only one gym period a week. The best way to force the district to handle the problem was for the teachers to avoid easing the crisis for the district administration. The teachers stood firm.

When teachers talked about conflicts, they reflected their habits of interaction. Collectively empowered, they could resist policies that they found oppressive or unjust. When they privatized their concerns, they either searched for individual solutions or accepted working conditions they disliked. All these ways of managing conflict involved talk. The more open and public the talk, the more institutionally broad the resolution. More private talk about conflict led to smaller-scale resolutions in the school. But even these resolutions could be implemented for a classroom of children.

CONCLUSION

Teachers' everyday lives in schools centered around their relationships with each other as well as the children. These relationships rested not only on what the teachers did with each other but on how they talked about what they did. Talk about community and conflict preserved their relationships with each other over the course of a school year.

Teachers moved closer to each other when they asked each other for advice and talked clinically or socially together. When a teacher defended someone who was broadly criticized by many, she prevented the teacher's ostracism. In this way, most teachers were kept in the circle of relationships. These different kinds of talk drew upon educational and psychological discourses aimed at keeping a balance between amity and discord.

When teachers confronted conflicts, their talk positioned them in relation to their resolution. Unhappy compliance brought no resolution and reinforced to teachers their lack of power. The standoff was a mediating strategy that preserved equanimity in the face of disagreements that were contextually irresolvable. Resistance in different forms enabled teachers to grow intellectually as it sometimes improved working conditions.

Teachers thought about the ways in which they spoke to each other. When teachers disagreed, they might look for something to talk about on another occasion where they could connect. Teachers looked for ways to enhance their teaching when they lost arguments. Even though covert resistance did not produce large-scale change, it benefited particular children. In the case of the kindergarten teachers, it also strengthened their determination to step out of the press of the first-grade team, and united them as a team.

Some of the conflicts teachers engaged in reflected not just determination that one pedagogical strategy was to be preferred, but also the complexity of being a teacher. Christine Bart wanted to be perceived as "structured and warm." Was this possible? Sandra Miller wanted her students to do as well on standardized tests as Christine Bart's students did. Bart had no trouble with structure, but struggled with warmth. Miller was continually warm but wondered how to fit in structure with her freedom. The standoff enabled these two teachers to function together on a first-grade team in a school where no process existed for talking through differences. Could they have ever struggled together with their concerns?

There were also many spaces where individual differences could flourish. Some teachers could include children labeled autistic even if others refused. Teachers who promoted alternative methods found each other and talked strategies. Rigid methods for teaching Distar were actually flexible. In many niches, in other words, teachers engaged with each other intellectually over what it meant to be a good teacher at Vista City Elementary. At the same time, teachers made choices about when to talk, when not to talk, and with whom they would or would not talk. These possibilities provided agency even as they minimized the teachers' interrogation of what was possible. Teachers wanted more space for talk. When they did not get it, their resistance sometimes went underground.

Gender was implicated in all the examples of the different strategies of talking through conflict and community. These moments included balancing being "nice" and strong women, avoiding gossip in order to be professional, or being exuberantly supportive. Whatever these teachers said about feminism, they continually negotiated their gendered situations, feeling comfortable neither with acquiescence nor an elaborated resistance. They wanted to resist without being critiqued as aggressive. When they acquiesced, they spoke self-criticism because they lacked agency. Negotiating gender meant finding a location from which they could speak and act.

CHAPTER 8

Conclusion:
Gender, Discourse, and Feminism

I have examined cultural constructions of teachers, putting gender at the center of that construction. I have argued that we have only recently begun to look beyond taken-for-granted notions of women in teaching. We take them seriously by listening to their perspectives about their work and by treating the concerns that arise in their talk as markers of occupational conditions, rather than interpreting these concerns as representations of the insignificance of work in their lives.

In the Introduction to this book I drew from Toni Morrison to discuss how to frame a study. Toni Morrison suggested that even though enslaved women attempted to make the sites where they worked in plantation homes their own, through such practices as placing a flowering sprig in their kitchens, the power of slavery was so strong that such endeavors disguised but did not disrupt their oppression. Morrison did not abandon empathy with such decorative acts because they emphasize human agency. Reading her in relation to my own work on teachers, I took her to mean that we must study more than the placing of the sprig, an activity whose meanings must be read in the context of the larger discursive systems that framed such actions. While I did not look upon gender as a system of slavery, I made connections to Morrison's metaphor.

I wanted to study how women who taught tried to make elementary schoolteaching their own, while at the same time examining how gender systems confined and constructed them. Over the years it took to complete this work, I came to think of gender arrangements as discursive practices to be negotiated. To attend to the issues in this way, I had to study daily life as well as the larger discursive issues that framed the enactment of daily life, calling upon different sorts of methodological work to do so. These included participant observation, in-depth interviewing, textual analysis, and archival research.

This book brings ethnographic data—particular to a certain school, in a defined geographic region, and collected over a limited two-year

171

period—together with archival and fictional data that situate teachers in different times and circumstances. Originally, the participant-observational data were central, and the historical, fictional, and other cultural data were to serve contextual purposes. Over time, however, the weights accorded the data shifted to form a kind of equal relationship.

This study is both empirical and interpretive. It is grounded in the close analysis of fieldnotes and interview transcripts, and dependent on the words of nineteenth- and early-twentieth-century teachers written in their diaries and letters. The interpretive work of reading fiction about teachers needed grounding in the political, economic, and social events of the period. Therefore, I read two novels about teaching published in the 1950s against the political climate of the times.

In this last chapter I do not want to lay out a plan for, say, a feminist professionalism. I would most like for teachers to think critically about the meanings gender has in their lives, and to examine where this analysis takes them. It seems to me that the most effective efforts at social change come not from the application of models developed elsewhere, but from the taking of ideas explored, applied, or charted at another place, and talking and acting to make them one's own. Empirical work is specific to the contexts where it was gathered, even as it may reach general conclusions that are applicable to other settings.

This book suggests two principal conclusions about the cultural construction of teaching. First, in fiction, the gendered demands on women are intertwined with teaching. When teaching seemed too much like dreary housekeeping, was too confining or repetitious, women complained of it. Additionally, how teachers were portrayed was firmly embedded in the particular historical moment when the characters were written. Miss Dove, for example, was written during the Cold War; the Cold War is never mentioned, but the "wholesale firing" of teachers through McCarthyite tactics during this period suggested the politicization of teaching (Belfrage, 1973, p. 112).

Second, being a teacher has come to have particular cultural meanings. In gendered terms, it meant for many decades that teaching was an occupation compatible with women's major responsibilities for raising children. The sociologists from whom I attempted to rescue teachers reflected these cultural constructions of teaching, which were sometimes taken up by the women themselves. Currently, women teachers draw on cultural constructions of teaching that diminish it in light of other professions women are now able to enter, as they explain their circumstances.

Some of the women at Vista City Elementary had taken up this earlier cultural construction, which they then had to renegotiate when feminism emphasized the status of work for women's importance.

They found themselves in a contradictory position because they got pleasure from the actual work itself while decrying its status. They learned from it, tried new things to "reach" a child or effect a curriculum change, but at the same time might hide what they did. The contradictions were expressed in the life of Carrie Amundsen, who had fought to get into teaching and who was a resource room teacher, informal adviser to the principal, and a well-regarded, influential teacher. Yet Amundsen either lied about her occupation or refused to reveal it when she was in social situations with other people whose jobs held more prestige. Caught between the lived reality of her work and its public representation and diminishment, she chose a private enjoyment and public acquiescence that did not challenge or resist.

These teachers came to read a whole series of interactions as markers of their diminished value. These included their conflicts with mothers, their vulnerability to specialists with the authority to have students taken from their classrooms at particular, even if inconvenient, times, and the lack of understanding the public had for their work. Therefore, the gendered construction of teaching was continually produced in the classrooms of these teachers even if they did not refer to it as gendered.

The rest of this chapter will accomplish two tasks. First, it examines other discourses in the school that gender intersected. Second, it explores the uses of feminism for studying and thinking about gender and teaching.

GENDER, EDUCATIONAL DISCOURSES, AND WORK

Gender is intertwined with discourses about schooling, work, and life that shape how women analyze the meaning of their work. These discourses directly relate to schooling and education. Teachers draw on them to explain their positions to themselves, and use them toward different ends. These discourses are of many different kinds—professional, clinical, pedagogical, feminine, regulatory, service-related, political—and include the discourse of possibility. Except for the discourse of possibility, I frame these discourses in terms of their control and restraint, examining how teachers negotiate and contest them.

Discourses of Professionalism

Central to understanding the work of women teachers in schools is the discourse of professionalism. I have elaborated on how this discourse works in Chapters 2, 6, and 7, so I will give it short shrift here.

Teachers drew upon the discourse of professionalism to understand their work. While teachers did not share a definition of professionalism, they all underscored its importance. Professionalism explained teachers' relationships to children, parents, and each other.

When teachers have conflicts with parents, it is not as though parents' perspectives are unconstructed by discourse. It is neither that parents are right and the teacher is wrong, nor that parents have more intimate views regarding their children's education. Within the discourse of professionalism, parents' knowledge is evaluated as experiential and therefore not intrinsically reliable, while the professional's knowledge is represented as disinterested and supported by technologies (of testing, assessment, and clinical evaluation). How race and class position the parents also shapes what parents know.

The difficulties of asserting agency in a world of bureaucracy and institutional anomie suggest the attractions of professionalism. It has seemed particularly important to teachers who have been marginalized as less than professionals. But the dangers are also apparent. Parents have to prove their worth in order to be taken as experts. Teachers want the power of professionalism and understand the expertise that backs individual judgments.

Clinical Discourses

Teaching is improved when children are clinically observed and discussed; observation, testing, and evaluation (of one kind or another) enable teachers to know children better. This aspect of clinical discourse is connected to interventions. When problems with individual children occur, teams of adults can look at the child more closely. After their observations, the different personnel who have looked at the child can discuss what is happening with him or her; what the causes are of the problems; and what strategies might be most useful to intervene to contain the problem and expand the child's repertoire of coping, learning, and interacting skills. A social worker might investigate to see what is happening with the child's family; a school psychologist might observe the child or give the child some tests; another teacher on a team, the instructional specialist, or the principal might come into the classroom to look for patterns in the child's behavior in the classroom, or whether there is something in the student–teacher relationship that is amiss.

This kind of clinical discussion happens not just when large problems might invite the magnitude of resources brought in above (if these resources were available), but also as part of daily practice. When one Vista City teacher had a series of conflicts with a child that made her worry that she was losing her mind about whether or not the child had handed in work (or the teacher had lost it, as the child accused), she spoke to the child's teacher from the previous year. The previous teacher described a similar series of incidents that had happened to her. The current teacher decided that the student was successfully "manipulating" teachers. The teacher had not lost the work; the student had never handed it in. Teachers also talk to parents and others at the school to figure out what children are like.

The sixth-grade team ate lunch together every day in order to talk about the children. They did this for several reasons. First, they wanted to pool their knowledge about particular children. A homeroom teacher might have some particular information to which the math or English teacher did not have access. Second, they could understand behavior better through talk with others in the same situation whom they trusted and with whom they worked. These team members had very different individual styles, but they trusted each other and each other's interpretations. They would negotiate interpretations together; the atmosphere of trust enabled them to shift from one way of making meaning of a situation to another. Third, talk about difficulties they had with children enabled them to get over their anger, discomfort, or irritation with particular students and so continue to interact for the afternoon. The clinical talk seemed to mediate individual relationships teachers had with children.

Clinical discourses were oriented toward the management of children in school, but teachers sometimes tried to make a space for children to have more freedom through dependence on clinical discourses. Once teachers decided, through meetings, evaluations, informal discussions, or consultations, what particular students were like, they applied this knowledge in their interactions with them. Some teachers would identify problem behaviors in students and then help students overcome these behaviors. At the end of the year they might talk of the child's "growth." Other teachers pegged children by their interactions with them, so that the children came to be known by the behavior that troubled the teacher. Teachers might choose to ignore particular behaviors or react in a variety of ways. They might, like the sixth-grade team, realize that talk about children also freed them from overreacting or overpersonalizing what their students did. Clinical discourses construct a diagnosis response rather than a questioning perspective toward students.

Discourses of Pedagogy

Not all of what teachers did in their classrooms or during their workday counted as teaching. Teachers shared an understanding that teaching did not include disciplining students. Teaching also did not include heavy doses of paperwork for attendance, lunches, IEPs, or demographic data collection. Teachers "had" to do these things because the school or the bureaucracy or downtown (or however they designated it) insisted, and assumed they would.

This understanding meant that teachers wanted to divide these daily nonteaching labors between themselves and other staff in order to dispense with them. If teachers could stick to teaching, they argued, they would be better at what they did and enjoy their work more. Those teachers who could divest themselves of these labors because they had help in the classroom did so. Others complained. "Teaching" meant immediate connections to children's learning, or the planning for it.

Discipline also meant close interactions with children, either individually or in groups, but teachers excluded this practice from their definitions of teaching. This way of understanding major discipline problems could also be a code that pointed to cultural and other differences between the student and the teacher. Pedagogy meant offering students cultural capital (Bourdieu, 1990), as well as depending on the students' cultural capital for evaluating their behavior. When many students in a class did not accept the teacher's authority, some teachers worried that they did not know how to keep their authority because of the students' ethnic or class backgrounds. Conflicts around different cultural interpretations of adult authority (Delpit, 1988) made teachers less sure of their abilities to "teach," and challenged their sense of themselves as competent teachers.

Teachers both sought after and critiqued expert knowledge. The origins of the knowledge made a difference to its believability. Teachers who worked with university professors tended less to see the university as out of touch with schools. They were willing to criticize professors for specific ideas rather than construct the university as an ivory tower. Teachers who were not engaged with university faculty as colleagues were more willing to see the university as out of touch with schools and school-based knowledge. In school discourses about pedagogy, for example, prepackaged curriculum plans and guides were considered as aiding rather than diminishing teaching.

Both clinical and pedagogical discourses rested on a construction of child development that represented the range of normative behaviors. Child development discourse was so intrinsic to pedagogy that its centrality was never problematized.

Discourses of Femininity

Femininity is a cultural construct about gender that yokes together a particular set of perspectives and characteristics. These relate to nurture, help, certain kinds of attention to bodily presentation, and a specific relationship to men. For teachers, femininity and gender intersected in specific ways. Issues relating to particular aspects of family and personal life were treated and celebrated in traditional fashion. To celebrate engagements, births, adoptions, and sometimes anniversaries, teachers threw showers for each other. Teachers who became pregnant (or who adopted children) handled their pregnancies (and the getting of the child) in different ways, but all the women took primary responsibility for their children. Part of femininity included maternal discourses. Some women took leaves of absence for six weeks or a semester or a year. These women were able to return to the positions they had left. Others departed from teaching altogether, until their own children entered elementary school. Even then, separation from their own children was difficult. One teacher described how painful it was for her to teach kindergarten when her own child was a kindergarten student. Maternal discourses encouraged women to think about the relationship between the children they taught and their own children in terms of a finite amount of nurturance that was available. The work of mothering and serving men and others was important talk among teachers.

Changes in family status perceived as negative did not engender particular ways of marking or relating to these occurrences. There was so little space for individual emotional privacy in the classroom that teachers who were going through personal traumas such as divorce, illness, or the death or illness of a parent found it difficult to "get through the days." These events required personal, almost spontaneous responses, rather than the clear-cut ways of marking more happy times. Teachers depended on team members in these circumstances to relieve the pressures of constant face-to-face contact with the children. The teacher's body is literally always in the range of children's view; a depressed body still had to be engaged, cheerful, and interpersonal.

Other domestic and feminine constructions could be seen in the talk about food and cooking and in the decorations of classrooms. Teachers circulated Tupperware booklets and order forms, and ordered items for their own personal use. Holidays such as St. Valentine's Day,

St. Patrick's Day, and Thanksgiving engendered the making of traditional crafts and cards. That this was part of the discourse of femininity was not acknowledged. It was seen as what is done in elementary school.

Many teachers also saw teaching (though particularly elementary schoolteaching) as a feminine occupation, drawing on discourses that connected women with small children. One of the teachers' husbands, for example, had originally been a salesman for a pharmaceutical company. Although successful, he did not like it. "The more you sell, the higher your quotas are. He did not want to excel just in order to make a higher quota." Some children in his family had had Down syndrome, and because of that he had wanted to go into special education. Originally, this teacher had not wanted her husband to teach because "it wasn't a job for a man." She drew on discourses of femininity to position work.

Teachers also drew on particular discourses of femininity in relation to their dressing and grooming. At Vista City Elementary, teachers dressed in quite varied and different styles. Many of the women wore pants and other loose, comfortable clothing. A few teachers wore jeans. Other women wore dresses or skirts every day, although even here, fashion styles differed dramatically. Teachers complimented each other on their clothing and appearance. There was a real range of relationship to clothing. For some teachers it played a very small role in their discussions and relationships with others; for others it played a larger role. When women teach in front of a classroom, their appearance is noticed by students.

Teachers' bodies are objects of the student gaze. When women recall their elementary schoolteachers, one of the primary things they remember is their teachers' appearance (Biklen, 1973). Students take note of their teachers and describe their appearance to others. These descriptions are often based on gendered considerations of appearance and personality. One of the teachers in this study started teaching a sixth-grade class in the middle of the year when the teacher she replaced left to get married. One of the first things she spoke of was how difficult it was to follow the "beautiful Miss Judge," who "had the kids wrapped around her little finger." The teacher recognized the effects of this gaze. Good looks formed a currency with which teachers could trade.

The feminist movement caused some teachers to resist this construction of the feminine. This resistance took pedagogical and other forms. There was a small group of teachers who were known for their interest in feminism. One teacher in particular included feminist teaching in her curriculum. She tried to get her fifth-grade class to analyze the use of women's bodies as objects to sell consumer items. A large activity she organized as part of feminist resistance to the discourses of femininity was the substitution of a celebration of Susan B. Anthony's birthday for Valentine's Day. All of the fifth-grade students dressed up as a figure in the feminist movement of Susan B. Anthony's time. All introduced themselves; a few students dressed as Anthony, Lucretia Mott, or Frederick Douglass gave short speeches. Some parents, other teachers, and the school administrators attended, as did the local press. Rich praise for the activity was countered with some parental complaints for being too "strident." Each time an accepted discourse was resisted, teachers had to explain themselves more than they had ever predicted.

The teachers did not set up the feminist and feminine oppositionally to each other. Both were part of the discourse of gender. Feminism, for example, critiqued not the maternal but social discourse about the maternal, which relegated maternal thinking (Ruddick, 1989) to the margins.

Discourses of Regulation

School rules regulate both students and teachers. Teachers' bodies are regulated by the very restrictions they establish for the children. Since elementary schoolchildren usually pass their days in some proximity to an adult, adults' days were controlled by needing, during all except free time, to be placed in some supervisory position in proximity to children. When Sara Lawrence Lightfoot refers to how the occupation of teaching small children "infantalizes" teachers, this kind of monitoring is relevant (Lightfoot, 1978).

The body of the adult is larger than the bodies of those with whom she spends most of the day. Therefore, aside from the taken-for-granted notion that teachers must control children in order for education to take place, whatever the nature of that control, the adult's larger body gives her a means to assert control over children. The larger body gives the teacher some force to back up her words, her ways of relating to children. This larger body size does not mean that the teacher will be harsh or repressive to children. It means that classrooms are structured so that small bodies are under the charge of a larger body.

In the history of women in teaching, the relative lack of strength in a woman's body, compared to a man's body, was a concern when women became teachers. Could women "manage" larger boys in rural schools? Women who teach in inner-city schools have also been concerned about questions of "safety." This relationship of the larger body and the smaller bodies shifts when the smaller bodies get bigger and stronger. Women teachers begin to worry about the safety of their own bodies in addition to their ability to manage their students. Racism has an ideological influence on the representation of teachers' fears, but body size and strength is certainly an issue.

A second issue about the bodies of women teachers involves the regulation of their movement around a school. When elementary students are in the classroom, teachers, or some designated substitute, must be in the room with them. The nature of teaching as work means that teachers' movements are regulated by the necessity of the continual viewing of their students. Teachers need to regulate their own bodily functions in the same way that they regulate their students' functions. Teachers do not have to ask their students for permission to use the toilets, but they need either their students' cooperation or a designated stand-in to take their place if they have to attend to personal bodily needs when students are in class. Regulations create the conditions for requiring permission.

What happens in this relationship? Teachers need to attend to bodily functions such as menstruation. When regard for their bodies becomes intertwined with the management of children, then they consider how their teaching practices provide for the time or space to attend to their needs. Teachers sometimes had to develop strategies that would keep students occupied in order to attend to body functions.

This need for close proximity in elementary school also influenced teachers' abilities to participate in districtwide decisionmaking about curriculum and policy. Teachers could only attend meetings at the central office if the principal were willing to arrange some substitute coverage for the teacher during that time. Teachers had to depend on the goodwill of the principal to facilitate their involvement. One teacher was very involved in the committee that chose the textbooks for teaching reading and needed the principal's cooperation. That she had to ask for coverage rather than arrange for it suggested to her that she was overregulated.

Vista City Elementary School served students from many different neighborhoods who understood the nature and expectations of schools and who were understood and treated by teachers in different ways. Managing all of these students under one roof and providing for their safety and education meant that for the teachers and administrators a certain degree of orderliness was necessary. Teachers drew on discourses of regulation and control for many aspects of their daily work.

There were rules for how students would walk from their classroom to other locations. There were rules for cafeteria behavior. There were rules for how to behave on the playground, how to speak to teachers and other adults, how to manage a desk and other spaces where personal property was stored. There were rules for how much talking was allowed in classrooms. It was not that these rules were unnecessary or even unfair. Rather, it was that the teachers had to enforce these rules. The ways these were enforced, particularly around levels of talk in the classroom, represented conflicting ways of understanding teaching and the teacher's relationship to children. Two questions seemed central to this conflict. Did children learn "as much" or "enough" when the classroom rules seemed more lax? Was the teacher "in control?" The relationship of control to learning was negotiated differently by teachers.

In addition to drawing upon the discourses of regulation to enact their own work in schools, teachers were also regulated by those occupying higher status than they had. The teaching of sixth-grade social studies was regulated by the state education department. The wishes of those teachers who wanted to continue to teach world communities instead of economic geography, as I described earlier, were not taken into account.

Teachers' lives are also regulated by the architecture of school buildings. How space is defined for pedagogy, recreation, and all-school activities shapes teachers' daily lives and their sense of their work. Many teachers at Vista City recognized the importance of the architectural redesign of the school and wanted to take a central position in shaping the changes.

Discourses of Service

Teaching is associated with discourses of service, though this connection varies according to the worker's relationship to education. The discourse of service explains teaching as a form of giving to others. Teaching is like neither the law nor the factory because part of teaching involves influencing the lives and futures of children. Young children need intellectual stimulation, nurturing, and monitoring. This need for teachers to continually be in the presence of children means that teachers must give up some of their personal needs in order to be present for children. Teaching, in other words, has some element of sacrifice involved in it. Teaching is a kind of human service. How teachers related to the service element of their work varied.

Some teachers in the study looked upon their work as jobs. The children, their students, were one part of that job. Other parts included paperwork, meetings, and collegial interactions. I use "job" here not to distinguish it from "labor," "career," or other status-differential terms, but rather to indicate that these teachers made an occupational choice from among many possible occupational choices. They liked receiving a salary, and valued working, colleagues, and students. They may or may not have excelled at their work. In this scenario, children were one (important) part of the job.

Other teachers' discussion of their work revolved more directly and consistently around the children. They liked being with children, finding that part of their job central and necessary. They took children, their needs, development, and feelings, very seriously. They felt much less strongly about other aspects of their work: For them, teaching meant their students. In fact, they may have classified most aspects of work occurring outside their classrooms as interference. Some of these teachers had theorized about what education should be for children. They were teachers because of a commitment to certain educational philosophies. Did this represent a missionary attitude? It certainly involved dedication and service. They had more difficulty assimilating bad parts of their worklife outside of the classroom. These teachers saw conflict between intra- and extra-classroom life most clearly.

I viewed many of the teachers who defined their work most centrally around the students as loners. They were loners because they appeared as adults isolated from other adults but surrounded by children. Two teachers in particular provided good examples. Both women held reputations as excellent teachers. Both women put significant time into their work. One woman, in fact, felt she had "neglected" her family. Neither of them, however, spent any time in the teachers' lounge, both described themselves as "loners," and each complained of lacking "community" and a "sharing" atmosphere. Both wanted more communication among teachers at the school, and the lack of it disappointed them both. Yet neither of them "hung out" with other teachers during their free time. One of these teachers said that she stayed away from the "politics."

While many issues came into play, one defining feature was the understanding of the discourse of service. Some teachers who spent time in the teachers' lounge smoked and went there for that purpose. (At the time there was only one teachers' lounge; later there were two, one for smokers and one for nonsmokers.) It was not as if teachers with time to waste frequented the lounge while others did not. Teachers in the school with excellent reputations spent time in the lounge. It was a place where casual interchange, encountering others, and teamwork (in the form of talk) took place.

The teachers who defined themselves as loners saw the lounge as a place where more gossip and small talk than they wanted occurred. Since these two women defined their goals as becoming great teachers to the children they taught, they centered all of their energies on this goal.

The discourse of service is constructed around both the giving of self and some forms of self-denial. When Vera Brittain volunteered as a nurse during World War I, she described her first hospital assignment in London:

> It never then occurred to us that we should have been happier, healthier, and altogether more competent if the hours of work had been shorter, the hostel life more private and comfortable, the daily walks between hostel and hospital eliminated, the rule against sitting down in the wards relaxed, and off-duty time known in advance when the work was normal. Far from criticizing our Olympian superiors, we tackled our daily duties with a devotional enthusiasm now rare amongst young women. (Brittain, 1933/1978, p. 210)

The nurses would have been able to work harder were the conditions of work better, even though as workers they never questioned the conditions. The discourse of service centers others.

The principal linked service to burnout. She argued that the loners could "burn out easily" because they gave "too much to their jobs." She said, "I often want to say to them, 'Don't work so hard,' because they really work too hard." These teachers did not appear to take things "easily" enough. They did not want the day-to-day work of teaching to mitigate their original ideals.

The larger argument concerns the relationship between service to others and needs of the self. On many occasions teachers have been accused of attending too much to their self-interests and not enough to the children they serve. Sometimes these criticisms have taken the form of teachers reproducing inequalities in the society, while on other occasions they suggest that unionization sets up rigidity. Susan Moore Johnson's (1982) work on schools where teachers are unionized argued that where principals were available and giving, teachers were, too, regardless of union rules. Those teachers for whom teaching means improving the lives of their students search for ways to serve children on the one hand, and rebel against an oppressive institution on the other. The rhetoric of school-based management at least mentions the concerns of service and need.

Discourses of Possibility

Schools are where children — those who are included — spend much of their time. Because schools sort and offer advantages to these children, educational reformers from many perspectives see the school as a site for social change. Many teachers have themselves considered the school a place to do "good work" for a just society, and have had to negotiate the tensions inherent in the institutional constraints of schooling with the possibilities of how to teach for children. Recent texts have examined feminist teachers' efforts to work for social change (Casey, 1993; Middleton, 1993; Weiler, 1988). A legacy of autobiographical accounts of Euro-American male teachers working against racism during the period of the Vietnam War (Herndon, 1968; Holt, 1964; Kohl, 1976; Kozol, 1967) has been expanded through ethnographic and journalistic accounts that pay more attention to gender (Delpit, 1988; Fine, 1988; Foster, 1993; Kozol, 1991). Writing from critical theory perspectives, authors have framed teachers as "transformative intellectuals" (Giroux, 1988), as radical pedagogues, and as progressive educators. Mainstream reform efforts, including school-based management models and programs in such places as Philadelphia and Chicago (Fine, 1992), include teachers as well as parents as central players in the design of change. The discourses of possibility have a rich legacy.

Social movements sometimes galvanized teachers' energies and focused their attention on particular change issues. I have already spoken of ways teachers drew upon feminist discourses in their work. The disability rights movement was another important source of progressive change in Vista City Elementary. Several teachers and the school principal actively promoted inclusive classrooms for children with moderate and severe intellectual disabilities. When this research was in process the program was at an early stage and later became much more extensive. In these instances, teachers joined together to improve the conditions of education for all students.

Teachers also worked individually on change, but they encountered more difficulty. The teacher who tried to implement the English open-education classroom had no allies with whom to do work. She had supporters, but no one with whom to collaborate. She became isolated. An African-American teacher who emphasized antiracist education also tended to work alone. All the other African-American personnel were not, at that time, teaching in the classroom; they had administrative positions. She closely related to other teachers but did not have colleagues with whom to implement curricular ideas.

Other change efforts were less formal. Teachers often encountered ideas that they wanted to implement in the classroom. One sixth-grade teacher had read Paulo Freire and was interested in applying some of his ideas to the teaching of reading with students who were behind. Teachers had a greater disposition toward change when they had opportunities to try out curricula or pedagogical methods that attracted them and in that they had some investment. Institutionally, the school had no focus on a progressive education agenda, so other teachers resisted change efforts and continued to teach in traditional ways. The space for change, however, had a secure location there.

All of these discourses were active in the social construction of the school. They were often taken to be part of the common sense of teaching. Their contribution to this book rests on their insistence that gender is entangled with other arrangements in schools.

Most of the chapters isolate gender in order to pay it particular attention. In this chapter I have tried to compensate for this distortion by navigating through other discursive practices that also contributed to teachers' sense of their work. We must pay attention to gender, but it is difficult to pay attention to gender all by itself. Additionally, although gender is an issue for all women who teach, it is not the same issue. We cannot assume that gender affects all women teachers in the same ways. It emerges differently in women's lives because it hooks onto other markers such as race, class, sexual orientation, and age.

FEMINISM, TEACHING, AND CHANGE

These chapters have raised questions about the meaning of feminism for relationships between teachers, between mothers and teachers, and between teachers and the principal. Feminists, from different theoretical perspectives, improve relationships between these parties because they force the examination of gender at work. Feminists insist that gender is a central issue rather than a peripheral one. Elementary school-teaching particularly, where so many of the faculty are women, where the work is connected to children, and where interactions with mothers are common, needs to confront the operation of gender arrangements.

Conventionalism will be confronted. Khayatt (1992) discusses the impact of feminine standards on the work of lesbian teachers, but the implications are broader than sexual orientation:

Teachers in general are hired in conformity with an assumed standard. They are expected, to some extent, to reflect a conventionality
that corresponds with the state's ideologically sanctioned model of
behavior. Not only are teachers often perceived as the "formal" trans-
mitters of a hegemonic ideology in a capitalist system that needs to
reproduce a labor force preferably complicit with the status quo, but
as unofficial representatives of the state, they are commonly assumed to embody the dominant values of the society that hires
them. (p. 5)

Women take these regulations and incorporate them into their own
stories. When teachers come to resist gender conventions and conformity, they must work to change their narratives.

Feminism compels us to interrogate the usefulness of particular
ways of framing how we come to know teachers. How do different
vocabularies work? This book has engaged the vocabularies of "voice,"
"resistance," and "difference." It has not examined "civil rights." These
partial truths about teachers narrate one story while ignoring another,
a story a lawyer might tell.

It is impossible to tell a story about teachers that does not speak
from a particular location. As Donna Haraway (1991) so forcefully
claims:

> I am arguing for politics and epistemologies of location, positioning,
> and situating, where partiality and not universality is the condition
> of being heard to make rational knowledge claims. These are claims
> on people's lives; the view from a body, always a complex, contradic-
> tory, structuring and structured body, versus the view from above,
> from nowhere, from simplicity. (p. 195)

My partial story has emphasized the culture of teaching while ignoring
its economy.

This story of teaching has examined some of the ways teachers
have tried to place their flowering sprigs. It has, at the same time,
explored how gender arrangements provoked particular placements,
and how the institutional practices of the school often made individual
efforts ineffectual.

A feminist discourse of possibility cannot separate justice in the
lives of women who teach school from justice for all of their students.
The complications of feminisms in this moment—that feminism does
not mean any single thing for women—coincide with the messy contradictions of teachers' lives. These contradictions need to be explored
rather than repressed. As researchers, we are attentive to gendered

modes of describing and cataloging women's lives that sometimes mask the effective negotiations that go on. Questions that teachers talk over together about gender will weaken the effects of a gender system—a system that perpetuates hostilities between mothers and teachers, and that maintains gender conventions. These questions bring to the surface ideological foundations that are central to the occupation, moving them from the subtext into the text. Once in the text, they can be revised.

References

Acker, S. (1989). *Teachers, gender & careers*. New York: Falmer Press.

Aldrich, B. S. (1919, August). A long distance call from Jim. *American Magazine, 88*, 48–50, 164–166.

Allmendinger, D. (1979, Spring). Mount Holyoke students encounter the need for life-planning. *History of Education Quarterly, 19*, 27–46.

Altenbaugh, R. (1993). *The teacher's voice*. London: Falmer Press.

American Association of University Women. (1992). *How schools shortchange girls*. Washington, DC: Author.

Ames, M. (1969). *A New England woman's diary in Dixie in 1865*. New York: Negro Universities Press.

Anonymous. (1864). *Diary*. Unpublished manuscript, Bancroft Library, University of California, Berkeley.

Antler, J., & Biklen, S. K. (Eds.). (1990). *Changing education: Women as radicals and conservators*. Albany: SUNY Press.

Appiah, K. A. (1993). "No bad nigger": Blacks as the ethical principle in the movies. In M. Garber, J. Matlock, & R. Walkowitz (Eds.), *Media spectacles* (pp. 77–90). New York: Routledge.

Apple, M. (1983, Spring). Work, gender and teaching. *Teachers College Record, 84*, 611–662.

Apple, M. (1986, Fall). Teaching and "women's work": A comparative historical and ideological analysis. *Journal of Education, 86*, 455–473.

Bakhtin, M. (1981). Discourse in the novel. *The dialogic imagination: Four essays* (pp. 259–422). Austin: University of Texas Press.

Barry, K. (1988). *Susan B. Anthony: A biography of a singular feminist*. New York: New York University Press.

Bartlett, F. J. M. (1891). Letter to family. Papers of Frances Jane McCulloh Bartlett in the McCulloh Family papers, Bancroft Library, University of California, Berkeley.

Baxandall, R., Gordon, L., & Reverby, S. (Eds.). (1976). *America's working women: A documentary history: 1600 to the present*. New York: Vintage.

Becker, H. S. (1952/1970). The career of the Chicago public school teacher. *American Journal of Sociology, 57* (March), 470–477. Reprinted in Becker, H. S., *Sociological work* (pp. 165–175). New Brunswick, NJ: Transaction Books.

Becker, H. S. (1962/1970). The nature of a profession. *Education for the profes-*

sions, *Sixty-first Yearbook of the National Society for the Study of Education, Part II* (pp. 27–46). Distributed by the University of Chicago Press. Reprinted in Becker, H. S., *Sociological work* (pp. 87–103). New Brunswick, NJ: Transaction Books.

Becker, H. S. (1970). *Sociological work.* New Brunswick, NJ: Transaction Books.

Belfrage, C. (1973). *The American inquisition, 1945–1960.* Indianapolis: Bobbs-Merrill.

Bell, S. (1988). Becoming a political woman: The reconstruction and interpretation of experience through stories. In A. Todd and S. Fisher (Eds.), *Gender and discourse: The power of talk* (pp. 97–124). Norwood, NJ: Ablex.

Belsey, C. (1980). *Critical practice.* London: Methuen.

Benveniste, E. (1971). *Problems in general linguistics.* Miami: University of Miami Press.

Berg, B. (1978). *The remembered gate: Origins of American feminism.* Oxford, England: Oxford University Press.

Berry, M. A. N. (1862–1867). *Mary Ann Nearing Berry diary.* Berry Family Papers, Asa Fitch Collection, Cornell University, Ithaca, NY.

Biklen, S. K. (1973). *Lessons of consequence: Women's perceptions of their elementary school experience; A retrospective study.* Unpublished doctoral dissertation, University of Massachusetts, Amherst.

Biklen, S. K. (1985, Winter). Can elementary schoolteaching be a career? A search for new ways of understanding women's work. *Issues in Education, 3,* 215–231.

Biklen, S. K. (1987a, Spring). Teachers, professionalism and gender. *Teacher Education Quarterly, 14,* 17–24.

Biklen, S. K. (1987b). Women in elementary schoolteaching: Perspectives from a case study. In P. Schmuck (Ed.), *Women educators: Employees of schools in western countries* (pp. 223–243). Albany: SUNY Press.

Biklen, S. K. (1990). Confiding woman: A 19th century teacher's diary. *History of Education Review, 19*(2), 24–35.

Biklen, S. K., & Brannigan, M. (Eds.) (1980). *Women and educational leadership.* Lexington, MA: Lexington Books.

Bledstein, B. (1976). *The culture of professionalism.* New York: Norton.

Boehm, M. (1947). Autonomy. *Encyclopaedia of the Social Sciences* (Vol. 1). New York: Macmillan.

Bogdan, R., & Biklen, S. K. (1992). *Qualitative research for education* (2nd ed.). Boston: Allyn and Bacon.

Bourdieu, P. (1990). *In other words: Essays towards a reflexive sociology* (Matthew Adamson, Trans.). Stanford, CA: Stanford University Press.

Bourne, B. G., & Wilker, N. J. (1982). Commitment and the cultural mandate: Women in medicine. In R. Kahn-Hut, A. K. Daniels, & R. Colvard (Eds.), *Women and work* (pp. 111–122). New York: Oxford University Press.

Bourne, E. (1974). *Ranch schoolteacher.* Tucson: University of Arizona Press.

Bradford, M. (1932). *Memoirs.* Evansville, WI: Antes Press.

Breines, W. (1986, Winter). The 1950s: Gender and some social science. *Sociological Inquiry, 56,* 69–92.

Breines, W. (1992). *Young, white, and miserable: Growing up female in the fifties*. Boston: Beacon Press.

Brittain, V. (1933/1978). *Testament of youth*. London: Wideview.

Britzman, D. (1991). *Practice makes practice*. Albany: SUNY Press.

Brown, L. M., & Gilligan, C. (1992). *Meeting at the crossroads: Women's psychology and girls' development*. Cambridge: Harvard University Press.

Burt, C. (1875-1889). *Journal*. Unpublished document, Bancroft Library, University of California, Berkeley.

Butler, J. (1990). *Gender trouble: Feminism and the subversion of identity*. New York: Routledge.

Byars, J. (1991). *All that Hollywood allows*. Chapel Hill: University of North Carolina Press.

Cannon, C. J. (1930). *Heirs*. Boston: Little, Brown.

Carnegie Forum on Education and the Economy. (1986). *A nation prepared: Teachers for the 21st century*. New York: Author.

Casey, K. (1993). *I answer with my life: Life histories of women teachers working for social change*. New York: Routledge.

Chambers-Schiller, L. V. (1984). *Liberty, a better husband; Single women in America: The generations of 1780-1840*. New Haven: Yale University Press.

Cherryholmes, C. (1988). *Power and criticism: Poststructural investigations in education*. New York: Teachers College Press.

Chesnutt, C. W. (1899/1967). The bouquet. In *Wife of his youth and other stories of the color line*. Ridgewood, NJ: Gregg Press.

Chopin, K. (1969). Aunt Lympy's interference. In P. Seyersted (Ed.), *Complete works*. Baton Rouge: Louisiana State University Press. (Original work published in *Youth's Companion*, August 12, 1897)

Christman, J. (1989). *The inner citadel*. New York: Oxford University Press.

Clark, S. (1962). *Echo in my soul*. New York: Dutton.

Clifford, G. (1981). *Teaching as a seedbed of feminism*. Paper presented at the 5th Berkshire Conference on History of Women, Vassar College, Poughkeepsie, NY.

Clifford, G. (1983). "Daughters into teachers": Educational and demographic influences on the transformation of teaching into "women's work" in America. *History of Education Review 12*(1), 15-28. Reprinted in A. Prentice & M. Theobald (Eds.). (1991). *Women who taught* (pp. 115-135). Toronto: University of Toronto Press.

Clifford, G. (1987). 'Lady teachers' and politics in the United States, 1850-1930. In M. Lawn & G. Grace (Eds.), *Teachers: The culture and politics of work* (pp. 3-30). London: Falmer Press.

Clifford, J. (1986). Introduction: Partial truths. In J. Clifford and G. Marcus (Eds.), *Writing culture*. Berkeley: University of California Press.

Clinton, C. (1984). *The other civil war*. New York: Hill & Wang.

Cockrell, M. (1965). *The revolt of Sarah Perkins*. New York: Bantam.

Cogan, M. (1953, Winter). Toward a definition of a profession. *Harvard Educational Review, 23*, 33-50.

Conant, M. P. (1931). *A girl of the eighties*. Boston: Houghton Mifflin.

Connell, R. W. et al. (1985). *Teachers' work*. Sydney, Australia: Allen & Unwin.

Cooke, H. B. (1861). *Memories of my life work*. New York: Robert Carter & Bros.

Coser, R. L., & Rokoff, G. (1970). Women in the occupational world: Social disruption and conflict. *Social Problems, 18*, 535–554.

Cott, N. (1975, Fall). Young women in the Second Great Awakening in New England. *Feminist Studies, 3*, 15–29.

Cott, N. (1977). *Bonds of womanhood*. New Haven, CT: Yale University Press.

David, M. (1989). Schooling and the family. In H. Giroux & P. McLaren (Eds.), *Critical pedagogy, the state, and cultural struggle* (pp. 50–65). Albany: SUNY Press.

Davies, D. (1988, April). Poor families and schools. Paper presented at the annual meeting of the American Educational Research Association, New Orleans. ERIC document 294 939.

Delpit, L. (1988, August). The silenced dialogue: Power and pedagogy in educating other people's children. *Harvard Educational Review, 58*, 280–298.

Delta Kappa Gamma Society. (1955). *Pioneer women teachers of Arkansas*. Imboden, AR: Kappa State of Delta Kappa Gamma.

DeVault, M. (1990, February). Talking and listening from women's standpoint: Feminist strategies for interviewing and analysis. *Social Problems, 37*, 96–116.

Downing, B. L. (1951, October). Teaching in the Keeler "deestrict" school. *Vermont Quarterly, A Magazine of History, 19*, 233–243.

Dreeben, R. (1970). *The nature of teaching*. Glenview, IL: Scott Foresman.

Eagleton, T. (1991). *Ideology*. London: Verso.

Edna. (1866). Edna to Lizzie, December 6, 1866. Lizzie Ives Collection. Olin Library, Cornell University, Ithaca, NY.

Ellison, R. C. (1951, October). Caroline Lee Hentz's Alabama diary, 1836. *The Alabama Review, 4*, 254–269.

Engstrand, S. (1940). *Miss Munday*. New York: Dial Press.

Epstein, J. (1986, January). Parent reaction to teacher practices on parent involvement. *Elementary School Journal, 86*, 277–294.

Estler, S. (1975). Women as leaders in public education. *Signs: Journal of Women in Culture and Society, 1*(2), 363–386.

Etzioni, A. (Ed.). (1969). *The semi-professions and their organization*. New York: Free Press.

Evans, A. (1870). *Beulah*. New York: Carleton.

Fine, M. (1988, February). Sexuality, schooling, and adolescent females: The missing discourse of desire. *Harvard Educational Review, 58*, 29–53.

Fine, M. (1992). *Disruptive voices*. Ann Arbor: University of Michigan Press.

Flax, J. (1990). *Thinking fragments: Psychoanalysis, feminism, & postmodernism in the contemporary west*. Berkeley: University of California Press.

Flexner, A. (1910). *Medical education in the United States and Canada* (Bulletin no. 4). New York: Carnegie Foundation for the Advancement of Teaching.

Flexner, A. (1915). Is social work a profession? *Proceedings of the National Conference of Charities and Correction* (pp. 577–578). Chicago: Hildman Printing Co.

Forten, C. (1961). *Journal, a free Negro in the slave era* (R. Billington, Ed.). New York: Collier.

Foster, M. (1993). Resisting racism: Personal testimonies of African-American teachers. In L. Weis & M. Fine (Eds.), *Beyond silenced voices: Class, race, and gender in United States schools* (pp. 273–288). Albany: SUNY Press.

Foucault, M. (1977). *Discipline and punish*. New York: Pantheon.

Foucault, M. (1984). Truth and power. In P. Rabinow (Ed.), *The Foucault reader* (pp. 51–57). New York: Pantheon.

Fox, M. F., & Hesse-Biber, S. (1984). *Women at work*. Palo Alto, CA: Mayfield.

Fox-Genovese, E. (1988). *Within the plantation household*. Chapel Hill: University of North Carolina Press.

Fuller, A. (1892). The schoolmarm. In *Pratt portraits*. New York: G. P. Putnam's Sons.

Fuller, W. (1982). *The old country school: The story of rural education in the middle west*. Chicago: University of Chicago Press.

Gal, S. (1991). Between speech and silence: The problematics of research on language and gender. In M. di Leonardo (Ed.), *Gender at the crossroads of knowledge: Feminist anthropology in the postmodern era* (pp. 175–203). Berkeley: University of California Press.

Gilder, G. (1989). The real American heroes (business people who reduce prices and enhance quality). *Chief Executive* (January/February).

Gilligan, C. (1980). *In a different voice*. Cambridge, MA: Harvard University Press.

Giroux, H. (1988). *Teachers as intellectuals*. New York: Bergin & Garvey.

Glasgow, E. (1963). Romance and Sally Byrd. In R. Meeker (Ed.), *The collected stories of Ellen Glasgow* (pp. 217–238). Baton Rouge: Louisiana State University Press. (Originally published 1924)

Glass, J. (1990, March). The impact of occupational segregation on working conditions. *Social Forces, 68*, 779–798.

Goldman, M. (1981). *Gold diggers and silver miners: Prostitution and social life on the Comstock Lode*. Ann Arbor: University of Michigan Press.

Goode, W. (1957, April). Community within a community: The professions. *American Sociological Review, 22*, 194–200.

Gordon, E. E. (1934). *A little bit of a long story*. Humboldt, IA. Micropublished in *Western Americana: Frontier history of the trans-Mississippi West, 1550–1900*. (1975). New Haven, CT: Research Publications, Inc., No. 2220, no page numbers.

Gordon, L. (1988). *Heroes of their own lives*. New York: Penguin.

Greenwood, E. (1957, July). Attributes of a profession. *Social Work, 2*, 45–55.

Grumet, M. (1988). *Bitter milk: Women and teaching*. Amherst: University of Massachusetts Press.

Gulliford, A. (1984). *America's country schools*. Washington, DC: Preservation Press.

Hall, O. (1948, March). The stages of a medical career. *American Journal of Sociology, 53*, 243-253.

Hall, O. (1966). The social structure of the teaching profession. In F. Lutz & J. Azzarelli, (Eds.), *Struggle for power in education* (pp. 35-48). New York: Center for Applied Research in Education.

Haraway, D. (1991). Situated knowledges: The science question in feminism and the privilege of partial perspective. In *Simians, cyborgs, and women: The reinvention of nature* (pp. 183-201). New York: Routledge.

Hatheway, E. (1852). Elizabeth Hatheway to her sister. Unpublished manuscript, Hatheway family papers, Asa Fitch Collection, Cornell University.

Hatheway, E. (1853). Annie Devlin to Elizabeth Hatheway. Unpublished manuscript, Hatheway family papers, Asa Fitch Collection, Cornell University.

Henderson, A. (1985). *The evidence grows*. Columbia, MD: National Committee for Citizens in Education.

Herndon, J. (1968). *The way it spozed to be*. New York: Simon and Schuster.

Higbee, D. (1864-1867). *Dema Higbee diary*. Unpublished manuscript, Schlesinger Library, Radcliffe College, Cambridge, MA.

Higginbotham, E. (1992, Winter). African American women's history and the metalanguage of race. *Signs: Journal of Women in Culture and Society, 17*, 251-274.

Hoffman, N. (Ed.). (1981). *Women's true profession: Voices from the history of teaching*. New York: Feminist Press.

Holmes, F. K. (1836-1839). *Diary*. Unpublished manuscript, Schlesinger Library, Radcliffe College, Cambridge, MA.

Holmes, F. K. (1839). Letter to Anna. Fannie Kingman Holmes Papers, Schlesinger Library, Radcliffe College, Cambridge, MA.

Holmes Group. (1986). *Tomorrow's teachers*. East Lansing, MI: Author.

Holt, J. (1964). *How children fail*. New York: Putnam.

hooks, b. (1989). *Talking back*. Boston: South End Press.

Huber, J. (1990, February). Macro-micro links in gender stratification. *American Sociological Review, 55*, 1-10.

Hughes, E. (1937, November). Institutional office and the person. *American Journal of Sociology, 43*, 404-413.

Hughes, E. (1971). *The sociological eye*. Chicago: Aldine.

Humphrey, L. M. (1955). *Aggie*. New York: Vantage Press.

Husband, M. (Ed.). (1974). Nellie Carnahan Robinson: The recollections of a schoolteacher in the disappointment Creek Valley. *The Colorado Magazine, 51*(2), 141-156.

Ives, L. (1866). Lizzie Ives paper, Olin Library, Cornell University, Ithaca, NY.

Jackson-Coppin, F. (1913). *Reminiscences of school life*. Philadelphia: A. M. E. Book Concern.

Johnson, M. (1980, Summer). Antoinette Brevost, a schoolmistress in early Pittsburgh. *Winterthur Portfolio, 15*, 151-168.

Johnson, S. M. (1982). *Teacher unions and the schools*. Harvard University Graduate School of Education: Institute for Policy Studies.

Jones, J. (1980). *Soldiers of light and love: Northern teachers and Georgia blacks, 1865–1973.* Chapel Hill: University of North Carolina Press.

Jones, J. (1985). *Labor of love, labor of sorrow.* New York: Random House.

Joseph, P., & Burnaford, G. (Eds.). (1994). *Images of schoolteachers in twentieth century America.* New York: St. Martin's Press.

Kaestle, C. (1983). *Pillars of the republic.* New York: Hill & Wang.

Kahn-Hut, R., Daniels, A. K., & Colvard, R. (Eds.). (1982). *Women at work.* New York: Oxford University Press.

Kaledin, E. (1984). *Mothers and more: American women in the 1950s.* Boston: Twayne.

Kaplan, C. (1985). Subjectivity, class and sexuality. In G. Greene & C. Kahn (Eds.), *Making a difference: Feminist literary criticism* (pp. 146–176). London: Methuen.

Kaufman, P. (1984). *Women teachers on the frontier.* New Haven, CT: Yale University Press.

Kellogg, C. (1923, December). Not eighteen. *Atlantic Monthly, 132,* 797–807.

Khayatt, M. D. (1992). *Lesbian teachers: An invisible presence.* Albany: State University of New York Press.

Kohl, H. (1976). *36 children.* New York: New American Library.

Kondo, D. (1990). *Crafting selves: Power, gender, and discourses of identity in a Japanese workplace.* Chicago: University of Chicago Press.

Kozol, J. (1967). *Death at an early age.* Boston: Houghton Mifflin.

Kozol, J. (1991). *Savage inequalities.* New York: Crown.

Kress, G. (1985). Ideological structures in discourse. In T. A. Van Dijk (Ed.), *Handbook of discourse analysis, Vol. 4,* (pp. 27–42). London: Academic Press.

Krieger, S. (1984). Fiction and social science. *Studies in Symbolic Interaction, 5,* 269–286.

Kundsin, R. (Ed.). (1974). *Women and success.* New York: William Morrow.

Langer, E. (1972). Inside the New York Telephone Company. In W. O'Neill (Ed.), *Women at work* (pp. 307–360). Chicago: Quadrangle Books.

Larcom, L. (1889/1961). *A New England girlhood.* New York: Corinth Books.

Lareau, A. (1987, April). Social class differences in family-school relationships: The importance of cultural capital. *Sociology of Education, 60,* 73–85.

Larson, M. S. (1977). *The rise of professionalism: A sociological analysis.* Berkeley: University of California Press.

Lensink, J. (1989). *"A secret to be burried": The diary and life of Emily Hawley Gillespie, 1858–1888.* Iowa City: University of Iowa Press.

Levin, M. (1987). Parent-teacher collaboration. In D. Livingstone (Ed.), *Critical pedagogy and cultural power* (pp. 269–291). South Hadley, MA: Bergin & Garvey.

Lightfoot, S. L. (1977, Winter). Family-school interactions: The cultural image of mothers and teachers. *Signs: Journal of Women in Culture and Society, 3,* 395–408.

Lightfoot, S. L. (1978). *Worlds apart: Relations between families and schools.* New York: Basic Books.

Lines, A. A. (1982). *To raise myself a little, the diaries and letters of Jennie, a Georgia teacher, 1851–1886* (T. Dyer, Ed.). Athens: University of Georgia Press.

Lipsitz, G. (1990). *Time passages: Collective memory and American popular culture*. Minneapolis: University of Minnesota Press.

Little, J. W. (1990). Teachers as colleagues. In A. Lieberman (Ed.), *Schools as collaborative cultures: Creating the future now* (pp. 165–193). New York: Falmer.

Lortie, D. (1959, Fall). Laymen to lawmen: Law schools, careers and professional socialization. *Harvard Educational Review, 29*, 352–369.

Lortie, D. (1975). *Schoolteacher*. Chicago: University of Chicago Press.

Ludlow, H. (1886). *Memoir of Mary Anna Longstreth*. Philadelphia: J. B. Lippincott.

Lundberg, F., & Farnham, M. (1947). *Modern woman: The lost sex*. New York: Harpers.

Lynch, M. A. (1843). Letter to brother and sister, April 8, 1843. Atkins Family Papers; Obituary, *The Cleveland Leader*, October 24, 1882; Bancroft Library, University of California, Berkeley.

Marsh, A. S. T. (1845–1851). Letters. Marsh Family Papers, Bancroft Library, University of California, Berkeley.

Marsh, A. S. T. (1846). Letter to Rev. Z. P. Wild, Unionville, MA. Marsh Family Papers, Bancroft Library, University of California, Berkeley.

Marston, M. A. (n.d.) *The lady of the diary or the little Yankee goes South*. Unpublished manuscript, Asa Fitch Collection, Cornell University, Ithaca, NY.

Mason, W. S. (1961). *The beginning teacher: Status and career*. Washington, DC: U.S. Government Printing Office.

Matthaei, J. A. (1982). *An economic history of women in America*. New York: Schocken Books.

May, E. T. (1988). *Homeward bound: American families in the cold war era*. New York: Basic Books.

McClellan, G. M. (1906/1975). A Creole from Louisiana. In *Old Greenbottom Inn*. New York: AMS Press.

McPherson, G. (1972). *Small town teacher*. Cambridge, MA: Harvard University Press.

Metzger, M. T., & Fox, C. (1986, November). Two teachers of letters. *Harvard Educational Review, 56*, 349–354.

Middleton, S. (1993). *Educating feminists*. New York: Teachers College Press.

Miller, J. (1990). *Creating spaces and finding voices: Teachers' collaborating for empowerment*. Albany: SUNY Press.

Mills, C. W. (1959). *The sociological imagination*. New York: Oxford University Press.

Modleski, T. (1991). *Feminism without women: Culture and criticism in a "postfeminist" age*. New York: Routledge.

Morrison, T. (1987). *Beloved*. New York: Knopf.

Mudge, M. (1854). *Diary*. Unpublished manuscript, Schlesinger Library, Radcliffe College, Cambridge, MA.

Mulvey, L. (1975, Autumn). Visual pleasure and narrative cinema. *Screen, 16,* 6–18.

National Education Association. (1972). *Status of the American public-school teacher, 1970–1971.* Washington, DC: Author.

Nieva, V., & Gulick, B. (1981). *Women and work.* New York: Praeger.

Orner, M. (1992). Interrupting the calls for student voice in "liberatory" education: A feminist poststructuralist perspective. In C. Luke & J. Gore (Eds.), *Feminisms and critical pedagogy* (pp. 74–89). New York: Routledge.

Padgett, J. A. (Ed.). (1937). A Yankee school teacher in Louisiana, 1853–1937: The diary of Caroline B. Poole. *Louisiana Historical Quarterly, 20,* 651–679.

Parker, A. S. (n.d.). *A pioneer school mistress.* Unpublished manuscript, Bancroft Library, University of California, Berkeley.

Parsons, T. (1959, Fall). The school class as a social system. *Harvard Educational Review, 29,* 297–318.

Patton, F. G. (1954). *Good morning, Miss Dove.* New York: Dodd, Mead.

Perkins, L. (1987). *Fanny Jackson Coppin and the Institute for Colored Youth.* New York: Garland.

Popkewitz, T. (1992). Culture, pedagogy and power: Issues in the production of values and colonialization. In K. Weiler (Ed.), *What schools can do: Critical pedagogy and practice* (pp. 133–148). Albany: SUNY Press.

Prentice, A. (1975). The feminization of teaching in British, North America and Canada 1845–1875. *Social History, 8*(15), 5–20.

Prentiss, E. P. (1882). *Life and letters.* New York: Anson D.F. Randolf & Co.

Reese, W. (1978, November). Between home and school: Organized parents, club women and urban education in the Progressive Era. *School Review,* 3–26.

Richards, C. (1984). Teaching school in Fort Wayne in the 1830s. *Old Fort News, 47*(3), Allen County-Fort Wayne Historical Society, 3–15.

Rist, R. (1987). *The invisible children.* Cambridge, MA: Harvard University Press.

Roberts, H., & Barker, R. (1989, March). What are people doing when they grade women's work? *British Journal of Sociology, 40,* 130–146.

Rose, W. L. (1964). *Rehearsal for reconstruction: The Port Royal experiment.* New York: Vintage.

Rosenstone, R. A. (1975). *Romantic revolutionary.* New York: Alfred A. Knopf.

Roth, J. (1974, February). Professionalism: The sociologist's decoy. *Sociology of Work and Occupations, 1,* 6–23.

Ruddick, S. (1989). *Maternal thinking.* Boston: Beacon Press.

Sanford, M. D. (1959). *The journal of Mollie Dorsey Sanford in Nebraska and Colorado Territories, 1857–1866.* Lincoln: University of Nebraska Press.

Sarason, S. (1974). *The psychological sense of community.* San Francisco: Jossey-Bass.

Sarason, S. (1982). *The culture of school and the problem of change* (2nd ed.). Boston: Allyn and Bacon.

Sayre, N. (1978). *Running time: Films of the cold war.* New York: Dial Press.

Schlossman, S. (1976, August). Before "Home Start": Notes toward a history of parent education in America, 1897-1929. *Harvard Educational Review, 46,* 436-467.

Sengstacken, A. (1942). *Destination West.* Portland, OR: Binfords & Mort.

Shakeshaft, C. (1985). *Teaching as a radicalizing activity for women.* Paper presented at the 10th annual Research on Women and Education conference, Boston.

Simpson R., & Simpson, I. (1969). Women and bureaucracy in the semi-professions. In A. Etzioni, (Ed.), *The semi-professions and their organization* (pp. 196-265). New York: Free Press.

Sklar, K. K. (1973). *Catherine Beecher, a study in American domesticity.* New York: Norton.

Sleeper, S. (1843). *Memoir of Martha Hazeltine Smith.* Boston: Freeman and Bolles.

Small, S. (1979, August). The Yankee schoolmarm in Freedmen's Schools: Analysis of attitudes. *The Journal of Southern History, 45,* 381-402.

Smith, D. (1987). *The everyday world as problematic.* Boston: Northeastern University Press.

Smith, H. W. (1879). *John M. Whitall, the story of his life.* Philadelphia: Printed for the family.

Sneller, A. (1964). *A vanished world.* Syracuse, NY: Syracuse University Press.

Specht, R. (1976). *Tisha: The story of a young teacher in the Alaska wilderness.* New York: St. Martin's.

Spring, J. (1986). *The American school.* New York: Longman.

Sterling, D. (Ed.). (1984). *We are your sisters: Black women in the nineteenth century.* New York: W. W. Norton.

Stoddard, A. J. (1860). *Diary.* Unpublished manuscript, Schlesinger Library, Radcliffe College, Cambridge, MA.

Swint, H. W. (Ed.). (1966). *Dear ones at home, letters from contraband camps.* Nashville, TN: Vanderbuilt University Press.

Swint, H. (1967). *The Northern teacher in the South, 1862-1870.* New York: Octagon Books.

Teachers are in trouble. *Newsweek,* April 27, 1981, 78-84.

Tevis, J. (1878). *Sixty years in a school-room: An autobiography.* Cincinnati: Western Methodist Book Concern.

Turnbull, A. (1925, October). In such a night. *American Magazine, 100,* 29-31, 191-195.

Tyack, D. (1974). *The one best system.* Cambridge, MA: Harvard University Press.

Tyack, D., & Hansot, E. (1982). *Managers of virtue.* New York: Basic Books.

Van Maanen, J. (1988). *Tales of the field.* Chicago: University of Chicago Press.

Walker, M. (1944). *Winter wheat.* New York: Harcourt Brace Jovanovich.

Waller, W. (1932). *The sociology of teaching.* New York: John Wiley.

Webber, A. (1972). The diary of Anna Webber: Early day teacher of Mitchell County. *The Kansas Historical Quarterly, 38*(3), 320–337.

Wester, L. (1952). *Memories of mine*. Austin, TX: Author.

Weeks, E. (1954, October). Review of *Good morning, Miss Dove* and two other books. *The Atlantic Bookshelf, 194*, 90.

Weiler, K. (1988). *Women teaching for change*. South Hadley, MA: Bergin & Garvey.

Whitefield, S. (1991). *The culture of the Cold War*. Baltimore: Johns Hopkins.

Wilson, L. (1942). *The academic man*. New York: Oxford University Press.

Winston, E. (1980). The autobiographer and her readers: From apology to affirmation. In E. Jelinek (Ed.), *Women's autobiography, Essays in criticism*. Bloomington: Indiana University Press.

Woodburn, M. B. (1937). *Miss Lizzie, A portrait of a New England teacher*. Boston: Chapman and Grimes.

Woody, T. (1929). *A history of women's education in the United States*, Vol. 1. New York: Science Press.

Index

Pedagogy, discourses of, 176–177
Perkins, Arozina, 77
Perkins, L., 16, 58
Physical conditions, of nineteenth-
    century teachers, 63–64
Poates, Sara Fitch, 54
Poole, Caroline, 64
Popkewitz, T., 81
Power, of teachers, 19–20, 39–40, 45, 94,
    95–103, 179–181
Prentice, A., 50
Prentiss, Elizabeth Payson, 54, 57, 62
Principals
    and burnout of teachers, 183
    and institutional talk, 145–148
    teacher conflict with, 160–161
Process talk, 149
Professionalism, 26–27, 41–46, 52, 138,
    139
    discourses of, 173–174
    as obstacle to community, 156–159

Race
    African-American teachers and, 18, 36–
        37, 47–48, 110–111, 119–123, 184–
        185
    in fiction, 110–111, 116–125
    and gender of teachers, 35–37
Reed, John, 4
Reese, William, 128
Regulation, discourses of, 179–181
Relational talk, 150
Religious ideals, of teachers, 54–58
Resistance
    covert, 164–166
    open, 166–169
    by teachers, 19, 40, 101–103, 164–169
Reverby, S., 16
Revolt of Sarah Perkins, The (Cockrell),
    82, 92–93, 94–95
Richards, C., 72
Richardson, Sylvia, 34, 153, 160
Rist, Ray, 127
Roberts, H., 27
Robinson, June, 145–148, 151, 154, 165
Rokoff, G., 5
Romantic love, 60–61
Rose, W. L., 48
Rosenstone, R. A., 4
Roth, J., 41
Royce, Charlotte, 162, 165–166
Ruddick, Sara, 29, 179

Samuels, Heather, 151–152, 154,
    158
Sanford, M. D., 72
Sarason, Seymour, 28, 127, 150
Sayre, N., 114–115
Schlossman, S., 128
Schoolmarm, The (Fuller), 86–87
School size, and nineteenth-century teach-
    ers, 64–65
Schoolteacher (Lortie), 7, 8
Selover, Esther, 72
*Semi-Professions and Their Organization,
    The* (Etzioni), 7
Sengstacken, A., 72
Service, teachers and, 55–58, 94, 181–
    184
Shakeshaft, C., 17, 49
Simpson, I., 7
Simpson, R., 7
Sklar, K. K., 16, 50, 55
Sleeper, S., 57
Small, S., 56
Smith, Dorothy, 129–130
Smith, H. W., 53
Sneller, A., 72
Snow, Electra, 83–84
Social class, and parent-teacher relation-
    ships, 128–129, 141–142
Social discourses, 20
Social movements, 184
Social talk, 153–154
Social work, 41
Sociological Imagination, The (Mills),
    114
Sociology of Teaching, The (Waller), 124
Spear, Elizabeth "Miss Lizzie," 53
Specht, R., 82, 89–91
Spring, J., 115
Stand and Deliver (film), 1, 3
Standoffs, in conflict situations, 161–
    163
*Status of the American Public-School
    Teacher* (National Education
    Association), 8
Sterling, D., 16
Stoddard, Ann, 73
Stone, Lucy, 17
Student examinations, and nineteenth-
    century teachers, 65–67
Students, teacher relationships with, 68–
    70
Swint, H. W., 56, 58

About the Author

Sari Knopp Biklen is a professor in Cultural Foundations of Education at Syracuse University. She is also faculty in the Women's Studies Program. Earlier books include *Gender and Education* (with Diane Pollard), *Qualitative Research for Education* (with Robert Bogdan), and *Changing Education: Women as Radicals and Conservators* (with Joyce Antler). She has won the Willystine Goodsell Award of the American Educational Research Association for her research on women.